P9-DFO-452

VIOLENCE AGAINST WOMEN

Gender & Society Readers

Sponsored by Sociologists for Women in Society

Gender & Society Readers address key issues in contemporary gender studies informed by feminist writing, theory, and research. Readers are based on articles appearing in, and special theme issues of, the scholarly journal *Gender & Society*, sponsored by Sociologists for Women in Society.

Titles in this series:

Judith Lorber and Susan A. Farrell (eds.)
   THE SOCIAL CONSTRUCTION OF GENDER (1991)
Pauline B. Bart and Eileen Geil Moran (eds.)
   VIOLENCE AGAINST WOMEN: The Bloody Footprints (1993)

VIOLENCE AGAINST WOMEN
The Bloody Footprints

Edited by
Pauline B. Bart and
Eileen Geil Moran

A *Gender & Society* Reader
Published in cooperation with
Sociologists for Women in Society

 SAGE Publications
International Educational and Professional Publisher
Newbury Park   London   New Delhi

Copyright © 1993 by Sociologists for Women in Society

All rights reserved. No part of this book may be reproduced or utilized in any form or by any means, electronic or mechanical, including photocopying, recording, or by any information storage and retrieval system, without permission in writing from the publisher.

For information address:

SAGE Publications, Inc.
2455 Teller Road
Newbury Park, California 91320

SAGE Publications Ltd.
6 Bonhill Street
London EC2A 4PU
United Kingdom

SAGE Publications India Pvt. Ltd.
M-32 Market
Greater Kailash I
New Delhi 110 048 India

Printed in the United States of America

Library of Congress Cataloging-in-Publication Data

Violence against women: The bloody footprints / [edited by Pauline B. Bart,
    Eileen Geil Moran].
        p.   cm.   —(A gender & society reader)
    Includes bibliographical references.
    ISBN 0-8039-5044-6 (cl).   —ISBN 0-8039-5045-4 (pb)
    1. Women—United States—Crimes against.   2. Violent crimes—
United States.   3. Abused women—United States.   4. Rape—United
States.   I. Bart, Pauline B.   II. Moran, Eileen Geil.   III. Series.
HV6250.4.W65V54   1993
364.1'555'082—dc20   92-34839
                                                                    CIP
93   94   95   96   10   9   8   7   6   5   4   3   2   1

Sage Production Editor: Judith L. Hunter

Contents

22.75

86923

Dedicated to Boris Astrachan, M.D., chair of the Department of Psychiatry, University of Illinois, who saved me from the Cossacks, kapos, and "Good Germans"; to Catharine A. MacKinnon, who gave me the analysis that made this book possible, and whose uncompromising life gives us hope that we do not have to be complicit with evil; to the Chicago Women Law Teachers and Friends Colloquium; and to my grandchildren, Rebecca and Anna, with the hope, but not the expectation, that their world will not consist of endemic violence against women.

Pauline B. Bart

To my mother and to Don for their unlimited faith in me and to all my sisters, from the South Bronx to politics to the academy, whose lives have been diminished by sex inequality, but who struggle on in spite of it.

Eileen Geil Moran

Foreword

Pauline Bart suggested a special issue of *Gender & Society* on violence against women in spring 1986, arguing that a journal of feminist theory that did not address systemic gendered violence would be incomplete. At that time, I thought we would be addressing a pervasive problem that lurked on the underside of everyday life, but that tended to be put up with by women as part of "the routine." But in 1989, as we were reading manuscripts for the special issue, the hell of women's experience of violence broke loose in New York City. In every newspaper and magazine, on everyone's television set, in everyone's conversation, throughout the world it seemed, first Lisa Steinberg, Hedda Nussbaum, and Joel Steinberg played out the horror. Then came the "Central Park rape." And the familiar litany—is it race, is it class, is it pathology? Feminists looked at each other and said over and over, "What about gender? Why doesn't everyone realize this is a *gender* issue?"

Certainly, race and class were blatant in the attention paid to White, middle-class experience. The week in which a White investment banker jogging in Central Park in New York City was brutally beaten and gang-raped (April 16-22, 1989), 28 girls and women, aged 8 to 51, mostly Black or Hispanic, were raped—in the street, waiting for a train, visiting a friend (Terry, 1989). Two weeks after the headline-grabbing event, a 38-year-old Black woman was forced up to the roof of a four-story building, raped, beaten, and thrown off. She was badly injured, but lived. No headlines.

In the United States, the FBI estimates there is one rape every 6 minutes. These statistics do not include forcible rapes by dates, boyfriends, and husbands, most of which get into the news only when the *man* is famous, as in the cases of William Kennedy Smith or Mike Tyson. When men batter their wives and lovers, it doesn't get turned into a TV movie; when wives kill their batterers, that's drama. Sexual propositions and "dirty talk" addressed to junior and senior women in workplaces all over the Western world and embarrassing sexual remarks or jokes in the school-room are such common "microinequities" that it took years before women could see them as a form of discrimination against them (Benokraitis & Feagin, 1986). And again, it took the Anita Hill-Clarence Thomas hearings to draw public attention to what every woman—heterosexual or lesbian, Black, Latina, Asian, Native American, or White—knows, and what homosexual men and men of color experience for their sexual orientation or race and ethnicity, not for their *gender.*

These are all sex crimes against women—aggressive acts of sexual-ized violence that range from obscene, intrusive phone calls and side-walk salaciousness to Jack-the-Ripper serial murders and the massacre of "feminists" by men who feel their dominance challenged.

Reading the papers submitted for the special issue raised my own consciousness as to the importance of gendered violence for feminist theory and practice. In conversations with friends and family members, particularly young ones, I make constant use of the insights these papers present. This book, which not only touches on the enormity of the every-day violence women experience, but which lays out the institutional structure, politics, and research implications, should make you angry at the injustice. But then you must turn to the other women and men who also feel outrage, and with them, speak out, act out, and turn that anger into political power.

Judith Lorber
Founding Editor
Gender & Society

REFERENCES

Benokraitis, N. V., & Feagin, J. R. (1986). *Modern sexism: Blatant, subtle, and covert discrimination.* Englewood Cliffs, NJ: Prentice-Hall.

Terry, D. (1989, May 29). A week of rapes: The jogger and 28 not in the news. *New York Times,*

Preface

I don't understand mens like that. . . . She see how the world is. Mens like that
shouldn't have the right to live. I don't think they're sick. It's their egos. It's bad
on her. Someone invaded her body just to take stuff. Things have changed. Think
somebody damn cruel. . . . See how dogs men be.

—Mother of an 11-year-old girl raped by her cousin's friend

Fourteen women were massacred in Montreal on the day the original
issue of *Gender & Society* on violence against women, which this book
augments, arrived. This Montreal femicide, with the "selection" sepa-
rating females from males, the former to be shot, recalled the selection
on the train platform at the Auschwitz concentration camp where Dr.
Mengele separated those who would live from those who would die. In
both cases, people were condemned to death because of ascribed characteristics. Although the Montreal killer said that he murdered the
women because he hated feminists, the debate that followed attributed
his behavior simply to psychopathology, ignoring the fact that he was
a woman-hating man reinforced by a woman-hating society.

Misogynist violence is common in our society. Between July 1991
and April 1992, a series of such acts were reported in the media, demonstrating not only male power over women, but men's ability to harass
women with impunity. We will note five publicized cases:

1. St. John's University athletes were acquitted of the gang rape of an African-
   American woman.

2. The African-American judge Clarence Thomas was confirmed by the U.S. Senate as a Supreme Court justice in spite of the African-American professor Anita Hill's credible testimony about his sexual harassment of her, including the use of pornography (see cartoon, p. 66), and the Senate failed to call other women who had accused Thomas of similar behavior.

3. William Kennedy Smith was acquitted of acquaintance rape, at least in part because of the judge's failure to allow his sexual history to be admitted as evidence of a tendency to commit such crimes. The judge also refused to allow expert witnesses on rape trauma to testify. That the judge was biologically female not only shows that those members of subordinate groups who reach positions of power do so by internalizing the values of the dominant groups, but as the feminist law professor Catharine A. MacKinnon says, "The good news is that it isn't biological."

Even the surprise conviction of the heavyweight boxing champion Mike Tyson, currently being appealed by the liberal law professor Alan Dershowitz, can be explained by the victim being what is considered "rapable," that is, young, "moral," having a witness to Tyson's harassment, and reporting the assault to the police immediately. That Tyson's every court appearance was greeted with cheers supports Jane Caputi's concept of "the heroic rapist" (see p. 13). Indeed, Tyson denied doing any harm at all because he didn't blacken the raped woman's eye or break her ribs. This "neutralization," as sociologists call it, is substantiated in the chapters by Patricia Hill Collins and Diana Scully in greater depth.

4. Another striking example of unpunished misogyny, this time committed by Harvard Law School students—"the best and the brightest"—is the vicious parody of the feminist legal scholar Mary Jo Frug's article that appeared in the *Harvard Law Review* on the anniversary of her brutal stabbing death on the streets of Cambridge. The parody appeared on everyone's plate, including that of her husband, at the *Harvard Law Review*'s gala banquet. "It depicted Ms. Frug as a humorless, sex-starved mediocrity and dubbed her the 'Rigor Mortis Professor of Law' " (New York Times, 4/17/92; David Margolick, "At the Bar"). Frug had maintained in her article, as most feminist jurisprudence and critical legal theory scholars do, that the law perpetuates the subjugation of women. These graduating students with distinguished appointments to assist such jurists as Justice Scalia illustrated her point by their behavior.

5. A husband was found not guilty of raping his wife, in spite of the jury having seen a videotape he made showing his wife pleading with him not to tie her up, which he did, and screaming at him not to rape her, which he did. He slapped her and taped her eyes and mouth with duct tape after

showing her a videotape depicting similar events. His attorney told the jury her screams could be screams of pleasure—the message of pornography (Washington Post, A2, April 18, 1992). The incident also demonstrates the desensitization to women's pain that results from watching pornography.

It should be noted that the jury in the Rodney King case, to which a videotape was shown of the police beating King, also found the perpetrators not guilty and implied that King had "asked for it" by not being more docile. Dominant groups' versions of reality provide the filter through which jurors who identify with those groups construct "reality."

We see in these events that we haven't come a long way, that woman hating is alive and well, and those women who ignore it may help their careers, but hurt their analyses (see the "Not Andrea" sections of Dworkin's Mercy [Prologue, pp. 1-4 and Epilogue, pp. 114-342] for a brilliant portrait of such academic feminists). This distancing from real women's real pain is reinforced by the rehabilitation of Freud, whether in the French or North American versions, in feminist theory (e.g., Gallup, Chodorow). Psychoanalytic feminism is an oxymoron like "friendly fire," "family vacation," and "Justice Thomas." Taking women's experience seriously, dealing with our concrete experiences and validating them, rather than grounding our work in male seminal thinkers such as Freud and Lacan and the deconstructionists with all their mystifying jargon, frequently results in rejection by the academic community. For example, Pauline Bart's work has been called politics and not sociology by male academics.

Although this book expands the coverage of the original *Gender & Society* issue on which it is based, space limitations precluded addressing important issues such as marital rape, pornography, prostitution, rape avoidance strategies, women in prison, and unnecessary surgery, including genital mutilation, although we have tried to provide some coverage of these issues in the introduction.

In this book, we do not define women as simply victims who have no agency or coping strategies, although the issue is usually presented as either one or the other. Women use agency in coping with our lives, including our exploitation, though women have considerably less power in institutional relationships than men. One does not negate the other, although for some feminist theorists the term *victim* is taboo. In fact, Bart and O'Brien (1985) found that a substantial number of women felt strengthened by their avoidance of rape when attacked and even by the assault itself. Yet our lives are at best constrained and at worst seriously damaged by violence and fear of violence.

We want the results of these studies to be incorporated into public policy. Policymakers usually want allegedly valid and reliable large-scale surveys answering questions such as How many? Who? Where? How bad are the consequences? and How much will it cost (Miller, 1989)? In these times, cost is a particularly important issue, and the backlash against women undercuts compelling arguments about these issues. Yet in spite of these biases, some headway is being made; for example, Carole Warshaw's work on emergency room treatment of battered women was abstracted in the *Journal of the American Medical Association* and brought to the attention of the U.S. Surgeon General, who contacted her.

Currently, both in journals and in policy statements, violence against women is considered a serious public health problem, and a recent issue of the *Journal of the American Medical Association* is devoted to "family" violence. One relevant example of the funding biases discussed above is that in spite of numerous criticisms, some in this volume, some in other journals (e.g., Dobash & Dobash, 1992), the Conflict Tactics Scale, which is a national survey to find the number of noncontextual violent incidents in families, keeps getting funded and replicated. Moreover, feminist analyses, particularly when qualitative, as most of those in this book are, are not considered "objective" and thus are less likely to be approved by peer review for funding. One such alleged peer turned down a grant application on rape from Bart because she wasn't "objective" about rape. Another "peer" reviewer did not understand what it meant to be a rape victim advocate. Perhaps if Bart had a rapist as coinvestigator, the proper balance would be attained and the grant would be approved. (See MacKinnon's chapter for a critique of "objectivity.")

When you finish reading this book, you will never watch television or read newspapers or observe male-female interactions the same way again. In fact, you will never see the world the same way again. This will not make you happier; as the saying goes, "The truth will set you free. But first it will make you miserable."

Acknowledgments

This book is built on the special issue of *Gender & Society* on violence against women that was published by Sage in December 1989. We are grateful to the authors whose work appeared in the special issue and in subsequent issues of *Gender & Society*. For addressing important aspects of this problem, we gratefully acknowledge the original contributions of Kathleen J. Ferraro and Elizabeth Anne Stanko along with the authors and publishers who permitted us to reprint their work. We particularly appreciate the contributions of Andrea Dworkin, Lynda J. Barry, and Jules Feiffer.

We wish to give special thanks to Patricia Miller, who helped conceive this project and assisted with the literature search to supplement the work from the special issue, and to Judith Lorber, SWS, and Bettina Huber for their continuous support for this book. We also appreciate Maren Carden's asking the right questions and Barbara Katz Rothman's apt, always politically correct, editorial suggestions.

Pauline B. Bart
Eileen Geil Moran
Editors

Part I

Types of Violence Women Experience

Introduction

That some men rape, some batter, some commit incest, some sexually harass, some make obscene phone calls, and some murder is not surprising in a society in which dominance and subordination are eroticized. What is surprising is that some men do not. In the United States and Great Britain, as Jane Caputi shows in "The Sexual Politics of Murder" (Chapter 1) most men's male significant others, backed up by the media, or sometimes the other way around, steadily feed them the message that they are entitled to goods and services from women as a class; not only should we provide such services, including our bodies and the orifices thereof, but that is what we are for. And we enjoy it. As one rapist said to his victim, "You want it. I can tell. You really want it." The chapters in this section address the types of violence women experience, running the gamut from pornographic phone calls to femicide, but all the acts described terrorize and control women and girls.

The major theme of this book is that all forms of violence against women are interrelated, coalescing like a girdle to keep women in our place, which is subordinate to men. This is not a conscious male plot. The controversial feminist analysis of pornography and sexual harassment, as put forward by MacKinnon and Dworkin, runs through this section.

Caputi highlights the relationship between pornography and mass murder of women by showing how misogyny is reflected in the culture. Diana Scully and Joseph Marolla (Chapter 2) also recognize the cultural and structural factors that encourage rape; they thus undermine the popular image of rape as the act of a "sick man." In interviewing convicted rapists they identified the "rewards of rape," such as revenge or punishment: "These men perceive rape as a rewarding, low risk act"—given that women frequently don't report rape.

Whereas Scully and Marolla base their analysis on interviews with men who rape, Judith Herman's analysis comes from interviewing survivors of a different form of abuse. What incest survivors tell us is another part of the same story. Herman's early work on incest (1977, 1981) together with Florence Rush's (1974) work formed the basis for the feminist analysis of Freud's perfidy. Freud claimed that his female patients were fantasizing when they told him the truth of their lives. The excerpts from Herman's work in Chapter 3 illuminate the link between the patriarchal family and the sexual abuse and exploitation of daughters.

Beth Schneider's chapter supports the analysis that workplace sexual harassment is also about sex and eroticized dominance. In a discussion shedding light on the Hill-Thomas hearings,[1] Schneider points out the few options available to women and that any response other than accommodation is regarded as deviant. As MacKinnon (1987) has stated:

> The moment we physically embody our complaint, and they can see us, the pornography of the process starts in earnest. I have begun to think that a major reason that many women do not bring sexual harassment complaints is that they know this. They cannot bear to have their personal account of sexual abuse reduced to a fantasy they invented, used to define them and to pleasure the finders of fact and the public. . . . I hear that they—in being publicly sexually humiliated by the legal system, as by the perpetrator—are pornography. The first time it happens, it is called freedom; the second time, it is called justice. (p. 111)

As the chapters move from murder, to rape, to incest, to harassment—with less and less physical violence to be seen—the theme of dominance, terror, and intimidation remains powerful. This shows clearly in Carole Sheffield's chapter, in which there is no physical violence, nor even physical contact. Voice alone serves to intimidate even terrorize. Sheffield states in Chapter 5: "The reactions of the women who felt physically and psychologically threatened by the calls support Dworkin's contention that women 'fear the languages of the rapist' as well as the rapist." Ironically but predictably, the phone companies' remedy for those phone calls, Caller ID, is opposed by all battered women's groups and most antirape groups because it endangers women. Needless to say, the phone companies benefit, exploiting our fear of crime without reducing our risk.

Taken together, the chapters in Part I set the stage for the case being made in this book that all these violations against women are connected; whether with a knife or a word, these violations serve to constrain the lives of women.

Pauline Bart's poem, "Prior Restraint," written while she took MacKinnon's course on the First Amendment at the UCLA law school and lived in an unfamiliar neighborhood, expresses the censorship women employ every day to avoid assaults. As of press time, Bart has been forbidden to teach classes in sociology or women's studies at her university, stemming from a 1992 incident with a male student who attempted in class to invalidate women's experience of violence. The poem was written in 1985.

NOTE

1. "Judge Clarence Thomas, . . . won confirmation as an Associate Justice of the Supreme Court . . . by one of the narrowest margins in history, . . . barely surviving an accusation by one of his assistants (Professor Anita Hill) that he had sexually harassed her." *The New York Times*, Oct.16, 1991.

REFERENCES

Apple, R. W., Jr. (1991, October 16). Senate confirms Thomas, 52-48, ending week of bitter battle: Time for healing. *The New York Times*, p.1.
Herman, J., with Hirschman, L. (1977). Father-daughter incest. *Signs, 2*(4),
Herman, J., with Hirschman, L. (1981). *Father-daughter incest.* Cambridge, MA: Harvard University Press.
MacKinnon, C. A. (1987). *Feminism unmodified.* Cambridge, MA: Harvard University Press.
Rush, F. (1974). The sexual abuse of children: A feminist point of view. In N. Connell & C. Wilson (Eds.), *Rape: The first sourcebook for women.* New York: New American Library.

Prior Restraint

Every day I censor myself
Pinning my blouse so "nothing" shows
Checking my clothes so I don't look vulnerable
Thinking of putting up my hair
So I don't resemble a mark
Putting out trash in the morning
So I won't be in the alley at night
Parking in well-lit places
Leaving my office while there are still people
Remembering what happened last weekend
Taking my cleaning in early
So I won't have to run the male gauntlet
Like last week.
I am censored constantly
My "free speech" cut from 25 to five minutes
My titles changed
Destroying the meter
And the politics
My articles expurgated of wit
So they will pass "peer review"
(the editors tell me)
Being canceled from conferences
And cut off the air
Because I might tell the truth
About the Chicago election.
Being threatened by my brother-in-law
Because I might tell the truth
About the men in my family.
I may not be asked to speak to sex educators on pornography
I may not say that pornography leads to desensitization
Leading to violence
Against women and children
Pornographers have protected speech
Leading to women to having unprotected lives
My speech is not protected
Because my speech
May lead to
Censorship.

© 1992 Pauline B. Bart (revised)

1 The Sexual Politics of Murder

JANE CAPUTI
University of New Mexico

When is an act sexed? When do you kill, or die, as a member of your gender, and when as whoever else you are? Are you ever anyone else?
—Catharine A. MacKinnon (1982b, p. 703)

Those of us who are . . . so much influenced by violence in the media, in particular pornographic violence, are not some kind of inherent monsters. We are your sons, and we are your husbands, and we grew up in regular families.
—Ted Bundy (Lamar, 1989, p. 34)

They made me out to be a monster . . . but, even my worst enemies admit that I was a good father.
—Joel Steinberg (Gross, 1989, p. 72)

In her book, *The Demon Lover: On the Sexuality of Terrorism*, Robin Morgan (1989) relates an incident that occurred during a civil rights movement meeting in the early 1960s. A group composed of members of both the Congress of Racial Equality (CORE) and the Student Nonviolent Coordinating Committee (with men outnumbering women three to one) had gathered in the wake of the disappearance of three civil rights workers in Mississippi. The FBI, local police, and the national guard had been dredging local lakes and rivers in search of the bodies. During

AUTHOR'S NOTE: I would like to thank Patricia Murphy, Gordene MacKenzie, Elena Ortiz, Mary Caputi, Elizabeth McNamara Caputi, and Shari Weinstein for their help in finding the news stories necessary for researching this chapter. Thanks also to Judith Lorber and Pat Miller for editorial suggestions. I dedicate this chapter to the memory of Elizabeth Ann Landcraft, Frankie Bell, and Althea Oakeley.

this search, the mutilated parts of an estimated 17 unidentified bodies were found, all but one of whom were women. Morgan recalls that a male CORE leader, upon hearing that news, agonized: "There's been a whole goddamned lynching we never even *knew* about. There's been some brother disappeared who never even got *reported*." When Morgan asked, Why only one lynching and what about the other 16 bodies, she was told: "Those were obviously *sex* murders. Those weren't political" (pp. 223-224).

Twenty years later, that perception still holds sway. For example, in the spring of 1984, Christopher Wilder raped and murdered a still unknown number of women. About to be apprehended by the police, he shot himself. The *Albuquerque Tribune* (April 14, 1984) commented:

Wilder's death leaves behind a mystery as to the motives behind the rampage of death and terror. With plenty of money, soft-spoken charm, a background in photography, and a part-time career on the glamorous sports car racing circuit, Wilder, 39, would have had no trouble attracting beautiful women. (p. 2)

This man not only murdered women but first extensively tortured them. Although the FBI refuses to release all the details of that abuse, it was revealed that Wilder had bound, raped, repeatedly stabbed his victims, and tortured them with electric shocks. One woman (who survived the attack) had even had her eyelids glued shut. Obviously, Wilder did not wish to date, charm, or attract women; his desire was to torment and destroy. From a feminist perspective there is no mystery behind Wilder's actions. His were sexually political murders, a form of murder rooted in a system of male supremacy in the same way that lynching is based in white supremacy. Such murder is, in short, a form of patriarchal terrorism.

That recognition, however, is impeded by longstanding tradition, for, as Kate Millett (1970) noted in her classic work, *Sexual Politics:*

We are not accustomed to associate patriarchy with force. So perfect is its system of socialization, so complete the general assent to its values, so long and so universally has it prevailed in human society, that it scarcely seems to require violent implementation. . . . And yet . . . control in patriarchal societies would be imperfect, even inoperable, unless it had the rule of force to rely upon, both in emergencies and as an ever-present instrument of intimidation. (pp. 44-45)

Early feminist analysts of rape (Brownmiller, 1975; Griffin, 1983; Russell, 1975) asserted that rape is not, as the common mythology insists, a crime of frustrated attraction, victim provocation, or uncontrollable biological urges. Nor is it one perpetrated only by an aberrant fringe. Rather, rape is a direct expression of sexual politics, a ritual enactment of male domination, a form of terror that functions to maintain the status quo. MacKinnon (1982a) further maintains that rape is not primarily an act of violence but is a *sexual* act in a culture where sexuality itself is a form of power, where oppression takes sexual forms, and where sexuality is the very "linchpin of gender inequality" (p. 533).

The murders of women and children—including torture and murder by husbands, lovers, and fathers, as well as that committed by strangers —are not some inexplicable evil or the domain of "monsters" only. On the contrary, sexual murder is the ultimate expression of sexuality as a form of power. Sex murder (what the FBI also terms "recreational murder") is part of a tradition that Mary Daly first named as gynocide (1973, p. 73). As further defined by Andrea Dworkin (1976), gynocide is "the systematic crippling, raping, and/or killing of women by men . . . the relentless violence perpetrated by the gender class men on the gender class women." She adds, "Under patriarchy, gynocide is the ongoing reality of life lived by women" (pp. 16, 19).

It is only through an extraordinary numbing that such a reality can be denied, for the terrible reminders are everywhere: in the ubiquitous posters pleading for information about women who have "disappeared"; in the daily newspaper reports of various public and private atrocities. In January and February 1989, along with all the grimly usual stories, three others demanded my attention. The first was the conviction of Joel Steinberg—the batterer, child killer, familiar family member, and self-proclaimed "good father"—for the death of his illegally adopted daughter. The second was the execution of the serial sex killer Ted Bundy, the ultimate stranger and paradigmatic "good son." The third also is related to serial murder: Hundreds of women, many of whom police say were working as prostitutes, have been murdered in the past 7 years on the West Coast by killers such as Seattle's "Green River Killer" and the Los Angeles "South Side Slayer." Currently, in San Diego County, 39 women who have been categorized as "prostitutes, drug addicts, and street denizens" have been killed since 1985, and in Los Angeles, police are investigating the murders of 69 prostitutes and the killings of 30 other women in what they term "street murders" (Overend & Wood, 1989;

Serrano, 1989). In this chapter, I will look at some of the issues raised
by these three separate but related gynocidal events.

MIXED SIGNALS[1]

He was giving me mixed signals. He would praise me and build my ego. On the
other hand, he was constantly critical. And he would strike me.

—Hedda Nussbaum (Hackett, 1989, p. 60)

On November 1, 1987, 6-year-old Lisa Steinberg was brought to a
hospital emergency room unconscious and with injuries that led to her
death 4 days later. The two people who had been raising her in their
Greenwich Village apartment—Joel Steinberg, a lawyer who had illegally adopted the child, and Hedda Nussbaum, the former children's
book editor he lived with and battered for some 12 years—were brought
in by the police for questioning. Suspicion was directed at Steinberg in
part because upon being told that the child had suffered at the very
least "permanent brain damage," he joked that "Lisa would never be an
Olympic athlete." At first, both Nussbaum and Steinberg were charged
with second-degree murder, but a year later, as the trial began, the
prosecution dropped the charges against Nussbaum. No longer a defendant, she became the key witness in the state's case. The trial was tele-
vised, and for 7 days, Nussbaum told of her abusive relationship with
Steinberg; videotapes of her extensively and permanently damaged body
and face were introduced as evidence. Massive national attention was
focused on the trial, with Nussbaum and Steinberg routinely described
as "national symbols" of domestic abuse. On January 30, 1989, Steinberg
was convicted of a lesser charge, first-degree manslaughter, in the death
of Lisa Steinberg.

Steinberg has consistently refused to admit his guilt; he denies that
either Lisa or Nussbaum was abused, claims that Lisa's death was
accidental or that Nussbaum killed her, and proclaims himself to be "a
victim." Yet, no matter how reprehensibly Steinberg behaves, he has
largely been overshadowed, particularly among feminists, by the troubling and controversial figure of Hedda Nussbaum. In part, this is due
to the enormous media attention; millions watched on live television as
the disfigured Nussbaum told her story of their mutual cocaine abuse,
his increasingly bizarre and torturous beatings over a period of 10 years,
her desire to protect and remain loyal to her batterer, and her overwhelming adoration of him. This case has opened up debate among

feminists as to the culpability of Nussbaum herself, her moral responsibility in the murder of the child. After beating Lisa into unconsciousness, Steinberg went out for 3 hours. During that time, Nussbaum did not call for emergency help because, as she testified, she was afraid such an action would show disloyalty to and distrust of Steinberg. When he returned, they freebased cocaine together and did not call for help until the following morning. Some feminists are now asking, Was Nussbaum victim or collaborator?

Steinberg had used not only physical force but also elaborate psychological manipulation to control Nussbaum. In 1982, Nussbaum lost her editor's job; the battering had caused her to miss too much work. By 1984, 8 years after they began living together, Nussbaum's physical appearance had deteriorated to such an extent that she rarely left the apartment. Thus isolated, she was particularly prey to Steinberg's mind games. Aided by cocaine, he convinced her that her friends and family (and eventually even the two children) were part of a hypnotic cult that was out to get them. Ironically, of course, the only cult involved was the cult of one that Steinberg was forming around himself. She later recalled: "I loved to listen to him talk. Basically, I worshiped him. He was the most wonderful man I had ever met. I believed he had supernatural, godlike power" (Hackett, 1989, p. 60). As in other patriarchal cults and religions, the female supplicant provided fodder for the pornographic fantasies of the empowered, god-identified man. Nussbaum recalled: "Many days and nights, Joel (Steinberg) would push me to fantasize about the cults, about the sexual encounters he said I had with all these people, and about pornographic videos I had supposedly made. Joel got me to believe these things happened, but I never had any recollection of them" (Weiss & Johnson, 1989, p. 90).

The battering of Nussbaum's body was clearly recapitulated in Steinberg's simultaneous battering and disfigurement of her memory and mind. That psychological manipulation took shape not only in the bizarre cult delusion but also in the quotidian mixed signals he consistently sent to her. Many who have studied or experienced abusive men would agree that such behavior is common, perhaps dramatized most vividly in the show of love and affection that often follows a beating. Indeed, contradictory messages—for example, dress glamorously, but if you are raped, you were asking for it—frequently riddle patriarchal communications. Not insignificantly then, one of the most blatant of such mixed messages can be found in the February 13, 1989, issue of *People Weekly.* The cover itself shows a large photo of an unsmiling and clearly disfigured Nussbaum, flanked by two smaller pictures of Steinberg and Lisa. Above, we read "Hedda's Story;" underneath, the copy asks the haunting question, "How could any mother, no matter how battered, fail to help her dying child?" In the story, told by a "close friend," Nussbaum is presented as the largely pathetic victim of a sadistic monster. We are told in great detail of the horrors of Steinberg's abuse:

> Steinberg had kicked her in the eye, strangled her, beaten her sexual organs, urinated on her, hung her in handcuffs from a chinning bar, lacerated a tear duct by poking his finger in the corner of her eye, broken her nose several times and pulled out clumps of hair while throwing her about their apartment. "Sometimes he'd take the blowtorch we used for freebasing and move it around me, making me jump. . . . I have burn marks all over my body from that. Joel told me he did this to improve my coordination." (Weiss & Johnson, 1989, pp. 89-90)

This last quote from Nussbaum is reiterated in a blown-up section on the left side of a two-page spread. On the right (p. 91) is an advertisement for Neutrogena soap. It features a large photo of a grinning woman, Cathy Guisewite, cartoonist and creator of the strip "Cathy," as well as a highlighted quote from the woman herself:

> I know all about eating a cheesecake after a bad date. People say, "You know exactly how I feel; I'm so relieved that somebody else sits in the closet and eats a cheesecake after a bad date." I think I verbalize for a lot of women the anxieties and insecurities we live out every day, like I'll buy anything that will promise me a miracle. But, I've bought the 25-step skin care and it's still in the bottom drawer, because I never have the energy even to get to Step Two. I always go back to Neutrogena Soap, because it's so simple. I mean, I stagger into the bathroom, I wash my face, and I can handle it. It's the one thing I don't have to torture myself about.

In order to understand the mode of communication here, it is useful to borrow a concept from television criticism. Raymond Williams (1974) has described a central characteristic of the television experience to be that of *flow*—that is, TV programs are surrounded by commercials and other programs, an uninterrupted following of one thing by another. One result of this flow is a powerful tendency to blur the contents together, a result encouraged by programmers "so that one program leads effortlessly into the next" (Adler, 1976, p. 7). Commercial advertisements that accompany programs also participate in this flow pattern.

Cognizant of this media structure, we might consider the basic message that the juxtaposition of article and ad in *People Weekly* delivers. Key themes in each are torture, feminine insecurities, anxieties, and masochism. We move from a graphic description of the torture of a former successful career woman (Nussbaum) to the smiling confession of egregious self-torture by a current career woman (Guisewite). (We might note that Guisewite's "torture" also can be traced to an "abusive" man, the "bad date" on account of whom she locked herself in a closet.) Moreover, after reading "Hedda's Story" (Weiss & Johnson, 1989) including its mention of the six times Nussbaum left Steinberg (the lifelong "bad date") only to return, what can we make of these strategically placed and highly resonant words of Guisewite: *"I never have the energy. . . . I always go back . . . because it's so simple. I mean, I stagger into the bathroom, I wash my face, and I can handle it."*

Nussbaum's torture by a man she continued to live with is appalling (though fascinating enough to rivet the nation), but Guisewite's self-torment is pitched as normal, representative, and smilingly cute. Though the article's authors superficially abhor Nussbaum's battering (all the while describing it in titillating detail), the entire media package subtextually is an attempt to instill in women the very attitudes (insecurity, masochism, self-abuse) that result from abuse. This is a mixed message par excellence, replicating the typical pattern of the batterer.

The patriarchal construction of female victimization is at the heart of the debate over Nussbaum's collusion. Susan Brownmiller, in a *New York Times* editorial (1989a) as well as in an article in *Ms.* (1989b), has argued vehemently that feminists should not support "unquestioningly the behaviors and actions of all battered women. . . . The point of feminism is to give women the courage to exercise free will, not to use the 'brainwashed victim's' excuse to explain away the behavior of a woman who surrenders her free will. Victimhood must no longer be an acceptable or excusable model of female behavior" (1989b, p. 61). Brownmiller condemns Nussbaum as a "narcissist," "empty at the core" (1989a, p. A19), and finds her a "participant in her own and Lisa's destruction" (1989b, p. 61). In some ways, particularly if one assumes the perspective of the abused child, such an argument might be compelling. But this argument collapses in a number of significant ways. First of all, it takes the burden and the focus off Steinberg; once again, the question centers not on how the man could have done this rape, battery, murder, incest, and so on, but on how the woman could have let him. Second, it seeks the reason for battery in the personality of the woman, in this case her "narcissism," and not in male dominance. Finally, Nussbaum's failure to summon emergency aid for Lisa as she lay unconscious was abusive, but an understanding of that behavior must *first* be sought not in Nussbaum's personality, but in her oppression in the nuclear family and in her status as a torture victim (Russell, 1982, pp. 273-285).

In her *Times* editorial, Brownmiller (1989a) deplores what she finds to be a common feminine identification with Nussbaum as both "simplistic and alarming." She further observes: "Significantly, no man of my acquaintance has felt the need to proclaim that he, but for the grace of God, could have been a Joel Steinberg. Decent, honorable men rushed to put a vast distance between themselves and Lisa's convicted killer" (p. 19). Yet, in some ways, much of women 's vituperation against Nussbaum equally might stem from an identification with her, followed by a horrified denial and distancing. Furthermore, and this is my central point, *of course* men both decent and indecent will rush to disassociate themselves from a man who has been publicly shown up as a batterer and murderer. Prior to public humiliation, or in the case of fictional representatives of the type, some of those very same men frequently gush with admiration for and identification with the sexual criminal. This male rush to disassociate (especially after the fact) is characteristic of a patriarchal culture in which awareness of institutionalized male supremacy is repressed. Thus, in myriad ways, the culture regularly doublethinks a distance between itself and sexual violence, denying the fundamental *normalcy* of that violence in a male supremacist culture and trying to paint it as the domain of psychopaths and "monsters" only (Cameron & Frazer, 1987; Caputi, 1987). The career of the sex killer Ted Bundy is especially instructive on this point.

THE BOYS NEXT DOOR

Most men just hate women. Ted Bundy killed them.
—Jimmy McDonough (1984, p. 3)

At some point when I was writing my book *The Age of Sex Crime* (1987), an analysis of the contemporary phenomenon of serial sex murder, I had a dream that I was back living in the white, middle-class, suburban neighborhood I grew up in and that Ted Bundy had moved in a few houses down. This was but one of several such dreams I had while engaged in the writing. Still it made a deep impression on me. Certainly, it meant that my subject was getting closer and closer to my psyche. But it also was significant that the nightmare figure was Ted Bundy, for Bundy is almost universally hailed as the killer who represented the all-American boy, the boy next door who did not marry, but rather killed, the girl next door.

Ted Bundy committed serial murder, and FBI statistics show that this new type of murder has increased drastically in the United States in the last 20 years. In addition, in 1984, the Justice Department estimated that there were at the very least 35 and possibly as many as 100 such killers roaming the country. A Justice Department official, Robert O. Heck, summed up the general situation:

> We all talk about Jack the Ripper; he killed five people [sic]. We all talk about the "Boston Strangler" who killed 13, and maybe "Son of Sam," who killed six. But we've got people [sic] out there now killing 20 and 30 people and more, and some of them don't just kill. They torture their victims in terrible ways and mutilate them before they kill them. Something's going on out there. It's an epidemic. (Lindsey, 1984, p. 7)

Although Heck's statement is superficially correct, his language obscures what actually is going on out there, for the "people" who torture, kill, and mutilate in this way are men, whereas their victims are characteristically females—women and girls—and to a lesser extent younger males. As this hierarchy indicates, these are crimes of sexually political, essentially *patriarchal,* domination. So hidden is this knowledge, however, that the criminologist Steven Egger (1984), after first noting that all known serial killers are male, goes on to observe: "This sexual differentiation may lead researchers to study maleness and its socialization as an etiological consideration. However, the lack of this obvious distinction has apparently precluded such study" (p. 351). Yet most researchers have not yet made that so obvious distinction because to do so would inevitably introduce the issue of sexual politics into sexual murder.

Although sexual force against women is endemic to patriarchy, the 20th century is marked by a new form of mass gynocide: the mutilation serial sex murder. This "age of sex crime" begins with the crimes of "Jack the Ripper," the still unidentified killer who in 1888 murdered and mutilated five London prostitutes. Patriarchal culture has enshrined "Jack the Ripper" as a mythic hero; he commonly appears as an immortal figure in literature, film, television, jokes, and other cultural products.

The function of such mythicization is twofold: to terrorize women and to empower and inspire men.

The unprecedented pattern laid down during the Ripper's original siege is now enacted with some regularity: the single, territorial, and sensationally nicknamed killer; socially powerless and scapegoated victims; some stereotyped feature ascribed in common to the victims (e.g., all coeds, redheads, prostitutes, and so on); a "signature" style of murder or mutilation; intense media involvement; and an accompanying incidence of imitation or "copycat" killings. Ripper-type killers include the "Lipstick Killer," the "Boston Strangler," the "Son of Sam," the "Hillside Strangler," the "Green River Killer," and the "South Side Slayer," to name only a few.

The Ripper myth received renewed attention in 1988, the centennial year of the original crimes. That occasion was celebrated by multiple retellings of the Ripper legend. In England, Ripper paraphernalia, such as a computer game, T-shirts, buttons, and cocktails appeared (Cameron, 1988). Retellings included a British-produced massively promoted made-for-TV movie, *Jack the Ripper;* an exploitation thriller called *Jack's Back,* about a killer of prostitutes in contemporary Los Angeles; and scores of new books on the master killer.

Within months of this anniversary celebration for the mythic father of sexual murder, the focus effortlessly and eerily shifted to a figurative son of that very father—a man who himself was portrayed as a paradigmatic American son, the "handsome," "intelligent," and "charming" Ted Bundy. In 1979, he was convicted of 3 women's deaths and is suspected of being responsible for perhaps 47 more. Bundy, like "Jack the Ripper," was a sex criminal who spawned a distinctive legend and was attended by a distinctive revelry. In the days preceding his death, his story dominated the mass media, memorializing and further mythicizing a killer who had already been the subject of scores of articles, five books, and a made-for-TV movie (where he was played by Mark Harmon, an actor *People Weekly* once gushed over as the "world's sexiest man"). The atmosphere surrounding his execution was repeatedly described as a "carnival" or "circus." On the morning Bundy went to the electric chair, hundreds (from photographs of the event, the crowd seemed to be composed largely of men) gathered across the street from the prison. Many wore specially designed costumes, waved banners proclaiming a "Bundy BBQ" or "I like my Ted well done," and chanted songs such as "He bludgeoned the poor girls, all over the head. Now we're all ecstatic, Ted Bundy is dead." A common journalistic metaphor for the overall scene was that of a tailgate party before a big game. Indications of a spreading Bundy cult continue to appear: A student group at the University of New Mexico in April 1989 offered a program showing a tape of Bundy's final interview. The poster advertising that event displayed a likeness of the killer under the headline: "A Man With Vision. A Man With Direction. A Prophet of Our Times. . . . Bundy: The Man, the Myth, the Legend." This sort of spontaneous outpouring of folk sentiment regarding Ted Bundy was not without precedent. In the late 1970s, when he was awaiting trial for the murder of Caryn Campbell in Aspen, Colorado, Bundy managed to escape twice. The first time he was caught and returned to custody; the second time he was successful and traveled to Florida. But upon the news of his escapes (particularly the first) a phenomenal reaction occurred. All observers concur: "In Aspen, Bundy had become a folk hero" (Larsen, 1980, p. 182); "Ted achieved the status of Billy the Kid at least" (Rule, 1980, p. 255); "Aspen reacted as if Bundy were some sort of Robin Hood instead of a suspected mass murderer. A folklore sprang up out of the thin Rocky Mountain air" (Nordheimer, 1978, p. 46). T-shirts appeared reading, "Ted Bundy is a One Night Stand." Radio KSNO programmed a Ted Bundy request hour, playing songs like "Ain't No Way to Treat a Lady." A local restaurant offered a "Bundyburger," consisting of nothing more than a plain roll: "Open it and see the meat has fled," explained a sign. Yet after his second escape, the FBI took Bundy seriously enough to name him to their 10 Most Wanted list, seeking him "in connection with 36 similar-type sexual slayings throughout several Western states."

Just as Bundy's white, young, generally middle-class victims were stereotypically (and with marked racist and classist bias) universalized as "anyone's daughters," Bundy himself was depicted as the fatherland's (almost) ideal son—handsome, intelligent, a former law student, a rising star in Seattle's Republican party. And although that idealization falls apart upon close examination (Bundy's photographs show an ordinary face, and he had to drop out of law school due to bad grades), it provided an attractive persona for purposes of identification. As several feminist analysts (Lacy, 1982-1983; Millett, 1970; Walkowitz, 1982) have noted, a recurrent and vivid pattern accompanying episodes of sensationalized sex murder is ordinary male identification with the sex killer, as revealed in "jokes, innuendoes, veiled threats (*I* might be the Strangler, you know)" (Lacy, 1982-1983, p. 61).

After his first escape, the male identification was with Bundy as an outlaw rebel-hero. But subsequently, Bundy did the supremely unmanly thing of getting caught; moreover, at the last moment he confessed to his crimes and manifested fear of death. No longer qualifying as hero, Bundy was now cast into the alternate role of scapegoat. The "blood-thirsty revelers" outside the prison gates, through their objectification of the victims and lust for death, still mirrored Bundy, but now delight-edly demanded that the preeminent patriarchal son die as a token sacri-fice for his and their sins.

In the final days before his execution, Bundy spoke directly about his cultural construction as a sex killer, telling James Dobson, a psycholo-gist and religious broadcaster, that since his youth he had been obsessed with pornography. Bundy claimed that pornography inspired him to act out his torture and murder fantasies. Five years earlier, another inter-viewer (Michaud & Aynesworth, 1983) had reported a similar conver-sation with Bundy:

> He told me that long before there was a need to kill there were juvenile fantasies fed by photos of women in skin magazines, suntan oil advertise-ments, or jiggly starlets on talk shows. He was transfixed by the sight of women's bodies on provocative display. . . . Crime stories fascinated him. He read pulp detective magazines and gradually developed a store of knowledge about criminal techniques—what worked and what didn't. That learning remained incidental to the central thrill of reading about the abuse of female images, but nonetheless he was schooling himself. (p. 117)

Bundy also spoke for himself (although in the third person, as he had not yet decided to openly admit his guilt):

> Maybe he focused on pornography as a vicarious way of experiencing what his peers were experiencing in reality. . . . Then he got sucked into the more sinister doctrines that are implicit in pornography—the use, the abuse, the possession of women as objects. . . . A certain percentage of it [pornogra-phy] is devoted toward literature that explores situations where a man, in the context of a sexual encounter, in one way or another engages in some sort of violence toward a woman, or the victim. There are, of course, a whole host of substitutions that could come under that particular heading. Your girlfriend, your wife, a stranger, children—whatever—a whole host of victims are found in this literature. And in this literature, they are treated as victims. (p. 117)

Bundy's self-confessed movement from pornography (reportedly introduced to him at an early age by a grandfather who beat his wife, regularly
assaulted other people, and tormented animals) to actual sexual assault
is consistent with testimony from other sex offenders, including sex
murderers, who claim that viewing pornography affected their criminal
behavior (Caputi, 1987; Einsiedel, 1986).

Diana E. H. Russell (1988) has proposed a theoretical model of the
causative role of pornography in violence against women. Russell first
distinguishes between pornography and erotica, drawing upon a definition of pornography as "sexually explicit material that represents or
describes degrading or abusive sexual behavior so as to endorse and/or
recommend the behavior as described" (Longino, 1980, p. 44). She defines erotica as "sexual representations premised on equality" (Russell,
1993; Russell, 1988, p. 46). Using the findings from a range of social
research from the past decade, Russell argues that pornography predis-
poses or intensifies a predisposition in some men to rape women and
that it can undermine some men's internal or social inhibitions against
acting out sexually violent behavior. Bundy's testimony clearly supports that model.

Bundy's assertions released a wave of scorn, ridicule, and fury in the
mainstream press, with some commentators seemingly more angry at
his aspersions on pornography than at his crimes. As one columnist
(Leo, 1989) fulminated:

> As Bundy told it, he was a good, normal fellow, an 'all-American boy'
> properly raised by diligent parents, though one would have liked to hear
> more about his 'diligent' mother. While nothing of this mother-son rela-
> tionship is known, a hatred of women virulent enough to claim 50 lives
> does not usually spring full-blown from the reading of obscene magazines.
> (p. 53)

Once again, normalcy as well as "maleness and its socialization" are
vehemently discarded as an etiological consideration for sexual murder;
misogynist myth prevails and the finger of blame is pointed unswerv-
ingly at a woman. Since Bundy's execution, an extensive article has
appeared in *Vanity Fair*; predictably, it absolves pornography and instead condemns Louise Bundy as responsible for the evolution of her
son into a "depraved monster" (MacPherson, 1989).

A companion chorus of voices suggests that we cannot take Bundy
seriously because Dobson, the fundamentalist crusader, led Bundy to

his assertions to further his own agenda. Thus, once again, the feminist connection between violence against women and pornography is potentially discredited by its association with fundamentalism. Yet few feminists would agree with the religious Right's claim that pornography is the sole or root cause of violence against women. Rather, pornography (as well as its diffusions through mainstream culture) is a modern mode for communicating and constructing patriarchy's necessary fusion of sex and violence, for sexualizing torture. Clearly, that imperative has assumed other forms historically: the political operations of military dictatorships, the enslavement of Africans in the "new world," witch hunting and inquisitions by the Christian church and state, and so on. The basic elements for a gynocidal campaign—an ideology of male supremacy, a vivid imagination of (particularly female) sexual filth, loathing of eroticism, belief in the sanctity of marriage and the family, and the containment of women in male-controlled in-stitutions—structure fundamentalism's very self-serving opposition to pornography.

Finally, it was claimed that Bundy, a characteristic manipulator, was simply manipulating and lying one last time, trying to absolve himself in his 11th hour by blaming society. Yet a feminist analysis would not accept the equation that to recognize the responsibility of society for sexually political murder is to absolve the murderer. Rather, it would point to the connection between Bundy and his society, naming Bundy as that society's henchman (albeit, like other sex criminals, a freelancer) in the maintenance of patriarchal order through force. Indeed, we might further recognize Bundy as a martyr for the patriarchal state, one who after getting caught had to pay for his fervor, the purity of his misogyny, and his attendant celebrity with his life.

EVERYONE'S SISTERS

There was wide public attention in the Ted [Bundy] case . . . because the victims resembled everyone's [sic] daughter. . . . But not everybody relates to prostitution on the Pacific Highway.
—Robert Keppel, member of the Green River Task Force (Starr, 1984, p. 106)

The victims were universally described as runaways, prostitutes, or drug addicts who "deserved" to die because of how they lived. The distorted portrayal of the girls and women could be expected in a city notorious for its racism, but there was a particular sexist turn, because the victims were not only Black, but female.
—Barbara Smith (1981, p. 68; on a 1979 series of murders in Boston)

Some of the victims were prostitutes, but perhaps the saddest part of this case is that some were not.

—Sir Michael Havers, prosecuting counsel at the trial of Peter Sutcliffe, the "Yorkshire Ripper" (Holloway, 1981, p. 39)

There'd be more response from the police if these were San Marino house-wives. . . . If you're Black and living on the fringe, your life isn't worth much.

—Margaret Prescod, founder of the Black Coalition Fighting Back Serial Murders (Uehling, 1986, p. 28)

Ted Bundy's victims were young white women and were consistently described in the press as "beautiful" with "long, brown hair." We can recognize some of this description as a fetishization meant to further eroticize the killings for the public. But although some highly cele-brated killers such as Bundy or David Berkowitz, the "Son of Sam," chose victims on the basis of their correspondence to a pornographic, objectifying, and racist ideal, the majority of victims of serial killers are women who, as Steven Egger (1984) noted, "share common char-acteristics of what are perceived to be prestigeless, powerless, and/or lower socioeconomic groups" (p. 348), that is, prostitute women, run-aways, "street women," women of color, impoverished women, single and elderly women, and so on. The Bundy murders consistently aroused not only a unique folklore and ritual revelry but also a public display of mourning because in the first place mainstream men could readily identify with Bundy and also because sexual murder, like rape, is understood as a property crime. A far different societal response is forthcoming when the women killed are not white, not "family women," and not middle class. A pattern of police officials waiting an unreason-able amount of time before organizing a concentrated effort to catch a killer, failing to warn a community, refusing to initiate community involvement, prejudicially labeling victims, and ignoring community input has marked nearly all investigations of the murders of "prestige-less" women (Grant, 1988a, 1988b; Jones & Wood, 1989; Serrano, 1989).

In the "Jack the Ripper" crimes, all of the victims were prostitute women. The killer (or far more likely, someone pretending to be the killer) wrote to the press a letter that not only originated the famous nickname, but also boasted: "I am down on whores and I shan't quit ripping them until I do get buckled." In the late 1970s, a gynocidal killer was active in northern England; the first victims were all prostitute women. Perpetuating the myth of the immortal and recurring sex crim-inal, the men of the press nicknamed him the "Yorkshire Ripper." As in many cases involving the serial murder of prostitute women, including those of the "Green River Killer," the "South Side Slayer," and a current series of murders of "prestigeless" women in San Diego County, a great deal of controversy has attended police handling, or rather, mishandling, of the case (Serrano, 1989). In the wake of that controversy in Yorkshire, the British press has claimed that the major problem that the police faced in the early years of that investigation was "apathy over the killing of prostitutes." Police work, it was declared, depends upon public interest, cooperation, and support; and, as the London *Times* noted, "Such was the apathy at the time that it was virtually nil" (Osman & Ford, 1981, p. 5). Ironically, in Yorkshire, such open attitudes of hostility to prostitute women and apathy toward their murders were openly expressed not only by the public but also by the police themselves.

Four years after the first mutilation and murder, the killer had begun to target nonprostitute women, and West Yorkshire's Constable Jim Hobson issued an extraordinary statement as an "anniversary plea" to the killer: "He has made it clear that he hates prostitutes. Many people do. We, as a police force, will continue to arrest prostitutes." Here, Hobson matter-of-factly aligns Ripper motives and actions to larger social interests as well as police goals. He goes on, shifting voice to a direct appeal to the killer: "But the Ripper is now killing innocent girls. That indicates your mental state and that you are in urgent need of medical attention. You have made your point. Give yourself up before another innocent woman dies" (J. Smith, 1982, p. 11). From such official statements we learn that it is normal to hate prostitute women; the killer is even assured of social solidarity in this emotion. His deeds, it seems, only become socially problematic when he turns to so-called innocent girls. Over in the Americas, one consultant on the "Green River Killer" case, the psychiatrist John Liebert, offered his expert opinion that serial murderers either idealize women or degrade them, seeing women as "'angels or whores,' with no sensible middle ground" (Berger, 1984, p. 1). Once again, we are at an utter loss in distinguishing the point of view of the ostensibly deviant sex killer from that of his pursuers or his society. Moreover, the notion that this distinction has any abiding reality in the sex killer's mind is both erroneous and dangerous.

In the mid-1980s, at least 17 women, characterized by the police as prostitutes, were murdered within a 40-mile radius in South Central Los Angeles, a primarily African-American neighborhood; all but 3 of the victims were African-Americans. The police waited until 10 women were killed before notifying the public that a serial murderer was operating and then waited until there were 4 more deaths before forming a task force. In response to police and media neglect, Margaret Prescod, a long-time public spokeswoman for US PROS (a national network of women who work in the sex industry and their supporters) founded the Black Coalition Fighting Back Serial Murders. Rachel West (1987) notes:

> The Black Coalition has stated again and again that they are not convinced that all the women murdered were prostitutes and that the police have offered little evidence to support that claim. When the police could not dig up a prostitution arrest record on victim 17, they immediately said, "but she was a street woman." This statement reflects the attitude of the police toward poor women generally, especially if they are black. We all know only too well that any of us at any time can be labeled a prostitute woman, if we dare step out of line in the way we speak and dress, in the hours we keep, the number of friends we have, or if we are "sexual outlaws" of any kind. (p. 285)

West further observes that in many other instances of serial murder, the killer might begin with prostitute women, but then moves on to women of all types (as in the "Hillside Strangler" killings). When the police or press describe the murdered women as prostitutes, it lulls nonprostitute women into a false feeling of safety. It plays upon sexist and frequently racist prejudices to mute the seriousness of the murders, and—most effectively—it diverts the blame to the victim.

In October 1888, Charles Warren, police chief in charge of the "Jack the Ripper" case, pontificated to the press: "The police can do nothing as long as the victims unwittingly connive at their own destruction. They take the murderer to some retired spot, and place themselves in such a position that they can be slaughtered without a sound being heard" (Cameron & Frazer, 1987, p. 20). That sentiment was echoed, one century later, in a piece in the *Los Angeles Times* (Boxall, 1989) titled, "Prostitutes: Easy Prey for Killers." It portrays "drug-dazed" women, good daughters gone bad, and contains a quote from Commander William Booth of the Los Angeles police department: "I think that's the highest-risk occupation there is. Mercenaries are way behind prostitutes. . . . There is nothing that carries the risk with it, in peacetime, as streetwalking prostitution" (p. 1). The same article states: "Police sweeps have greatly reduced streetwalking in Hollywood, police say, leaving the gritty main drags of South-Central the city's streetwalking center. Elsewhere in Los Angeles, prostitution tends to take more sophisticated, expensive and less hazardous forms, such as escort services" (p. 23). Thus we can surmise that police actions have contributed toward creating a more dangerous city for South Central women; moreover, these women, targeted because of their race and class, are in far greater danger than women in moneyed, white areas. Clearly, the illegality of prostitution and institutionalized harassment by the police contribute to making prostitution such a "high-risk" occupation.

Although, as far as I know, there are no national statistics kept on the number of prostitutes murdered annually, the Los Angeles police claim that there have been 69 murders of prostitute women and 30 women killed in what they call "street murders" in the past 4 years. Assuredly, those numbers register appalling danger. Yet the Steinberg case might remind us that each year 30 percent of all women murdered are killed by their husbands and lovers, about 1,500 women per year (*Uniform Crime Reports,* 1987, p. 11), and that *at least* 1.8 million women are beaten by husbands and lovers annually (Summers, 1989, p. 54). Despite blandishments directed toward stereotypical "angels" and "good girls," wifehood seems to rank right up there with prostitution as an endemically unsafe occupation. Faced with such statistics, the invidious distinctions collapse, and we realize with Rachel West (1987) that "the rights of prostitute women are the rights of all women" (p. 285).

As I worked on the conclusion to this piece, I listened to a National Public Radio news program ("Morning Edition," June 7, 1989) reporting that nine women (all of whom were described as prostitutes or drug addicts) had been murdered in the past year in New Bedford, Massachusetts, the site of a notorious gang rape (Chancer, 1987). Two other women have been missing for months. A serial killer is suspected; "apathy" is said to be the primary response of the mainstream New Bedford community. Obviously, we have heard this story before. Yet the ascription of "apathy," so common in such cases, is really quite misleading. The reigning, though denied, mood is *hatred,* sexually political hatred. A "hate crime" is conventionally defined as "any assault, intimidation or harassment that is due to the victim's race, religion or ethnic background" (Malcolm, 1989, p. A12). That definition obviously must be expanded to include gender (as well as sexual preference). Vast numbers of women are now suffering and dying from various forms of hate crime worldwide, including neglect, infanticide, genital mutilation, battering, rape, and murder. What men might call "peacetime," researcher Lori Heise (1989) truthfully names a "global war on women."

NOTE

1. Part of this section previously appeared in my review of Susan Brownmiller's *Waverly Place* (Caputi, 1989).

REFERENCES

Adler, R. (1976). Introduction. In R. Adler & D. Cater (Eds.), *Television as a cultural force* (pp. 1-16). New York: Praeger.

Albuquerque Tribune. (1984, April 14). Blood trail ends: Brother says he's glad Wilder's killing is over. P. 2.

Berger, J. (1984, August 27). Traits shared by mass killers remain unknown to experts. *New York Times,* p. 1.

Boxall, B. (1989, March 21). Prostitutes: Easy prey for killers. *Los Angeles Times,* pp. 1, 23. Copyright 1989, *Los Angeles Times.* Reprinted by permission.

Brownmiller, S. (1975). *Against our will: Men, women and rape.* New York: Simon & Schuster.

Brownmiller, S. (1989a, February 2). Hedda Nussbaum: Hardly a heroine. *New York Times,* p. A19.

Brownmiller, S. (1989b, April). Madly in love. *Ms.,* pp. 56-61.

Cameron, D. (1988). That's entertainment? Jack the Ripper and the celebration of sexual violence. *Trouble and Strife, 13,* 17-19.

Cameron, D., & Frazer, E. (1987). *The lust to kill: A feminist investigation of sexual murder.* New York: New York University Press.

Caputi, J. (1987). *The age of sex crime.* Bowling Green, OH: Bowling Green State University Press.

Caputi, J. (1989, May). Stranger than fiction [Review of *Waverly Place*]. *Women's Review of Books, 6,* 10-11.

Chancer, L. S. (1987). New Bedford, Massachusetts, March 6, 1983-March 22, 1984: The 'before and after' of a group rape. *Gender & Society, 1,* 239-260.

Daly, M. (1973). *Beyond god the father: Toward a philosophy of women's liberation.* Boston: Beacon.

Dworkin, A. (1976). *Our blood: Discourses and prophecies on sexual politics.* New York: Harper & Row.

Dworkin, A. (1981). *Pornography: Men possessing women.* New York: Perigee.

Egger, S. A. (1984). A working definition of serial murder and the reduction of linkage blindness. *Journal of Police Science and Administration, 12,* 348-357.

Einsiedel, E. F. (1986). *Social Science Report* (Prepared for the Attorney General's Commission on Pornography). Washington, DC: U.S. Department of Justice.

Grant, J. M. (1988a, June). Who's killing us? Part one. *Sojourner: The Women's Forum,* pp. 20-21.

Grant, J. M. (1988b, July). Who's killing us? Part two. *Sojourner: The Women's Forum,* pp. 16-18.

Griffin, S. (1983). Rape: The all-American crime. In *Made from the earth: An anthology of writings* (pp. 39-58). New York: Harper & Row.

Gross, K. (1989, March 13). Denying his guilt, Joel Steinberg tells how he cared for the child he killed and the lover he beat. *People Weekly,* p. 72.

Hackett, G. (1989, December 12). A tale of abuse. *Newsweek,* p. 60.

Heise, L. (1989, April 9). The global war against women. *Washington Post,* Sec. B, p. 1.

Holloway, W. (1981). "I Just Wanted to Kill a Woman" Why: The ripper and male sexuality. *Feminist Review, 9,* 33-40.

Jones, J., & Wood, T. (1989, February 25). Sheriff's deputy held in prostitute's killings. *Los Angeles Times,* p. 1.

Lacy, S. (1982-1983, Fall/Winter). In mourning and in rage (with analysis aforethought). *Ikon,* pp. 60-67.

Lamar, J. V., Jr. (1989, February 6). "I Deserve Punishment." *Time,* p. 34.

Larsen, R. W. (1980). *Bundy: The deliberate stranger.* Englewood Cliffs, NJ: Prentice-Hall.

Leo, J. (1989, February 6). Crime: that's entertainment. *U.S. News & World Report,* p. 53.

Lindsey, R. (1984, January 21). Officials cite rise in killers who roam U.S. for victims. *New York Times,* p. 1.

Longino, H. E. (1980). What is pornography? In L. Lederer (Ed.), *Take back the night* (pp. 40-54). New York: William Morrow.

McDonough, J. (1984). I can teach you how to read the book of life. *Bill Landis' Sleazoid Express, 3,*(7), 3-5.

MacKinnon, C. A. (1982a). Feminism, Marxism, method, and the state: An agenda for theory. *Signs: Journal of Women in Culture and Society, 7,* 515-544.

MacKinnon, C. A. (1982b). Toward feminist jurisprudence. *Stanford Law Review, 34,* 703-737.

MacPherson, M. (1989, May). The roots of evil. *Vanity Fair,* pp. 140-448, 188-198.

Malcolm, A. (1989, May 12). New efforts developing against the hate crime. *New York Times,* p. A12.

Michaud, S. G., & Aynesworth, H. (1983). *The only living witness.* New York: Linden.

Millett, K. (1970). *Sexual politics.* Garden City, NY: Doubleday.

Morgan, R. (1989). *The demon lover: On the sexuality of terrorism.* New York: Norton.

Nordheimer, J. (1978, December 10). All-American boy on trial. *New York Times Magazine,* pp. 46ff.

Osman, A., & Ford, R. (1981, May 23). Lost chances, bad luck and malice of the tapes foiled untiring search. *The* (London) *Times,* p. 5.

Overend, W., & Wood, T. (1989, February 26). Deputy "devastated" by arrest in probe of prostitute deaths. *Los Angeles Times,* pp. CC1, 5.

Rule, A. (1980). *The stranger beside me.* New York: New American Library.

Russell, D.E.H. (1975). *The politics of rape: The victim's perspective.* New York: Stein & Day.

Russell, D.E.H. (1982). *Rape in marriage.* New York: Macmillan.

Russell, D.E.H. (1988). Pornography and rape: A causal model. *Political Psychology, 9,* 41-73.

Russell, D.E.H. (Ed.). (1993). *Making violence sexy: Feminist views on pornography.* New York: Teachers College.

Serrano, R. A. (1989, February 26). S. D. serial-killer probe mimics "error" pattern of Green River slayings. *Los Angeles Times* (San Diego County), Part II, p. 1.

Smith, B. (1981). Introduction to "Twelve black women: Why did they die?" In F. Delacoste & F. Newman (Eds.), *Fight back! Feminist resistance to male violence* (pp. 68-69). Minneapolis, MN: Cleis.

Smith, J. (1982, May/June). Getting away with murder. *New Socialist,* pp. 10-12.

Starr, M. (1984, November 26). The random killers. *Newsweek,* p. 106.
Summers, A. (1989, April). The Hedda conundrum. *Ms.,* p. 54.
Uehling, M. D. (1986, June 9). The LA slayer. *Newsweek,* p. 28.
Uniform Crime Reports. (1987). Washington, DC: U.S. Department of Justice, Federal Bureau of Investigation.
Walkowitz, J. R. (1982). Jack the Ripper and the myth of male violence. *Feminist Studies, 8,* 543-574.
Weiss, N., with Johnson, B. (1989, February 13). A love betrayed: A brief life lost. *People Weekly,* pp. 89-90.
West, R. (1987). US PROstitutes Collective. In F. Delacoste & P. Alexander (Eds.), *Sex work: Writings by women in the sex industry* (pp. 279-289). Pittsburgh, PA: Cleis.
Williams, R. (1974). *Television: Technology and cultural form.* Glasgow: Fontana/Collins.

2 "Riding the Bull at Gilley's": Convicted Rapists Describe the Rewards of Rape

DIANA SCULLY
JOSEPH MAROLLA
Virginia Commonwealth University

Over the past several decades, rape has become a "medicalized" social problem. That is to say, the theories used to explain rape are predicated on psychopathological models. They have been generated from clinical experiences with small samples of rapists, often the therapists' own clients. Although these psychiatric explanations are most appropriately applied to the atypical rapist, they have been generalized to all men who rape and have come to inform the public's view on the topic.

Two assumptions are at the core of the psychopathological model: that rape is the result of idiosyncratic mental disease and that it often includes an uncontrollable sexual impulse (Scully & Marolla, 1985). For example, the presumption of psychopathology is evident in the often cited work of Nicholas Groth (1979). Although Groth emphasizes the non-sexual nature of rape (power, anger, sadism), he also concludes, "Rape is always a symptom of some psychological dysfunction, either temporary and transient or chronic and repetitive" (Groth, 1979, p. 5). Thus, in the

AUTHORS' NOTE: This research was supported by a grant (R01 MH33013) from the National Center for the Prevention and Control of Rape, National Institute of Mental Health. We are indebted to the Virginia Department of Corrections for its cooperation and assistance in this research. Correspondence to: Scully, Department of Sociology/Anthropology, Virginia Commonwealth University, 312 Shafer Street, Richmond, Virginia 23284.
© 1985 by the Society for the Study of Social Problems. Reprinted from *Social Problems,* Vol. 32 No. 3 (February, 1985), pp. 251-263. Reprinted by permission.

psychopathological view, rapists lack the ability to control their behavior; they are "sick" individuals from the "lunatic fringe" of society.

In contradiction to this model, empirical research has repeatedly failed to find a consistent pattern of personality type or character disorder that reliably discriminates rapists from other groups of men (Fisher & Rivlin, 1971; Hammer & Jacks, 1955; Rada, 1978). Indeed, other research has found that fewer than 5 percent of men were psychotic when they raped (Abel, Becker, & Skinner, 1980).

Evidence indicates that rape is not a behavior confined to a few "sick" men but that many men have the attitudes and beliefs necessary to commit a sexually aggressive act. In research conducted at a midwestern university, Koss and her co-workers reported that 85 percent of men defined as highly sexually aggressive had victimized women with whom they were romantically involved (Koss & Leonard, 1984). A survey quoted in *The Chronicle of Higher Education* estimates that more than 20 percent of college women are the victims of rape and attempted rape (Meyer, 1984). These findings mirror research published several decades earlier that also concluded that sexual aggression was commonplace in dating relationships (Kanin, 1957, 1965, 1967, 1969; Kirkpatrick & Kanin, 1957).[1] In their study of 53 college males, Malamuth, Haber, and Feshback (1980) found that 51 percent indicated a likelihood that they, themselves, would rape if assured of not being punished.

In addition, the frequency of rape in the United States makes it unlikely that responsibility rests solely with a small lunatic fringe of psychopathic men. Johnson (1980), calculating the lifetime risk of rape to girls and women aged 12 and over, makes a similar observation. Using Law Enforcement Assistance Association and Bureau of Census Crime Victimization studies, he calculated that, excluding sexual abuse in marriage and assuming equal risk to all women, 20 to 30 percent of girls now 12 years old will suffer a violent sexual attack during the remainder of their lives. Interestingly, the lack of empirical support for the psychopathological model has not resulted in the demedicalization of rape, nor does it appear to have diminished the belief that rapists are "sick" aberrations in their own culture. This is significant because of the implications and consequences of the model.

A central assumption in the psychopathological model is that male sexual aggression is unusual or strange. This assumption removes rape from the realm of the everyday or "normal" world and places it in the category of "special" or "sick" behavior. As a consequence, men who rape are cast in the role of outsider and a connection with normative male behavior is avoided. Because in this view, the source of the behavior is thought to be within the psychology of the individual, attention is diverted away from culture or social structure as contributing factors. Thus, the psychopathological model ignores evidence that links sexual aggression to environmental variables and that suggests that rape, like all behavior, is learned.

CULTURAL FACTORS IN RAPE

Culture is a factor in rape, but the precise nature of the relationship between culture and sexual violence remains a topic of discussion. Ethnographic data from preindustrial societies show the existence of rape-free cultures (Broude & Green, 1976; Sanday, 1979), though explanations for the phenomena differ.[2] Sanday (1979) relates sexual violence to contempt for female qualities and suggests that rape is part of a culture of violence and an expression of male dominance. In contrast, Blumberg (1979) argues that in preindustrial societies women are more likely to lack important life options and to be physically and politically oppressed where they lack economic power relative to men. That is, in preindustrial societies relative economic power enables women to win some immunity from men's use of force against them.

Among modern societies, the frequency of rape varies dramatically, and the United States is among the most rape prone of all. In 1980, for example, the rate of reported rape and attempted rape for the United States was 18 times higher than the corresponding rate for England and Wales (West, 1983). Spurred by the women's movement, feminists have generated an impressive body of theory regarding the cultural etiology of rape in the United States. Representative of the feminist view, Griffin (1971) called rape "The All-American Crime."

In the feminist perspective rape is an act of violence and social control that functions to "keep women in their place" (Brownmiller, 1975; Kasinsky, 1975; Russell, 1975). Feminists see rape as an extension of normative male behavior, the result of conformity or overconformity to the values and prerogatives that define the traditional male sex role. That is, traditional socialization encourages males to associate power, dominance, strength, virility, and superiority with masculinity, and submissiveness, passivity, weakness, and inferiority with femininity. Furthermore, males are taught to have expectations about their level of sexual needs and expectations for corresponding female accessibility that function to justify forcing sexual access. The justification for forced sexual access is buttressed by legal, social, and religious definitions of women as male property and sex as an exchange of goods (Bart, 1979). Socialization prepares women to be "legitimate" victims and men to be potential offenders (Weis & Borges, 1973). Herman (1984) concludes that the United States is a rape culture because both genders are socialized to regard male aggression as a natural and normal part of sexual intercourse.

Feminists view pornography as an important element in a larger system of sexual violence; they see pornography as an expression of a rape-prone culture in which women are seen as objects available for use by men (Morgan, 1980; Wheeler, 1985). Based on his content analysis of 428 "adults only" books, Smith (1976) makes a similar observation. He notes that not only is rape presented as part of normal male/female sexual relations, but the woman, despite her terror, is always depicted as sexually aroused to the point of cooperation. In the end, she is ashamed but physically gratified. The message—women desire and enjoy rape—has more potential for damage than the image of the violence per se.[3]

The fusion of these themes—sex as an impersonal act, the victim's uncontrollable orgasm, and the violent infliction of pain—is commonplace in the actual accounts of rapists. Scully and Marolla (1984) demonstrated that many convicted rapists denied their crime and attempted to justify their rapes by arguing that their victim had enjoyed herself despite the use of a weapon and the infliction of serious injuries, or even death. In fact, many argued, they had been instrumental in making *her* fantasy come true.

The images projected in pornography contribute to a vocabulary of motive that trivializes and neutralizes rape and that might lessen the internal controls that otherwise would prevent sexually aggressive behavior. Men who rape use this culturally acquired vocabulary to justify their sexual violence.

Another consequence of the application of psychopathology to rape is it leads one to view sexual violence as a special type of crime in which the motivations are subconscious and uncontrollable rather than overt and deliberate as with other criminal behavior. Black (1983) offers an approach to the analysis of criminal and/or violent behavior that when applied to rape avoids this bias.

Black (1983) suggests that it is theoretically useful to ignore that crime is criminal in order to discover what such behavior has in common with other kinds of conduct. From his perspective, much of the crime in modern societies, as in preindustrial societies, can be interpreted as a form of "self-help" in which the actor is expressing a grievance through aggression and violence. From the actor's perspective, the victim is deviant and his own behavior is a form of social control in which the objective may be conflict management, punishment, or revenge. For example, in societies where women are considered the property of men, rape is sometimes used as a means of avenging the victim's husband or father (Black, 1983). In some cultures rape is used as a form of punishment. Such was the tradition among the puritanical, patriarchal Cheyenne where men were valued for their ability as warriors. It was the Cheyenne custom that a wife suspected of being unfaithful could be "put on the prairie" by her husband. Military confreres then were invited to "feast" on the prairie (Hoebel, 1954; Llewellyn & Hoebel, 1941). The ensuing mass rape was a husband's method of punishing his wife.

Black's (1983) approach is helpful in understanding rape because it forces one to examine the goals that some men have learned to achieve through sexually violent means. Thus, one approach to understanding why some men rape is to shift attention from individual psychopathology to the important question of what rapists gain from sexual aggression and violence in a culture seemingly prone to rape.

In this chapter, we address this question using data from interviews conducted with 114 convicted, incarcerated rapists. (For a complete discussion see Scully, 1990.) Elsewhere, we discussed the vocabulary of motive, consisting of excuses and justifications, that these convicted rapists used to explain themselves and their crime (Scully & Marolla, 1984).[4] The use of these culturally derived excuses and justifications allowed them to view their behavior as either idiosyncratic or situationally appropriate and thus reduced their sense of moral responsibility for their actions. Having disavowed deviance, these men revealed how they had used rape to achieve a number of objectives. We find that some men used rape for revenge or punishment whereas for others it was an "added bonus"—a last-minute decision made while committing another crime. In still other cases, rape was used to gain sexual access to women who were unwilling or unavailable, and for some it was a source of power and sex without any personal feelings. Rape was also a form of recreation, a diversion or an adventure, and finally, it was something that made these men "feel good."

METHODS[5]

Sample

During 1980 and 1981 we interviewed 114 convicted rapists. All of the men had been convicted of the rape or attempted rape (*n*=8) of an adult woman and subsequently incarcerated in a Virginia prison. Men convicted of other types of sexual offense were omitted from the sample. In addition to their convictions for rape, 39 percent of the men also had convictions for burglary or robbery, 29 percent for abduction, 25 percent for sodomy, and 1 percent for first- or second-degree murder; 12 percent had been convicted of more than one rape. The majority of the men had previous criminal histories but only 23 percent had a record of past sex offenses and only 26 percent had a history of emotional problems. Their sentences for rape and accompanying crimes ranged from 10 years to seven life sentences plus 380 years for one man. Twenty-two percent of the rapists were serving at least one life sentence. Forty-six percent of the rapists were white, 54 percent black. In age, they ranged from 18 to 60 years, but the majority were between 18 and 35 years. Based on a statistical profile of felons in all Virginia prisons prepared by the Virginia Department of Corrections, it appears that this sample of rapists was disproportionately white, and at the time of the research, somewhat better educated and younger than the average inmate.

All participants in this research were volunteers. In constructing the sample, age, education, race, severity of current offense, and past criminal record were balanced within the limitations imposed by the characteristics of the volunteer pool. Obviously the sample was not random and thus may not be typical of all rapists, imprisoned or otherwise.

All interviews were hand recorded using an 89-page instrument that included a general background; psychological, criminal, and sexual history; attitude scales; and 30 pages of open-ended questions intended to explore rapists' own perceptions of their crime and themselves. Each author interviewed half of the sample in sessions that ranged from 3 to 7 hours depending on the desire or willingness of the participant to talk.

Validity

In all prison research, validity is a special methodological concern because of the reputation inmates have for "conning." Although one goal of this research was to understand rape from the perspective of men who have raped, it was also necessary to establish the extent to which rapists' perceptions deviated from other descriptions of their crime. The technique we used was the same others have used in prison research; comparing factual information obtained in the interviews, including details of the crime, with reports on file at the prison (Athens, 1977; Luckenbill, 1977; Queen's Bench Foundation, 1976). In general, we found that rapists' accounts of their crime had changed very little since their trials. There was a tendency to understate the amount of violence they had used, however, and especially among certain rapists, to place blame on their victims.

FEIFFER

Figure 2.1. Copyright 1989 Jules Feiffer. Originally published in *The Washington Post.*

HOW OFFENDERS VIEW THE REWARDS OF RAPE

Revenge and Punishment

As noted earlier, Black (1983) suggests that a rapist might see his act as a legitimized form of revenge or punishment. Additionally, he asserts that the idea of "collective liability" accounts for much seemingly random violence. "Collective liability" suggests that all people in a particular category are held accountable for the conduct of each of their counterparts. Thus, the victim of a violent act may merely represent the category of individual being punished.

These factors—revenge, punishment, and the collective liability of women—can be used to explain a number of rapes in our research. Several cases will illustrate the ways in which these factors combined in various types of rape. Revenge rapes were among the most brutal and often included beatings, serious injuries, and even murder. Typically, revenge rapes included the element of collective liability. That is, from the rapists' perspective, the victim substituted for a woman they wanted revenge against. As explained elsewhere (Scully & Marolla, 1984), an upsetting event involving a woman preceded a sig- nificant number of rapes. When they raped, these men were angry because of a perceived indiscretion, typically related to a rigid, moralistic standard of sexual conduct, that they required from "their" woman, but in most cases, did not abide by themselves. Over and over these rapists talked abut using rape "to get even" with their wives or other significant women.[6] Typical is a young man who, prior to the rape, had a violent argument with his wife over what eventually proved to be her misdiagnosed case of venereal disease. She assumed the disease had been contracted through him, an accusation that infuriated him. After fighting with his wife, he explained that he drove around "thinking about hurting someone." He encountered his victim, a stranger, on the road where her car had broken down. It appears she accepted his offered ride because her car was out of commission. When she realized that rape was pending, she called him "a son of a bitch" and attempted to resist. He reported flying into a rage and beating her, and he confided,

> I have never felt that much anger before. If she had resisted, I would have killed her. . . . The rape was for revenge. I didn't have an orgasm. She was there to get my hostile feelings off on.

Although not the most common form of revenge rape, sexual assault continues to be used in retaliation against the victim's male partner. In one such case, the offender, angry because the victim's husband owed him money, went to the victim's home to collect. He confided, "I was going to get it one way or another." Finding the victim alone, he explained, they started to argue about the money and,

> I grabbed her and started beating the hell out of her. Then I committed the act.[7] I knew what I was doing. I was mad. I could have stopped but I didn't. I did it to get even with her and her husband.

Griffin (1971) points out that when women are viewed as commodities, "In raping another man's woman, a man may aggrandize his own manhood and concurrently reduce that of another man" (p. 33).

Revenge rapes often contained an element of punishment. In some cases, although the victim was not the initial object of the revenge, the intent was to punish her because of something that transpired after the decision to rape had been made or during the course of the rape itself. This was the case with a young man whose wife had recently left him. Although they were in the process of reconciliation, he remained angry and upset over the separation. The night of the rape, he met the victim and her friend in a bar where he had gone to watch a fight on TV. The two women apparently accepted a ride from him, but after taking her friend home, he drove the victim to his apartment. At his apartment, he found a note from his wife indicating she had stopped by to watch the fight with him. This increased his anger because he preferred his wife's company. Inside his apartment, the victim allegedly remarked that she was sexually interested in his dog, which he reported put him in a rage. In the ensuing attack, he raped and pistol-whipped the victim. Then he forced a vacuum cleaner hose, switched on suction, into her vagina and bit her breast, severing the nipple. He stated:

> I hated at the time, but I don't know if it was her [the victim]. [Who could it have been?] My wife? Even though we were getting back together, I still didn't trust her.

During his interview, it became clear that this offender, like many of the men, believed men have the right to discipline and punish women. In fact, he argued that most of the men he knew would also have beaten the victim because "that kind of thing [referring to the dog] is not acceptable among my friends."

Finally, in some rapes, both revenge and punishment were directed at victims because they represented women whom these offenders perceived as collectively responsible and liable for their problems. They used rape to prove their "manhood" by displaying dominance over a female and "to put women in their place." For example, one multiple rapist believed his actions were related to the feeling that women thought they were better than he was.

> Rape was a feeling of total dominance. Before the rapes, I would always get a feeling of power and anger. I would degrade women so I could feel there was a person of less worth than me.

Another, especially brutal, case involved a young man from an upper-middle-class background, who spilled out his story in a 7-hour interview conducted in his solitary confinement cell. He described himself as tremendously angry, at the time, with his girlfriend, whom he believed was involved with him in a "storybook romance," and from whom he expected complete fidelity. When she went away to college and became involved with another man, his revenge lasted 18 months and involved the rape and murder of five women, all strangers who lived in his community. Explaining his rape-murders, he stated:

> I wanted to take my anger and frustration out on a stranger, to be in control, to do what I wanted to do. I wanted to use and abuse someone as I felt used and abused. I was killing my girlfriend. During the rapes and murders, I would think about my girlfriend. I hated the victims because they probably messed men over. I hated women because they were deceitful and I was getting revenge for what happened to me.

An Added Bonus

Burglary and robbery commonly accompany rape. Among our sample, 39 percent of rapists had also been convicted of one or the other of these crimes committed in connection with rape. In some cases, the original intent was rape and robbery was an afterthought. However, a number of the men indicated that the reverse was true in their situation. That is, the decision to rape was made subsequent to their original intent, which was burglary or robbery.

This was the case with a young offender who stated that he originally intended only to rob the store in which the victim happened to be working. He explained that when he found the victim alone.

> I decided to rape her to prove I had guts. She was just there. It could have been anybody.

Similarly, another offender indicated that he initially broke into his victim's home to burglarize it. When he discovered the victim asleep, he decided to seize the opportunity "to satisfy an urge to go to bed with a white woman, to see if it was different." Indeed, a number of men indicated that the decision to rape had been made after they realized they were in control of the situation. This was also true of an unemployed offender who confided that his practice was to steal whenever he needed money. On the day of the rape, he drove to a local supermarket and paced the parking lot, "staking out the situation." His pregnant victim was the first person to come along alone and "she was an easy target." Threatening her with a knife, he reported the victim as saying she would do anything if he didn't harm her. At that point, he decided to force her to drive to a deserted area where he raped her. He explained:

> I wasn't thinking about sex. But when she said she would do anything not to get hurt, probably because she was pregnant, I thought, "Why not?"

The attitude of these men toward rape was similar to their attitude toward burglary and robbery. Quite simply, if the situation is right, "Why not?" From the perspective of these rapists, rape was just another part of the crime—an added bonus.

Sexual Access

In an effort to change public attitudes that are damaging to the victims of rape and to reform laws seemingly premised on the assumption that women both ask for and enjoy rape, many writers emphasize the violent and aggressive character of rape. Often such arguments appear to discount the part that sex plays in the crime. The data clearly indicate that from the rapists' point of view rape is in part sexually motivated. Indeed, it is the sexual aspect of rape that distinguishes it from other forms of assault.

Groth (1979) emphasizes the psychodynamic function of sex in rape, arguing that rapists' aggressive needs are expressed through sexuality. In other words, rape is a means to an end. We argue, however, that rapists view the act as an end in itself and that sexual access most obviously demonstrates the link between sex and rape. Rape as a means of sexual access also shows the deliberate nature of this crime. When a woman is unwilling or seems unavailable for sex, the rapists can seize what isn't volunteered. In discussing his decision to rape, one man made this clear.

> All the guys wanted to fuck her . . . a real fox, beautiful shape. She was a beautiful woman and I wanted to see what she had.

The attitude that sex is a male entitlement suggests that when a woman says no, rape is a suitable method of conquering the "offending" object. If, for example, a woman is picked up at a party or in a bar or while hitchhiking (behavior that a number of the rapists saw as a signal of sexual availability), and the woman later resists sexual advances, rape is presumed to be justified. The same justification operates in what is popularly called date rape. The belief that sex was their just compensation compelled a number of rapists to insist they had not raped. Such was the case of an offender who raped and seriously beat his victim when on their second date, she refused his sexual advances.

> I think I was really pissed off at her because it didn't go as planned. I could have been with someone else. She led me on but wouldn't deliver. . . . I have a male ego that must be fed.

The purpose of such rapes was conquest, to seize what was not offered.

Despite the cultural belief that young women are the most sexually desirable, several rapes involved the deliberate choice of a victim relatively older than the assailant.[8] As the rapists were themselves rather young (26 to 30 years of age on the average), they were expressing a preference for sexually experienced, rather than elderly, women. Men who chose victims older than themselves often said they did so because they believed that sexually experienced women were more desirable partners. They raped because they also believed that these women would not be sexually attracted to them.

Finally, sexual access emerged as a factor in the accounts of black men who consciously chose to rape white women.[9] The majority of rapes in the United States today are intraracial. However, for the past 20 years, according to national data based on reported rapes as well as victimization studies, which include unreported rapes, the rate of black on white (B/W) rape has significantly exceeded the rate of white on black (W/B) rape (LaFree, 1982).[10] Indeed, we may be experiencing a historical anomaly, because as Brownmiller (1975) has documented, white men have freely raped women of color in the past. The current structure of interracial rape, however, reflects contemporary racism and race relations in several ways.

First, the status of black women in the United States today is relatively lower than the status of white women. Further, prejudice, segregation, and other factors continue to militate against interracial coupling. Thus, the desire for sexual access to higher status, unavailable women, an important function in B/W rape, does not motivate white men to rape black women. Equally important, demographic and geographic barriers interact to lower the incidence of W/B rape. Segregation as well as the poverty expected in black neighborhoods undoubtedly discourages many whites from choosing such areas as a target for housebreaking or robbery. Thus, the number of rapes that would occur in conjunction with these crimes is reduced.

Reflecting in part the standards of sexual desirability set by the dominant white society, a number of black rapists indicated they had been curious about white women. Blocked by racial barriers from legitimate sexual relations with white women, they raped to gain access to them. They described raping white women as "the ultimate experience" and "high status among my friends. It gave me a feeling of status, power, macho." For another man, raping a white woman had a special appeal because it violated a "known taboo," making it more dangerous and, thus more exciting, to him than raping a black woman.

Impersonal Sex and Power

The idea that rape is an impersonal rather than an intimate or mutual experience appealed to a number of rapists, some of whom suggested it was their preferred form of sex. The fact that rape allowed them to control rather than care encouraged some to act on this preference. For example, one man explained,

Rape gave me the power to do what I wanted to do without feeling I had to please a partner or respond to a partner. I felt in control, dominant. Rape was the ability to have sex without caring about the woman's response. I was totally dominant.

Another rapist commented:

Seeing them laying there helpless gave me the confidence that I could do it. . . . With rape, I felt totally in charge. I'm bashful, timid. When a woman wanted to give in normal sex, I was intimidated. In the rapes, I was totally in command, she totally submissive.

During his interview, another rapist confided that he had been fantasizing about rape for several weeks before committing his offense. His belief was that it would be "an exciting experience—a new high." Most appealing to him was the idea that he could make his victim "do it all for him" and that he would be in control. He fantasized that she "would submit totally and that I could have anything I wanted." Eventually, he decided to act because his older brother told him, "Forced sex is great, I wouldn't get caught and, besides, women love it." Though now he admits to his crime, he continues to believe his victim "enjoyed it." Perhaps we should note here that the appeal of impersonal sex is not limited to convicted rapists. The amount of male sexual activity that occurs in homosexual meeting places as well as the widespread use of prostitutes suggests that avoidance of intimacy appeals to a large segment of the male population. Through rape men can experience power and avoid the emotions related to intimacy and tenderness. Further, the popularity of violent pornography suggests that a wide variety of men in this culture have learned to be aroused by sex fused with violence (Smith, 1976). Consistent with this observation, recent experimental research conducted by Malamuth et al. (1980) demonstrates that men are aroused by images that depict women as orgasmic under conditions of violence and pain. They found that for female students, arousal was high when the victim experienced an orgasm and *no* pain, whereas male students were highly aroused when the victim experienced an orgasm and pain. On the basis of their results, Malamuth et al., (1980) suggests that forcing a woman to climax despite her pain and abhorrence of the assailant makes the rapist feel powerful: He has gained control over the only source of power historically associated with women, their bodies. In the final analysis, dominance was the objective of most rapists.

Recreation and Adventure

Among gang rapists, most of whom were in their late teens or early twenties when convicted, rape represented recreation and adventure, another form of delinquent activity. Part of rape's appeal was the sense of male camaraderie engendered by participating collectively in a dangerous activity. To prove oneself capable of "performing" under these circumstances was a substantial challenge and also a source of reward. One gang rapist articulated this feeling very clearly,

> We felt powerful, we were in control. I wanted sex and there was peer pressure. She wasn't like a person, no personality, just domination on my part. Just to show I could do it—you know, macho.

Our research revealed several forms of gang rape. A common pattern was hitchhike-abduction rape. In these cases, the gang, cruising an area, "looking for girls," picked up a female hitchhiker for the purpose of having sex. Though the intent was rape, a number of men did not view it as such because they were convinced that women hitchhiked primarily to signal sexual availability and only secondarily as a form of transportation. In these cases, the unsuspecting victim was driven to a deserted area, raped, and in the majority of cases physically injured.

Sometimes, the victim was not hitchhiking; she was abducted at knife or gun point from the street, usually at night. Some of these men did not view this type of attack as rape either because they believed a woman walking along at night to be a prostitute. In addition, they were often convinced "She enjoyed it."

"Gang date rape" was another popular variation. In this pattern, one member of the gang would make a date with the victim. Then, without her knowledge or consent, she would be driven to a predetermined location and forcibly raped by each member of the group. One young man revealed this practice was so much a part of his group's recreational routine, they had rented a house for the purpose. From his perspective, the rape was justified because "Usually the girl had a bad reputation, or we know it was what she liked."

During his interview, another offender confessed to participating in 20 or 30 such gang date rapes because his driver's license had been revoked, making it difficult for him to "get girls." Sixty percent of the time, he claimed, "They were girls known to do this kind of thing," but "Frequently, the girls didn't want to have sex with all of us." In such cases, he said, "It might start out as rape, but then they [the women] would quiet down and none ever reported it to the police." He was convicted for a gang rape, which he described as "the ultimate thing I ever did," because unlike his other rapes, the victim in this case was a stranger whom the group abducted as she walked home from the library. He felt the group's past experience with gang date rape had prepared them for this crime in which the victim was blindfolded and driven to the mountains where, though it was winter, she was forced to remove her clothing. Lying on the snow, she was raped by each of the four men several times before being abandoned near a farmhouse. This young man continued to believe that if he had spent the night with her, rather than abandoning her, she would not have reported to the police.[11]

Solitary rapists also used terms like "exciting," "a challenge," "an adventure," to describe their feelings about rape. Like the gang rapists, these men found the element of danger made rape all the more exciting. Typifying this attitude was one man who described his rape as intentional. He reported:

> It was exciting to get away with it [rape], just being able to beat the system, not women. It was like doing something illegal and getting away with it.

Another rapists confided that for him "rape was just more exciting and compelling," than a normal sexual encounter because it involved forcing a stranger. A multiple rapist asserted, "It was the excitement and fear and the drama that made rape a big kick."

Feeling Good

At the time of their interviews, many of the rapists expressed regret for their crime and had empirically low self-esteem ratings. The experience of being convicted, sentenced, and incarcerated for rape undoubtedly produced many, if not most, of these feelings. What is clear is that, in contrast to the well-documented severity of the immediate impact, and in some cases, the long-term trauma experienced by the victims of sexual violence, the immediate emotional impact on the rapists is slight.

When the men were asked to recall their feelings immediately following the rape, only 8 percent indicated that guilt or feeling bad was part of their emotional response. The majority said they felt good, relieved, or simply nothing at all. Some indicated they had been afraid of being caught or felt sorry for themselves. Only 2 men out of 114 expressed any concern or feeling for the victim. Feeling good or nothing at all about raping women is not an aberration limited to men in prison. Smithyman (1978) in his study of "undetected rapists"—rapists outside of prison—found that raping women had no impact on their lives nor did it have a negative effect on their self-image.

Significantly, a number of men volunteered the information that raping had a positive impact on their feelings. For some the satisfaction was in revenge. For example, the man who had raped and murdered five women:

> It seems like so much bitterness and tension had built up and this released it. I felt like I had just climbed a mountain and now I could look back.

Another offender characterized rape as habit forming: "Rape is like smoking. You can't stop once you start." Finally one man expressed the sentiments of many rapists when he stated,

> After rape, I always felt like I had just conquered something, like I had just ridden the bull at Gilley's.

CONCLUSIONS

In this chapter we have explored rape from the perspective of a group of convicted, incarcerated rapists. The purpose was to discover how these men viewed sexual violence and what they gained from their behavior.

We found that rape was frequently a means of revenge and punishment. Implicit in revenge rapes was the notion that women were collectively liable for the rapists' problems. In some cases, victims were substitutes for significant women against whom the men desired to take revenge. In other cases, victims were thought to represent all women, and rape was used to punish, humiliate, and "put them in their place." In both cases women were seen as a class, a category, not as individuals. For some men, rape was almost an afterthought, a bonus added to burglary or robbery. Other men gained access to sexually unavailable or unwilling women through rape. For this group of men, rape was a fantasy come true, a particularly exciting form of impersonal sex that enabled them to dominate and control women by exercising a singularly male form of power. These rapists talked of the pleasures of raping—how for them it was a challenge, an adventure, a dangerous and "ultimate" experience. Rape made them feel good, and in some cases, even elevated their self-image.

The pleasure these men derived from raping reveals the extreme to which they objectified women. Women were seen as sexual commodities to be used or conquered rather than as human beings with rights and feelings. One young man expressed the extreme of the contemptuous view of women when he confided to the female researcher.

> Rape is a man's right. If a woman doesn't want to give it, the man should take it. Woman have no right to say no. Women are made to have sex. It's all they are good for. Some women would rather take a beating, but they always give in; it's what they are for.

This man murdered his victim because she wouldn't "give in."

Undoubtedly, some rapes, like some of all crimes, are idiopathic. However, it is not necessary to resort to pathological motives to account for all rape or other acts of sexual violence. Indeed, we find that men who rape have something to teach us about the cultural roots of sexual aggression. They force us to acknowledge that rape is more than an idiosyncratic act committed by a few "sick" men. Rather, rape can be viewed as the end point in a continuum of sexually aggressive behaviors that reward men and victimize women.[12] In the way that the motives for committing any criminal act can be rationally determined, reasons for rape can also be determined. Our data demonstrate that some men rape because they have learned that in this culture sexual violence is rewarding. Significantly, the overwhelming majority of these rapists indicated they never thought they would go to prison for what they did. Some did not fear imprisonment because they did not define their behavior as rape. Others knew that women frequently do not report rape and that in those cases that are reported conviction rates are low, and therefore they felt secure. These men perceived rape as a rewarding, low-risk act. Understanding that otherwise normal men can and do rape is critical to the development of strategies for prevention.

We are left with the fact that all men do not rape. In view of the apparent rewards and cultural supports for rape, it is important to ask why some men do not rape. Hirschi (1969) makes a similar observation about delinquency. He argues that the key question is not "Why do they do it?" but rather "Why don't we do it?" (p. 34). Likewise, we may be seeking an answer to the wrong question about sexual assault of women. Instead of asking men who rape, "Why?" perhaps we should be asking men who don't, "Why not?"

NOTES

1. Despite the fact that these data have been in circulation for some time, prevention strategies continue to reflect the "lunatic fringe" image of rape. For example, security on college campuses, such as bright lighting and escort service, is designed to protect women against stranger rape with little or no attention paid to the more frequent crime—acquaintance or date rape.

2. Broude and Greene (1976) list a number of factors that limit the quantity and quality of cross-cultural data on rape. They point out that it was not customary in traditional ethnography to collect data on sexual attitudes and behavior. Further, where data do exist, they are often sketchy and vague. Despite this, the existence of rape-free societies has been established.

3. This factor distinguishes rape from other fictional depictions of violence. That is, in fictional murder, bombings, robberies, etc., victims are never portrayed as enjoying themselves. Such exhibits are reserved for pornographic displays of rape.

4. We also introduced a typology consisting of "admitters" (men who defined their behavior as rape) and "deniers" (men who admitted to sexual contact with the victim but did not define it as rape). In this chapter we drop the distinction between admitters and deniers because it is not relevant to most of the discussion.

5. For a full discussion of the research methodology, sample, and validity, see Scully and Marolla (1984).

6. It should be noted that significant women, like rape victims, were also sometimes the targets of abuse and violence and possibly rape as well, although spousal rape is not

recognized in Virginia law. In fact, these men were abusers. Fifty-five percent of rapists acknowledged that they hit their significant woman "at least once," and 20 percent admitted to inflicting physical injury. Given the tendency of these men to underreport the amount of violence in their crime, it is probably accurate to say they underreported their abuse of their significant women as well.

7. This man, as well as a number of others, either would not or could not bring himself to say the word "rape." Similarly, we also attempted to avoid using the word, a technique that seemed to facilitate communication.

8. When asked toward whom their sexual interests were primarily directed, 43 percent of rapists indicated a preference for women "significantly older than themselves." When those who responded "women of any age" are added, 65 percent of rapists expressed sexual interest in women older than themselves.

9. Feminists as well as sociologists have tended to avoid the topic of interracial rape. Contributing to the avoidance is an awareness of historical and contemporary social injustice. For example, Davis (1981) points out that fictional rape of White women was used in the South as a postslavery justification to lynch Black men. And LaFree (1980) has demonstrated that Black men who assault White women continue to receive more serious sanctions within the criminal justice system when compared to other racial combinations of victim and assailant. Although the silence has been defensible in light of historical racism, continued avoidance of the topic discriminates against victims by eliminating the opportunity to investigate the impact of social factors on rape.

10. In our sample, 66 percent of Black rapists reported their victim(s) were white, compared to two White rapists who reported raping Black women. It is important to emphasize that because of the biases inherent in rape reporting and processing, and because of the limitations of our sample, these figures do not accurately reflect the actual racial composition of rapes committed in Virginia or elsewhere. Furthermore, since Black men who assault White women receive more serious sanctions within the criminal justice system when compared to other racial combinations of victim and assailant (LaFree, 1980), B/W rapists will be overrepresented within prison populations as well as overrepresented in any sample drawn from the population.

11. It is important to note that the gang rapes in this study were especially violent, resulting in physical injury, even death. One can only guess at the amount of hitchhike-abduction and gang date rapes that are never reported, or if reported, are not processed because of the tendency to disbelieve the victims of such rapes unless extensive physical injury accompanies the crime.

12. It is interesting that men who verbally harass women on the street say they do so to alleviate boredom, to gain a sense of youthful camaraderie, and because it's fun (Bernard & Schlaffer, 1984)—the same reason men who rape give for their behavior.

REFERENCES

Abel, G., Becker, J., & Skinner, L. (1980). Aggressive behavior and sex. *Psychiatric Clinics of North America, 3,* 133-151.

Athens, L. (1977). Violent crime: A symbolic interactionist study. *Symbolic Interaction, 1,* 56-71.

Bart, P. (1979). Rape as a paradigm of sexism in society—victimization and its discontents. *Women's Studies International Quarterly, 2,* 347-357.

Bernard, C., & Schlaffer, E. (1984). The man in the street: Why he harasses. In A. M. Jaggar & P. S. Rothenberg (Eds.), *Feminist frameworks* (pp. 70-73). New York: McGraw-Hill.

Black, D. (1983). Crime as social control. *American Sociological Review, 48,* 34-45.

Blumberg, R. L. (1979). A paradigm for predicting the position of women: Policy implications and problems. In J. Lipman-Blumen & J. Bernard (Eds.), *Sex roles and social policy* (pp. 113-42). London: Sage Studies in International Sociology.

Broude, G., & Greene, S. (1976). Cross-cultural codes on twenty sexual attitudes and practices. *Ethnology, 15,* 409-428.

Brownmiller, S. (1975). *Against our will.* New York: Simon & Schuster.

Davis, A. (1981). *Women, race and class.* New York: Random House.

Fisher, G., & Rivlin, E. (1971). Psychological needs of rapists. *British Journal of Criminology, 11,* 182-185.

Griffin, S. (1971, September 10). Rape: The all American crime. *Ramparts,* pp. 26-35.

Groth, N. (1979). *Men who rape.* New York: Plenum.

Hammer, E., & Jacks, I. (1955). A study of Rorschach flexnor and extensor human movements. *Journal of Clinical Psychology, 11,* 63-67.

Herman, D. (1984). The rape culture. In J. Freeman (Ed.), *Women: A feminist perspective* (pp. 20-39). Palo Alto, CA: Mayfield.

Hirschi, T. (1969). *Causes of delinquency.* Berkeley: University of California Press.

Hoebel, E. A. (1954). *The law of primitive man.* Boston: Harvard University Press.

Johnson, A. G. (1980). On the prevalence of rape in the United States. *Signs, 6,* 136-146.

Kanin, E. (1957). Male aggression in dating-courtship relations. *American Journal of Sociology, 63,* 197-204.

Kanin, E. (1965). Male sex aggression and three psychiatric hypotheses. *Journal of Sex Research, 1,* 227-229.

Kanin, E. (1967). Reference groups and sex conduct norm violation. *Sociological Quarterly, 8,* 495-504.

Kanin, E. (1969). Selected dyadic aspects of male sex aggression. *Journal of Sex Research, 5,* 12-28.

Kasinsky, R. (1975, September). Rape: A normal act? *Canadian Forum,* pp. 18-22.

Kirkpatrick, C., & Kanin, E. (1957). Male sex aggression on a university campus. *American Sociological Review, 22,* 52-58.

Koss, M. P., & Leonard, K. E. (1984). Sexually aggressive men: Empirical findings and theoretical implications. In N. M. Malamuth & E. Donnerstein (Eds.), *Pornography and sexual aggression* (pp. 213-232). New York: Academic Press.

LaFree, G. (1980). The effect of sexual stratification by race on official reactions to rape. *American Sociological Review, 45,* 824-854.

LaFree, G. (1982). Male power and female victimization: Towards a theory of interracial rape. *American Journal of Sociology, 88,* 311-328.

Llewellyn, K. N., & Hoebel, E. A. (1941). *The Cheyenne way: Conflict and case law in primitive jurisprudence.* Norman: University of Oklahoma Press.

Luckenbill, D. (1977). Criminal homicide as a situated transaction. *Social Problems, 25,* 176-187.

Malamuth, N., Haber, S., & Feshback, S. (1980). Testing hypotheses regarding rape: Exposure to sexual violence, sex difference, and the 'normality' of rapists. *Journal of Research in Personality, 14, 121-137.*

Meyer, T. J. (1984, December 5). "Date rape": A serious problem that few talk about. *Chronicle of Higher Education,* pp.

Morgan, R. (1980). Theory and practice: Pornography and rape. In L. Lederer (Ed.), *Take back the night: Women on pornography* (pp. 134-140). New York: William Morrow.

Queen's Bench Foundation. (1976). *Rape: Prevention and resistance.* San Francisco: Queen's Bench Foundation.

Rada, R. (1978). *Clinical aspects of rape.* New York: Grune & Stratton.

Russell, D.E.H. (1975). *The politics of rape.* New York: Stein & Day.

Sanday, P. R. (1979). *The socio-cultural context of rape.* Washington, DC: United States Department of Commerce, National Technical Information Service.

Scully, D. (1990). *Understanding Sexual Violence.* New York: Routledge.

Scully, D., & Marolla, J. (1984). Convicted rapists' vocabulary of motive: Excuses and justifications. *Social Problems, 31, 530-544.*

Scully, D., & Marolla, J. (1985). Rape and psychiatric vocabulary of motive: Alternative perspectives. In A. W. Burgess (Ed.), *Rape and sexual assault: A research handbook* (pp. 294-312). New York: Garland.

Smith, D. (1976). The social context of pornography. *Journal of Communications, 26,* 16-24.

Smithyman, S. (1978). *The undetected rapist.* Unpublished doctoral dissertation, Claremont Graduate School.

West, D. J. (1983). Sex offenses and offending. In M. Tonry & N. Morris (Eds.), *Crime and justice: An annual review of research* (pp. 1-30). Chicago: University of Chicago Press.

Weis, K., & Borges, S. (1973). Victimology and rape: The case of the legitimate victim. *Issues in Criminology, 8,* 71-115.

Wheeler, H. 1985. Pornography and rape: A feminist perspective. In A. W. Burgess (Ed.), *Rape and sexual assault: A research handbook* (pp. 374-391). New York: Garland.

3 Father-Daughter Incest*

JUDITH HERMAN
with LISA HIRSCHMAN

FATHER-DAUGHTER INCEST (HERMAN)

It is not possible to write dispassionately about incest. The subject is entirely enmeshed not only in myth and folklore, but also in ideology. We have found that a frankly feminist perspective offers the best explanation of the existing data. Without an understanding of male supremacy and female oppression, it is impossible to explain why the vast majority of incest perpetrators (uncles, older brothers, stepfathers, and fathers) are male, and why the majority of victims (nieces, younger sisters, and daughters) are female. Without a feminist analysis, one is at a loss to explain why the reality of incest was for so long suppressed by supposedly responsible professional investigators, why public discussion of the subject awaited the women's liberation movement, or why the recent apologists for incest have been popular men's magazines. (p. 3) . . .

Father-daughter incest is not only the type of incest most frequently reported but also represents a paradigm of female sexual victimization. The relationship between father and daughter, adult male and female child, is one of the most unequal relationships imaginable. It is no accident that incest occurs most often precisely in the relationship where the female is most powerless. The actual sexual encounter may be brutal or tender, painful or pleasurable; but it is always, inevitably, destructive to the child. The father, in effect, forces the daughter to pay with her

---

* For permission to photocopy this selection please contact Harvard University Press. Reprinted by permission of the publishers from *Father-Daughter Incest* by Judith Herman (with Lisa Hirschman), Cambridge, MA: Harvard University Press, Copyright © 1981 by the President and Fellows of Harvard College.

body for affection and care that should be freely given. In so doing, he destroys the protective bond between parent and child and initiates his daughter into prostitution. This is the reality of incest from the point of view of the victim. Measures can and must be taken to change that reality. (p. 4). . .

The sociologist David Finkelhor found impairment in "sexual self-esteem" compared with unabused peers. Carney Landis also found that women with a childhood history of sexual abuse complained of sexual difficulties in adult life. Women reporting sexual aggressions in childhood were "more apt to say that they were disgusted by all sexual subjects." The strongest emotional reactions were reported by women who had been molested by relatives, namely uncles, brothers, or fathers (Finkelhor, 1979). Incestuous abuse has also been frequently associated with a tendency toward repeated victimization in adult life. (p. 29) . . .

To summarize the question of harm: The preponderance of evidence suggests that for any child, sexual contact with an adult, especially a trusted relative, is a significant trauma that may have long-lasting deleterious effects. The sexual trauma does not necessarily lead to the development of a major mental illness; in fact, it does not necessarily lead to any permanent emotional damage. Many circumstances determine the course of a child's development, and the effect of a single trauma such as sexual abuse may be exacerbated or offset by other aspects of the child's environment. Nevertheless, sexual abuse does increase the risk that the victim will experience a variety of difficulties in later life. Most victims recall their experiences as upsetting and unpleasant, and a significant number feel themselves to be permanently scarred. Women who have been initiated into sex prematurely by an act of exploitation appear particularly vulnerable to a wide range of traditional female misfortunes. They have more than their share of difficulty developing a positive, self-respecting sexual identity and a rewarding sexual life. For too many, childhood sexual abuse is an introduction to a life of repeated victimization, an early and indelible lesson in woman's degraded condition. (p. 34).

Traditional psychiatric literature holds the mother responsible or "complicit" in incest. Implicit in these descriptions is a set of normative assumptions regarding the father's prerogatives and the mother's obligations within the family. The father, like the children, is presumed to be entitled to the mother's love, nurturance, and care. In fact, his dependent needs actually supersede those of the children, for if the mother fails to provide the accustomed attentions, it is taken for granted that some other female must be found to take her place. The oldest daughter is a frequent choice. The idea that the father might be expected to take on the mother's caretaking role is never entertained. The father's wish, indeed his right, to continue to receive female nurturance, whatever the circumstances, is accepted without question.

[Another] count in the indictment of the mother concerns her knowledge of and acquiescence in the affair. Some clinicians have gone so far as to assert that in every case, the mother is aware of the incestuous relationship (Kempe & Kempe, 1978). In the pornographic literature, one finds a similar assertion, sometimes with the added fillip that the mother gets her kicks by watching (Quigley, 1978).

The argument that all mothers are complicit in father-daughter incest is refuted by numerous examples of mothers who, upon discovering the incest, react with shock, outrage, and prompt action in defense of their daughters. In Narcyz Lukianowicz's study, for example, 16 out 26 mothers were found to be unaware of the incest until their daughters came forward to reveal the secret, and 2 mothers filed criminal charges against their husbands immediately upon being informed (Lukianowicz, 1972). (p. 48). . .

Even by patriarchal standards, the mother in the incestuous family is unusually oppressed. More than the average wife and mother, she is extremely dependent upon and subservient to her husband. She may have a physical or emotional disability that makes the prospect of independent survival quite impractical. Rather than provoke her husband's anger or risk his desertion, she will capitulate. If the price of maintaining the marriage includes the sexual sacrifice of her daughter, she will raise no effective objections. Her first loyalty is to her husband, regardless of his behavior. She sees no other choice. *"Maternal collusion in incest when it occurs is a measure of maternal powerlessness. As for the question of the mother's responsibility, maternal absence, literal or psychological, does seem to be a reality in many families where incest develops. The lack of a strong, competent, and protective mother does seem to render girls more vulnerable to sexual abuse"* (italics added).

Maternal disability of any sort represents a significant family stress and is perceived by all family members as a deprivation (p. 49). But no degree of maternal absence or neglect constitutes an excuse for paternal incest, unless one accepts the idea that fathers are entitled to female services within their family, no matter what the circumstances. Implicitly the incestuous father assumes that it is his prerogative to be waited upon at home, and that if his wife fails to provide satisfaction, he is entitled to use his daughter as a substitute. It is this attitude of entitlement—to love, to service, and to sex—that finally characterizes the incestuous father and his apologists. In a patriarchal society, the concept of the father's right to use female members of his family—especially his daughter—as he sees fit is implicit even in the structure of the incest taboo.

The families in which the informants grew up were conventional to a fault. Most were churchgoing and financially stable; they maintained a facade of respectability. They were for the most part unknown to mental health services, social agencies, or the police. Because they conformed to traditional family norms, their private disturbances were easily overlooked:

MARION: Yes, we were what you call an intact family. My mother lived at Church and Church functions. My father sang in the choir, and he molested me while my mother was at Sunday School class parties. There was no drinking or smoking or anything the world could see. Only God knows. 72 ff

The informants described their father as a perfect patriarch. The men were, without question, the heads of their household. Their authority within the family was absolute, often asserted by force. They were also the arbiters of the family's social life and frequently succeeded in virtually secluding the women in the family. But even as they were often feared within their family, they impressed outsiders as sympathetic, even admirable men.

In addition, the families of our informants adhered rigidly to the traditional sexual division of labor. Most of the mothers were full-time houseworkers who depended entirely upon their husband for their livelihood. Six mothers did some part-time work outside the home. Only three mothers had full-time jobs. None of the mothers had the working skills or experience that would have made independent survival a realistic option.

The mothers were considered inferior to the fathers, not only in their work achievements, but also simply in their status as women. These were families in which sex roles were rigidly defined, and male superiority was unquestioned:

CHRISTINE: My father just thought women were stupid. He had a very, very low opinion of women, and he never made my mother feel like she was worth anything. Nothing she could do was any good.

The preference for males was expressed in countless ways. Boys in the family were given more freedom and privileges than girls, or were excused from household chores. Some families paid for the education of their sons but not their daughters. One daughter recalled that with each of her mother's numerous pregnancies, her father proudly informed the relatives that his wife was expecting a boy.

In many families, it was considered a male prerogative to supervise and restrict the activities of the females. Fathers exercised minute control over the lives of their wives and daughters, often virtually confining them to the house. The boys in the family were sometimes enlisted as deputies in this policing role. Many daughters reported that their fathers discouraged their mothers from driving a car, visiting friends, or participating in activities outside the home:

YVONNE: My mother was a secretary when she met my father, and she became his secretary. After they were married, my parents moved away from my mother's birthplace, to Vermont. My father told my mother she should not work or drive there because it was too cold and too dangerous in the snow. She never drove or worked again.

Daughters were also deterred from establishing any independent social contacts. The fathers consolidated their power within the family by isolating their wives and children from the outside world:

SHEILA: We had no visitors. My father was very exclusive, and my mother was afraid to let people in when he had been drinking. People just didn't come to our house. I remember my best friend who lived across the street from me: People would float in and out of her house like it was Grand Central Station. I used to think, wouldn't it be nice to be able to do that.

One of the most significant distinguishing characteristics of the incestuous fathers was their tendency to dominate their family by the use of force. Half of the informants reported that their fathers were habitually violent and that they themselves had seen their mother beaten. Other children in the family were often beaten as well. The fathers were selective in their choice of targets: One child was often singled out as a scapegoat, whereas a more favored child was spared. This lesson was not lost on the daughters, who quickly recognized the advantages of being in their father's good graces. (p. 74). . .

Male professionals who are not themselves intimidated often find it hard to imagine how women and children might be. As one expert on chid abuse admits: "Many sexually abusive fathers are described as tyrants in the home. . . . Professionals who have worked with sexual abuse frequently encounter a father who has been described in those terms. When he enters the office for an interview, the professional is astonished to find this "violent and unpredictable" man to be 5'7", 150 pounds and neatly dressed. He is of a calm disposition and appears to be a rather anxious, harassed, and overburdened man, puzzled by recent events" (Lerman, 1980). A 5'7", 150-pound man out in public and on good behavior may not seem at all frightening to a larger man in a position of authority. But the same man may be quite large enough to terrorize his wife and children behind closed doors. (p. 76). . .

Although the fathers of our informants preserved a facade of competent functioning, the mothers were often unable to fulfill their traditional roles. Over half of the informants (55 percent) remembered that their mother had periods of disabling illness that resulted in frequent hospitalizations or in the mother's living as an invalid at home. Over a third (38 percent) of the daughters had been separated from their mother for some period of time during childhood. The separations occurred because the mothers either were hospitalized or felt unable to cope with their child care duties and temporarily placed their daughters in the care of relatives. Three mothers died before their daughters were grown, one by suicide. Another mother committed suicide after her daughter left home.

Depression, alcoholism, and psychosis were among the most common causes of the mothers' disability. Many daughters remembered their mother as suffering from mysterious ailments that made her seem withdrawn, peculiar, and unavailable. One daughter reported that when she was 10, her mother developed the delusion that she was dying of cancer and took to bed for a year. Many other daughters commented on their mother's strange maladies, which seemed to elude definition:

JANET: She was almost like a recluse. She was very alone. It was obvious to me by the time I reached high school that my mother was really strange. My sisters and I used to joke about it.

As in the case of the fathers, the mothers' psychiatric and medical problems usually went undiagnosed and untreated.

If the cause of the mother's ailment sometimes seemed obscure, in other cases it was only too obvious: repeated enforced pregnancies. The average number of children for this group of mothers was 3.6, well above the national mean of 2.2. Seventeen mothers had four children or more, and five had eight or more children. Although some daughters reported that their mother loved babies and had always wanted large families, in many cases the pregnancies were more or less imposed on women who felt helpless to prevent them. (p. 77). . .

These daughters . . . were alienated from their mothers, whom they saw as weak, helpless, and unable to nurture or protect them. They were elevated by their father to a special position in the family, in which many of the mothers' duties and privileges were assigned to them. They felt obligated to fulfill this role in order to keep their family together. Moreover, their special relationship with their father was often perceived as their only source of affection. Under these circumstances, when their father chose to demand sexual services, the daughters felt they had absolutely no option but to comply.

Most of the daughters (80 percent) were under 13 years of age when their father first approached them sexually. The average age was 9. The sexual conduct was limited at first to fondling and gradually proceeded to masturbation and oral-genital contact. Most fathers did not attempt vaginal intercourse, at least until their daughters had reached puberty. Force was rarely used. It was not necessary. (p. 83). . .

The father's explanation to our informants, if any was offered, always sounded silly in retrospect. Younger girls were told, "This is how we learn abut the birds and the bees," "This is our special game," or "Don't you want to make Daddy feel good?" Older girls were told, "I'm getting you ready for your husband," "You should feel comfortable about sex," or "You need me to teach you the facts of life." Many of the fathers seemed to consider it their parental prerogative to introduce their daughters to sex. (p. 85). . .

In no case was the incestuous relationship ended by the father [italics added]. The daughters put a stop to the sexual contact as soon as they could, by whatever means they could. But most felt that in their father's mind, the incestuous affair never ended, and that their father would gladly resume the sexual relationship if given an opportunity. Though all the daughters eventually succeeded in escaping from their family, they felt, even at the time of the interview, that they would never be safe with their father, and that they would have to defend themselves as long as their father lived. (p. 95). . .

Women who have been victimized are unanimous in their enthusiasm for consciousness raising among children. As one victim recalled:

> If there were some knowledge as a child, nine, ten years old, that fathers were not like that, were not sexual with their daughters. . . . I was ignorant, and I did not know whether fathers were really like that or not. And if I could have gotten some information when I was younger, I think that would have helped.

Another victim added: "I think if there was a big billboard out there when I was eight years old that said, 'If your father's bothering you call this number,' you know, I probably would have done it" (Murdock, 1949).

As most sexual abuse begins well before puberty, preventive education, if it is to have any effect at all, should begin early in grade school. Ideally, information on sexual abuse should be integrated into a general curriculum of sex education. In those communities where the experiment has been tried, it has been shown conclusively that children can learn what they most need to know about sexual abuse without becoming unduly frightened or developing generally negative sexual attitudes. In Minneapolis, Minnesota, for example, the Hennepin County Attorney's office developed an education program on sexual assault for elementary school children. The program was presented to all age groups in four different schools, some 800 children in all. The presentation opened with a performance by a children's theater group, illustrating the difference between affectionate touching and exploitative touching. The children's response to the skits indicated that they understood the distinction very well indeed. Following the presentation, about one child in six disclosed a sexual experience with an adult, ranging from an encounter with an exhibitionist to involvement in incest. Most of the children, both boys and girls, had not told anyone prior to the classroom discussion (Schneider, 1976). (p. 203). . .

As Sandra Butler put it in "Letter to a young victim": "Nobody, not even your parents, has the right to do anything to your mind or body that makes you feel bad or uncomfortable. And you are right to want to put an end to it. It is your body, and you can say no without feeling guilty" (Butler, 1978). This idea of the child's right to her own body is a radical one. In the traditional patriarchal family, there is no such concept. The child is the legal property of the father. Only in the last century have reforms in law and custom recognized the *mother's* custodial rights to her child (Abbott, 1938). The concept that the child too might have some individual rights or interests not represented by either parent is even more recent. (p. 204). . .

The painful hostility between mother and daughter so frequently observed in incestuous families is only an exaggeration of a common generational pattern among women. When mothers are powerless, their daughters are inevitably alienated from them. At present, too many girls learn by observation that oppression is their destiny and that to love a man is to be enslaved. If daughters are to be protected, they must learn from their mothers' example that they have the ability to fight and the right to defend themselves. When daughters see in their mothers an image of dignity and self-respect, they can more easily find in themselves the courage to resist abuse. Just as healing in incestuous families begins with the restoration of the mother-daughter bond, prevention of incest ultimately depends on strengthening that relationship to the point where the daughter would never feel the need to preserve the incest secret. (p. 207). . .

The integration of fathers into families cannot be carried out under the banner of "father power." Women have had quite enough of that. If it comes about, it will be as a result of the organized and self-conscious struggle of women to win for child care the dignity and respect that any essential human activity deserves. It will also have to be carried out gradually and with a certain amount of caution. Men cannot be expected to overcome their abusive tendencies or to develop their nurturant capacities overnight, and it makes no sense to expose children to the unsupervised care of men whose interest in them may be ambivalent at best, and perverse at worst. Women are going to have to be the teachers and the protectors for some time to come. (p. 216). . .

Incest is only one of the abuses that inevitably result from a patriarchal family structure. As long as mothers and children are subordinated to the rule of fathers, such abuses will continue. In the short term, mothers who seek to protect their children may have no choice but to fight to banish abusive fathers from the family. In the long run, most mothers would not wish for single parenthood, but would prefer to raise their children in partnership with a father who has learned to understand the needs of children, who can distinguish between sexuality and affection, and who recognizes the appropriate limits of parental love. If a mother's immediate defense rests on her power to exclude an incestuous father from the family, her ultimate hope lies in the possibility of transforming fatherhood so that such a defense would never become necessary.

As long as fathers retain their authoritarian role, they cannot take part in the tasks or the rewards of parenthood. They can never know what it means to share a work of love on the basis of equality, or what it means to nurture the life of a new generation. When men no longer rule their families, they may learn for the first time what it means to belong to one. (p. 218). . .

REFERENCES

Abbott, G. (1938). *The child and the state* (Vol. 1). Chicago: University of Chicago Press.
Butler, S. (1978). *Conspiracy of silence: The trauma of incest.* San Francisco: New Glide Publications.
Finkelhor, D. (1979). *Sexually victimized children.* New York: Free Press.
Kempe, R., & Kempe, H. C. (1978). *Child abuse.* Cambridge, MA: Harvard University Press.
Lerman, L. (1980, April). Civil protection orders: Obtaining access to court. *Response to Violence in the Family, 3,* 1-2.
Lukianowicz, N. (1972). Incest. *British Journal of Psychiatry, 120,* 201-212, 301-313.
Murdock, T. (1949). *Social structure.* New York: Macmillan.
Quigley, P. (1978, October). Incest. *Chic.*
Schneider, D. (1976). The meaning of incest. *Journal of Polynesian Society, 85,* 149-169.

4 Put Up and Shut Up:
Workplace Sexual Assaults

BETH E. SCHNEIDER
University of California, Santa Barbara

With the exception of Brodsky's (1976) description of five cases of rape at work, workplace sexual assaults have not been included in research on workplace deviance. The combination of the problems associated with the underreporting of all sexual assaults and some methodological difficulties in the sexual harassment literature result in limited attention to these particular incidents in feminist scholarship.

The fear of depersonalizing and humiliating institutional procedures and interpersonal hassles to which victims of rape and other sexual assaults are frequently subjected offers few encouragements to report and pursue a legal complaint (Beldin, 1979; Holmstrom & Burgess, 1978; MacKinnon, 1979; Weis & Borges, 1975). In the case of a workplace assault, the fact that a woman's livelihood may be jeopardized further exacerbates the tendency not to report to legal authorities, grievance officers, or workplace associates (MacKinnon, 1979; Silverman, 1976; United States Merit Systems Protection Board, 1981). Official reactions to men accused of sexual assault are less serious when the woman knew the offender and did not promptly report the incident (Holmstrom & Burgess, 1978; Sebba & Cahan, 1975; Williams, 1976). Assaults by

AUTHOR'S NOTE: This chapter is a revised version of a presentation given at the annual meeting of the American Sociological Association, San Antonio, Texas, August 1984. My thanks to Pauline Bart and Patricia Miller for comments on an earlier draft and to Judith Lorber for editing suggestions.

57

someone from work—almost always "acquaintance rape"—would un-derstandably be underreported.

Most of the research on the general problem of sexual harassment has been directed primarily toward highlighting its pervasiveness, gaining definitional clarity, and formulating the means by which women can curtail or eliminate such behaviors in their places of employment or education (Brewer, 1982). The available evidence makes it clear that sexual harassment is indeed a pervasive problem for women workers and students; estimates range from a low of 20 percent to a high of 100 percent, depending on the definition of harassment used and the setting (Benson & Thomson, 1982; Safran, 1976; Tangri, Burt, & Johnson, 1982). These studies indicate that few women report incidents to the appropri-ate or designated grievance authorities (Livingston, 1982). They dis-trust the institution and its ability to solve the problem (Jensen & Gutek, 1982), fear retaliation and an even more uncomfortable working envi-ronment (Alliance Against Sexual Coercion, 1981), wish to avoid public humiliation (MacKinnon, 1987), or observe that complaining brought no positive result (Benson & Thomson, 1982).

Methodologically, there is considerable inconsistency in the sexual harassment research in the examination of sexual assaults. Many of the early exploratory studies aggregated all incidents of harassment in an effort to demonstrate the enormity of the problem. *Unwanted physical contact* was typically used as a catchall phrase for touches, hugs, pinches, grabs, and sexual assaults, foreclosing separate analysis of distinct types of experiences (Benson & Thomson, 1982; Silverman, 1976). Occasion-ally, sexual assaults were omitted altogether from conceptualizations of the problem of sexual harassment (Crocker, 1983). Finally, studies that do discuss sexual assaults conceptualize the situation differently, mak-ing meaningful comparisons quite difficult. For example, the only per-petrators considered by Tangri et al. (1982) are persons employed at the workplace, whereas Lott, Reilly, and Howard (1992) allow for perpe-trators who are strangers.

In this chapter, I explore some of the general parameters of the work-place sexual assault experience for heterosexual women and lesbian workers and then focus on the "deviant" cases, those in which a woman worker either quit because of, or formally complained about, a workplace sexual assault. The analysis lays bare the process of informal deviance defining (Schur, 1984) in everyday life.

RESEARCH DESIGN

The analysis presented here is based on a sample of heterosexual and lesbian women workers who reported a workplace sexual assault incident in their employment history. The intent of the larger research project from which this subsample of the experiences of 64 women emerged was to examine in all its variety the incidence and consequences of the sexualization of the workplace for a representative sample of heterosexual women workers and a matched sample of lesbian workers (Schneider, 1982, 1984). Of the 64 women who reported workplace sexual assaults, 63 provided detailed answers to most, but not all, of the follow-up items used in this analysis.

Sample Selection

Two sampling procedures were used, one to generate a large lesbian sample, one to generate a representative sample of heterosexual women workers. A pool of 42 lesbian contacts who varied in age and in residential location throughout New England and the Middle Atlantic states were asked to identify women they personally knew who they assumed were lesbians, were 21 or older, and had been employed during the previous 5 years. Twenty-eight contacts provided a pool of 476 lesbians, an average of 17 per contact.

To obtain a heterosexual sample that would maximize the probability of obtaining a comparable spread in age and geographic location to that of the lesbian sample, street directories from five New England areas and the telephone directory from Manhattan (New York City) were used. The Manhattan directory was used to augment the number of women from large urban areas to match the lesbian sample more closely. In all instances, names were drawn through systematic sampling procedures. Although there are problems with street directories (rapid obsolescence, underestimation of both the very poor and the very rich, overestimation of the elderly, lack of indication of sexual orientation), they do list occupation; thus recent employment of women sampled was ensured. In all, 688 names were drawn from these sources.

Data Collection

Questionnaires were mailed to 386 women assumed to be heterosexuals and 294 women assumed to be lesbians.[1] A reminder letter was sent 2 weeks later. Both samples received the identical cover letter and questionnaire; included on the cover letter to all but 12 of the women identified by the lesbian contacts[2] was a handwritten note explaining that a contact had given the researcher the individual's name, thinking she would be interested in the study. As a consequence of this personal note of encouragement and the inaccuracies of the street directories, the return rates differed markedly: 36 percent of the heterosexuals, compared to 81 percent of the lesbians, returned completed questionnaires.

The difference in return rate of the two groups may have implications for this study of workplace sexual assault. It is clear from other analyses using these data that the heterosexual women in this sample were somewhat more reticent than the lesbians in reporting all types of sexual and physical experiences at work; the low return rate for the heterosexuals additionally suggests a self-selection process in this sample toward those willing to disclose sexual behavior. Consequently, no general inferences can be made about the underreporting of sexual assaults for this group. The data for this portion of the analysis come from the 20-page, self-administered questionnaire answered by both heterosexual and lesbian women workers. Through 316 precoded items, women were asked detailed questions about the characteristics of their work setting, their social and sexual experiences at work—friendships, committed sexual relationships, sexually harassing approaches—and sexual assaults.

Forty-three percent of the women in the main research project reported at least one type of sexual assault during their lifetime. Overall, 291 incidents were enumerated (38 heterosexuals, or 27 percent of the total heterosexual sample, reported 76 incidents; 122 lesbians, or 54 percent of the total lesbian sample, reported 215 incidents).

Sample Characteristics

Sexual identity was determined by a forced-choice, self-description measure. There were 144 self-identified current heterosexuals and 228 self-identified current lesbians in the resulting total samples. The lesbians had a median age of 29.4 (range: 21-58), compared to 35.0 for the heterosexuals (range: 21-77). At the time of the assault, 36 percent of the self-identified current lesbians considered themselves heterosexual. Ten percent of the total sample and 10 percent of the women who reported a workplace sexual assault were women of color.

For each group, 66 percent were employed in a professional or managerial occupational category, most in human services, health, or educational institutions. Approximately half (54 percent of the heterosexuals,

52 percent of the lesbians) were in workplaces with a predominance of women (55 percent or more). As women in factory and service employment were underrepresented and women in nonprofessional occupations experience higher and more severe levels of harassment than do other women (Silverman, 1976), there may have been fewer sexual assaults in this sample than in a more representative population.

In answer to the question, "Have you EVER experienced a sexual assault, or attempted sexual assault, or any kind of forced oral or anal sexual activity BY SOMEONE YOU KNEW FROM WORK?" 64 women (17 percent of the total study sample of 372) reported at least one completed or attempted workplace sexual assault. Fourteen percent of the current self-identified heterosexuals and 20 percent of the current self-identified lesbians had experienced a workplace sexual assault sometime during their employment history. Workplace sexual assaults accounted for 26.3 percent of the heterosexuals' reports and 20 percent of the lesbians' reports. By comparison, surveys of women federal workers between 1985 and 1987 indicate that 42 percent report sexual harassment, but only 0.8 percent of these incidents were actual or attempted rapes or assaults ("Feds in a pinch," 1988).

In each sample, approximately two thirds of the reported incidents were attempted assaults (63 percent for the heterosexuals, 69 percent for the lesbians). For those who were lesbians at the time of the assault, 89 percent reported an attempted assault. Of the completed sexual assaults, 62 percent were sexual intercourse, 38 percent were oral or anal sex.

The sexual assaults reported by this sample of women occurred from as recently as the year of the survey to 26 years before for one heterosexual woman. Many of these women were obviously no longer employed at the same workplace at which the assault had occurred. But at the time of the survey, 30 percent were still engaged by the same employer. Of these women, 77 percent were survivors of an attempted rape.

The phrasing of the question does not mean that the assault necessarily occurred at the workplace or during working hours, but rather that the assailant was someone with whom a woman worked. Therefore, the situational context is ambiguous. Although some studies do indicate that sexual assaults may indeed occur at the workplace during working hours (Brodsky, 1976), assaults by workplace acquaintances clearly also occur at many other locations. The workplace is a location at which employees interact and form social associations that may continue off-hours (Schneider, 1984). Some of these associations evolve into consensual sexual relationships; others, as the evidence on sexual assaults indicates, reflect patterns of violence against women common to the general population.

The lack of item specificity regarding the exact location of the assault does leave unanswered the extent to which the location of the assault may be a crucial factor in women's willingness to lodge a complaint or quit. But the assault was by someone with whom a woman was acquainted at her job; indeed, almost all assailants were either co-workers or supervisors rather than relatively unknown or temporary contacts, such as suppliers or consultants. It is the impact of this "acquaintance" aspect of the assaults that becomes prominent in analyzing the responses to them.

FINDINGS

Who Was Assaulted

The age range at the time of the assault was 16-42, but it is primarily women in their 20s who are sexually assaulted by supervisors or co-workers. At the time of the workplace assault, the mean age of heterosexuals was 23.1 years, of the lesbians, 24.8 years. Virtually all were single, separated, or divorced at the time of the assault.

The high proportion of young, unmarried women in the sample of workers who were sexually assaulted comes as little surprise; the findings are consistent with statistics on rape and other types of sexual harassment (Russell & Howell, 1983; Schneider, 1982; Schram, 1978; Tangri et al., 1982). Young, heterosexual women are considered more accessible, available, and sexually desirable than older ones, supporting MacKinnon's (1987) contention that rape is about sex and eroticized dominance. They are also vulnerable workers who typically lack sufficient job security, co-worker support, and the experience to manage difficult situations (Martin, 1980).

Who Assaulted

Approximately one half of the lesbians and 29 percent of the heterosexuals were assaulted by male co-workers. These data, unfortunately, cannot account for the difference between heterosexuals and lesbians in the status of the assailant. Although logical, no presumption can be made that the lesbian incidents arose from generalized hostility toward lesbians by their co-workers, as it is not known how open they were about their sexual identity at the time of the assault.

Bosses were responsible for nearly one half of both attempted and completed assaults. For the total sample, 49 percent involved persons with authority over the respondent's employment status (self-identified current heterosexuals, 57 percent; self-identified current lesbians, 45.5 percent). When marital status was known, the majority (67 percent) of all assailants were married men. None of the assailants was the subordinate of the woman assaulted.

Men in positions of authority were more likely to be involved in interactions leading to assaults than to less serious kinds of harassing approaches. Thus, although 49 percent of all lifetime workplace assaults were by a woman's boss or supervisor, they were responsible for only 8 percent of the sexual propositions, 9 percent of the pinches or grabs, and 31 percent of the jokes about women's bodies in the year of the survey (Schneider, 1982).

Types of Coercion

In many conceptualizations of sexual harassment, particularly those used in personnel policy and grievance procedures, the use of economic or educational threats or promises by the harasser can be crucial to the adjudication of a case. Indeed, without such coercion, a case is often considered unworthy of attention (Crocker, 1983). In everyday life, perceptions of seriousness of sexual harassment turn on whether threats or promises by the assailant are used. In 29 percent of the workplace incidents reported in this study, some form of economic promise or threat was employed, with promises outnumbering threats (21 percent to 8 percent). But economic pressures were far less common than either physical or emotional types of coercion. The threat or actual use of physical force was prevalent in a majority of the incidents; in more than one half of the assaults, whether attempted or completed, physical violence was employed. The attempted assaults were accompanied by more threats than were the rapes. Emotional appeals—pleas for sympathy or challenges to a woman's femininity—were consistently and commonly used (see Table 4.1 for a summary of these and the following findings). More threats but less actual physical force was used against the lesbians than the heterosexuals; they were, however, more likely to have their femininity challenged than were the heterosexuals.

TABLE 4.1 Workplace Sexual Assault Incident Characteristics (in percentages)

	Total[a] (N=63)	Attempted Assault (n=43)	Completed Assault (n=20)	At Time of Assault		At Time of Survey (1980)	
				Heterosexual[b] (n=35)	Lesbian[b] (n=28)	Heterosexual[b] (n=19)	Lesbian[b] (n=44)
Coercion by Assailant During Assault[c]							
Physical							
Threat of force	38.1	41.9	26.3	28.6	50.0	31.6	40.9
Use of force	58.7	58.1	57.9	65.7	50.0	68.4	54.5
Emotional							
Begging or pleading for sympathy	58.7	60.5	52.6	54.3	64.3	47.4	63.6
Challenges to femininity	49.2	48.8	47.4	42.9	57.1	42.1	52.3
Economic							
Promise of economic benefit	20.6	23.3	15.8	17.1	25.0	5.3	27.3
Threat of job or economic loss	7.9	11.6	0.0	2.9	14.3	5.3	9.1
Responses by Woman Worker During Assault[d]							
Verbally resisted	85.6	90.7	72.2	79.9	92.9	94.4	92.2
Physically resisted	74.0	79.1	62.5	69.7	82.1	68.8	75.6
Demanded to be left alone	63.3	69.7	43.8	56.3	71.4	56.2	65.9
Threatened to tell others at work	16.6	16.3	12.5	18.8	14.3	12.5	18.2
Went along with request	16.6	6.9	37.5	27.2	3.6	12.5	17.8
Actions by Woman Worker After Assault[e]							
Maintained formal work relationship	66.7	76.7	47.3	60.0	75.0	68.4	65.9
Talked with friends and family	60.3	62.8	52.6	60.0	60.7	63.2	59.1
Talked with co-workers	34.9	34.9	31.6	34.3	35.7	42.1	31.8
Complained through channels	20.6	16.2	31.6	20.0	21.4	31.2	18.2
Quit job	19.0	16.3	26.3	22.9	14.3	10.5	22.7
Caused a scene	7.9	9.3	5.3	5.7	10.7	0.0	11.4
Asked for transfer	6.3	7.0	5.3	5.7	7.1	10.5	4.5

a. Sixty-three of the 64 cases reporting a sexual assault provided data for these analyses; additional information is missing from 3 cases to the women's responses items.
b. Self-defined sexual identity.
c. In most cases, several types of coercion were used.
d. All but one woman employed one or more strategies in response to the assault.
e. Responses were multiple.

Bosses used economic pressures more than other assailants (39 percent to 19 percent). Consistent with expectations of the differential use of power by these two groups of assailants, threats and physical force were utilized more often by those without institutionalized economic means to force compliance. Physical coercion was present in 69 percent of all assaults by co-workers and outsiders, in contrast to 49 percent of assaults by bosses.

Hence, in a sizable number of the cases, the scenario represented what are considered the most serious conditions for sexual harassment: The assailant was a person with legitimate, institutionalized means to alter a woman's working or learning conditions or the assailant used intrusive physical actions or both (Loh, 1981; Reilly, Carpenter, Dull, & Bartlett, 1982; Weber-Burden & Rossi, 1982).

Figure 4.1. © 1991 Lynda Barry. Used with permission.

Women's Responses During Assault

During the assault, the women usually employed more than one response strategy, and 58 percent reported using three or four strategies. Most of the women (86 percent) verbally resisted the assailant, and 74 percent resisted physically. The attempted assaults were accompanied by greater levels of both types of resistance than were the rapes. The demand to be left alone was the only method of resistance significantly more frequent in attempts compared with rapes. The younger the woman, the more likely she was to threaten to reveal the incident to others at work ($r = -.27$, $p>.05$). These findings parallel research on rape avoiders that indicates that more strategies are used by those who deter an attack than by those who are eventually raped (Bart & O'Brien, 1985; Brodsky, 1976). A cautious inference from this evidence suggests that when women have less security of employment, fewer benefits, and less job tenure, they may be somewhat freer to risk their position than are women who have carefully developed such workplace protections. The nine women who reported that they "went along with the request" differed somewhat from the majority, in that the assailant was more often their boss (56 percent in contrast to 46 percent), and in six of these cases, the assault was completed. On this dimension, the sizable percentage difference between the heterosexual women and women who were lesbians at the time of the assault suggests that lesbians may have more practiced capacities for exercising control in everyday life. In these instances, "going along" is associated with greater use of physical force on the part of the assailant and neither verbal nor physical resistance by the woman ($r = -.36$, $r = -.32$, respectively). From the limited available data, these women seemed to feel compelled to succumb to the threats im- plicit in such an attack. Three of these women quit their jobs in the aftermath of the assault.

Women's Actions After Assault

Most (81 percent) of the women remained at their jobs in the aftermath of the workplace assault. Of those who continued, 67 percent reported maintaining a formal working relationship with their assailants. That is, similar to other women who have been raped, these women developed ways to cope with and minimize the continued contact with the perpetrator and the impact of the assault on their daily work lives (Kelly, 1988). Not surprisingly, relationships were maintained more often in attempted cases (77 percent) than in the rapes (47 percent). Continuation of the working relationship was more common when a supervisor was the assailant (74 percent, compared to 59 percent when the assailant was a co-worker or other at work). Here, too, the younger the woman, the less likely she was to maintain a formal working relationship with her assailant ($r = -.35$, $p>.01$).

TABLE 4.2 Women Workers' Actions After a Workplace Sexual Assault (in percentages)

	Quit (n=12)	Did Not Quit (n=51)	Complained (n=13)	Did Not Complain (n=50)
Forcible assault	42	28	46	26
Boss-as-assailant	67	45	31	54
Outsider-as-assailant	8	14	31	8*
Emotional coercion	83	69	85	68
Economic coercion	58	16*	23	24
Physical coercion	58	59	77	54
3 or more coercions used	68	42	62	44
Physical resistance	58	79	67	74
Verbal resistance (total)	83	86	92	84
Demanded to be left alone	75	60	67	63
Threatened to tell others	17	17	42	10*
Talked with friends or family	83	55*	62	60
Talked with co-workers	25	37	62	28*

*Statistically significant at $p<.05$.

Although 60 percent talked with friends or family members, only one third talked with co-workers about the incident. At the time of the assault, lesbians were equally as likely as the heterosexuals to communicate with their co-workers about the incident. Of the total, only 21 percent of the women who experienced a workplace sexual assault complained through appropriate workplace channels, and only 19 percent quit their jobs. Quitting and formal complaining were quite discrete acts. In only two cases did women complain and quit. Thus these two responses were unusual responses. An analysis of the conditions that account for quitting or complaining provides some indirect understanding of informal deviance defining in these situations.

Difference of proportions analyses yield one statistically significant difference between women who quit and women who did not: the use of economic coercion by the assailant (see Table 4.2). Rape and boss-assailant were not predictors of quitting a job, although the latter approaches statistical significance and was substantively important in understanding the situational context. Specifically, two thirds of those who quit had had an incident with a boss, although bosses had been involved in only 45 percent of the other cases. And being raped did not seem to matter. It took the blatant use of economic coercion to generate the circumstances that led the women who quit to leave their jobs. That is, once their jobs were held hostage, their choices seemed to be stay and continue to submit or leave.

There were no differences between those who complained and those who did not on the general verbal resistance measure, but there were in the type of verbal resistance. The indignant verbal response of threatening to tell others distinguishes the women who filed a formal complaint from those who did not. Thus, when a woman in the course of an assault had threatened to reveal the incident, she was quite likely to follow through.

None of the other major characteristics of the assault encounter, including the use of physical coercion, correlated significantly with lodging a complaint, except for the greater likelihood of filing a complaint against an outsider. Filing a formal complaint was thus an option mostly when the interpersonal dynamics of the workplace would not be severely damaged. Furthermore, a woman is more likely to find support among her colleagues when a stranger's behavior is called into question than when a boss or co-worker is accused. These formal complaints did not represent explicit sexual harassment grievances made through a person or office organized to handle such matters, as few existed prior to 1980, the period during which all of these assaults occurred. Although comparability with other sexual harassment research on use of grievance procedures is made problematic as a consequence, the rate of reporting is higher than is found in other, more representative studies. For example, the Equal Employment Opportunity Commission reports that in 1985 it received 436 official complaints from 2,100,000 government employees ("Feds in a pinch," 1988).

As for other sources of support, the women who quit were much more likely to talk with friends or family than those who did not quit, but they were not more likely to tell co-workers. The reverse is the case for those who complained. The women who filed a complaint were much more likely to talk with co-workers about the assault but no more likely to talk with friends and family. Nevertheless, most women avoided public revelation of the assault and suffered psychological, health, or job effects in silence.

Taken together, the findings on women's actions highlight the lack of options available to women following even an extreme instance of workplace sexual assault. Women who quit did not lodge a complaint; women who lodged a complaint did so for the most part in those rare instances in which an outsider was the assailant. Daily workplace interactions no doubt continued unchanged on the surface, and the woman worker adjusted to her situation unaided by interpersonal or institutional support.

The women's own feelings indicated considerable change: 40 percent reported they had "lost interest in their jobs"; an equal proportion believed they were "taken less seriously as a worker." These feelings were more likely when a woman had been raped than when she had avoided rape; for example, 58 percent of those who had been raped compared to 30 percent who had not been lost interest in their work. With regard to more concrete losses, 20 percent of the total sample believed they lost some career opportunity, 9 percent felt they lost an expected pay increase, and 10 percent believed they were not promoted when they thought they should have been. Lesbians more often reported concrete losses. Those who had avoided rape more often reported career losses than those who had been raped, but a greater proportion of those who had been raped quit their jobs. Quitting, of course, meant the loss of any advancement opportunities as well as income and work experience.

CONCLUSION

Although workplace sexual assault incidents resulting in women quitting or complaining are few in number, the examination of their characteristics is instructive in several ways. First, the combined effects of occupational segregation, employment discrimination, and economic dependency constrain women's choices and opportunities such that they remain in workplace situations that are decidedly threatening and coercive. Second, because few women report serious workplace assault experiences, less serious types of sexual harassment clearly go unreported. Although most of the cases examined here occurred prior to the publicity about sexual harassment generated by the women's rights and labor movements and before there were specific legal options available to redress such a grievance, there is little reason to assume enormous change in the proportion of cases reported once these avenues were in place (MacKinnon, 1987; Schneider, 1985) given the economic and social consequences to the woman worker.

Women, like other oppressed groups, adjust to unsatisfactory situations, losing some unspecified, but nevertheless real, freedom of choice and control in the process of making their lives tolerable (Adam, 1978; Schur, 1984). Quitting a job may be a rational solution, but it leaves intact the environment in which men are free to sexually harass. A woman who files a complaint may bring more attention to these incidents, but as the evidence suggests, a realistic assessment of the limits of co-worker support means a complaint is more likely to be lodged against outsiders, again leaving the men in the workplace untouched.

Whether a woman who has experienced a workplace sexual assault copes with and manages her situation by staying on, leaving her job, or filing a formal complaint, she is potentially subject to a process of informal deviance defining, in which those in a position to define a situation as problematic consider any response other than accommodation deviant activity and grounds for the further devaluation of the woman as a worker (Schur, 1984). Compelling support for the persistence of this process, particularly in assault cases, lies in an examination of the record of sexual harassment legal cases; MacKinnon (1987) found that "Many women who have been raped in the course of sexual harassment have been advised by their lawyers not to mention the rape because it would destroy their credibility" (p. 110). Hence sexual assaults at work continue to be a serious threat to economically vulnerable women workers.

NOTES

1. Street directories like telephone books more or less reflect the general population profile of an area. Researchers might reasonably assume that a listing of adult women from these sources in most locales would yield approximately 90 percent heterosexual women.

2. Among the lesbian contacts were a few who did not wish to be known to the women whose names they provided. These contacts were attempting to ensure their privacy or that of the woman they named. For those 12 names, no lesbian contact was mentioned.

REFERENCES

Adam, B. D. (1978). *The survival of domination: Interiorization and everyday life.* New York: Elsevier.

Alliance Against Sexual Coercion. (1981, July/August). Organizing against sexual harassment. *Radical America, 15,* 17-34.

Bart, P. B., & O'Brien, P. H. (1985). *Stopping rape: Successful survival strategies.* New York: Pergamon.

Beldin, L. (1979, September/October). Why women do not report sexual assault. *Aegis: Magazine on Ending Violence Against Women,* pp. 38-43.

Benson, D. J., & Thomson, G. E. (1982). Sexual harassment on a university campus: The confluence of authority relations, sexual interest, and gender stratification. *Social Problems, 29,* 236-251.

Brewer, M. B. (1982). Further beyond nine to five: An integration and future directions. *Journal of Social Issues, 38,* 149-158.

Brodsky, C. (1976). Rape at work. In M. Walker & S. Brodsky (Eds.), *Sexual assault: The victim and the rapist* (pp. 35-51). Lexington, MA: D. C. Heath.

Crocker, P. (1983). An analysis of university definitions of sexual harassment. *Signs, 8,* 696-707.

Feds in a pinch. (1988, December). *Playboy,* p. 64.

Holmstrom, L. L., & Burgess, A. W. (1978). *The victim of rape: Institutional reactions.* New York: John Wiley.

Jensen, I., & Gutek, B. (1982). Attributions and assignment of responsibility for sexual harassment. *Journal of Social Issues, 38,* 121-136.

Kelly, L. (1988). *Surviving sexual violence.* Minneapolis: University of Minnesota Press.

Livingston, J. A. (1982). Responses to sexual harassment on the job: Legal, organizational, and individual actions. *Journal of Social Issues, 38,* 5-22.

Loh, W. W. (1981). What has reform of rape legislation wrought? *Journal of Social Issues, 37,* 28-52.

Lott, B., Reilly, M. E., & Howard, D. R. (1982). Sexual assault and harassment: A campus community case study. *Signs, 8,* 296-319.

MacKinnon, C. A. (1979). *Sexual harassment of working women: A case of sex discrimination.* New Haven, CT: Yale University Press.

MacKinnon, C. A. (1987). *Feminism unmodified: Discourses on life and law.* Cambridge, MA: Harvard University Press.

Martin, S. E. (1980). *Breaking and entering: Policewomen on patrol.* Berkeley: University of California Press.

Reilly, T., Carpenter, S., Dull, V., & Bartlett, K. (1982). The factorial survey: An approach to defining sexual harassment on campus. *Journal of Social Issues, 38,* 99-110.

Russell, D.E.H., & Howell, N. (1983). The prevalence of rape in the United States revisited. *Signs, 8,* 688-695.

Safran, C. (1976, November). What men do to women on the job: A shocking look at sexual harassment. *Redbook,* p. 149.

Schneider, B. E. (1982). Consciousness about sexual harassment among heterosexual and lesbian women workers. *Journal of Social Issues, 38,* 75-97.

Schneider, B. E. (1984). The office affair: Myth and reality for heterosexual and lesbian women workers. *Sociological Perspectives, 27,* 443-464.

Schneider, B. E. (1985, July). Approaches, assaults, attractions, affairs: The policy implications of the sexualization of the workplace. *Population Research and Policy Review, 4,* 93-113.

Schram, D. D. (1978). Rape. In J. R. Chapman & M. Gates (Eds.), *The victimization of women* (pp. 53-79). Beverly Hills, CA: Sage.

Schur, E. M. (1984). *Labeling women deviant: Gender, stigma and social control.* New York: Random House.

Sebba, L., & Cahan, S. (1975). Sex offenses: The genuine and the doubted victim. In I. Drapkin & E. Viano (Eds.), *Victimology: A new focus* (pp. 29-46). Lexington, MA: Lexington.

Silverman, D. (1976). Sexual harassment: Working women's dilemma. *Quest: A Feminist Quarterly, 10,* 346-357.

Tangri, S., Burt, M. R., & Johnson, L. B. (1982). Sexual harassment at work: Three exploratory models. *Journal of Social Issues, 38,* 33-54.

United States Merit Systems Protection Board. (1981). *Sexual harassment in the federal workplace: Is it a problem?* Washington, DC: Government Printing Office.

Weber-Burden, E., & Rossi, P. H. (1982). Defining sexual harassment on campus: A replication and extension. *Journal of Social Issues, 38,* 111-120.

Weis, K., & Borges, S. (1975). Victimology and rape: The case of the legitimate victim. In L. G. Schultz (Ed.), *Rape victimology* (pp. 91-141). Springfield, IL: Charles C. Thomas.

Williams, K. M. (1976). The effect of victim characteristics on the disposition of violent crime. In W. F. McDonald (Ed.), *Criminal justice and the victim* (pp. 177-213). Beverly Hills, CA: Sage.

5 The Invisible Intruder: Women's Experiences of Obscene Phone Calls

CAROLE J. SHEFFIELD
William Paterson College

The conceptualization of male sexual violence against women has moved from singular analyses of particular forms of violence to frameworks that include many forms of male sexual violence. The analysis of male sexual violence as an integrated phenomenon rests on a theoretical premise that violence, and its threat, are the foundation of male domination. I call this phenomenon "sexual terrorism" (Sheffield, 1987, pp. 171-189; 1989, pp. 3-19). Sexual terrorism is the system by which men and boys frighten, and by frightening, dominate and control women and girls.

Sexual terrorism is manifested through both actual and implied violence. All females are potential victims—at any age, at any time, or in any place—through a variety of means—rape, physical abuse, incestuous assault, sexual harassment, prostitution, and pornography. Many forms of sexual intimidation are perceived as common, that is, ordinary, everyday occurrences. They are often readily dismissed by the women themselves and by agents of social control, and are the least studied. These common experiences, which include a range of verbal, visual, and physical intrusions, are the underpinning of sexual terrorism: They serve to remind women and girls that they are at risk and vulnerable to male aggression just because they are female.

In this chapter, I will examine the phenomenon of obscene telephone calls as a particular manifestation of sexual terrorism. In doing so, I will examine women's reactions to these types of phone calls. The definition of an obscene telephone call is elusive. Ostensibly, obscene phone calls are regarded by the legal system and the providers of telephone service as unwelcome, if not illegal, intrusions. For example, all telephone directories in the United States include a consumer rights and responsibilities section that discusses harassing or obscene phone calls. In the *New Jersey Bell Telephone Directory* (1989), consumers are advised to "hang up at the first obscene word or if the caller doesn't say anything the second time you say hello," to "give no information such as your name and address until the caller has been identified," and to advise children to "give no information to strangers." Moreover, the guide informs consumers that

> New Jersey law provides that a person commits a petty disorderly persons offense if, with the purpose to harass another, he or she makes or causes to be made, a communication anonymously or at extremely inconvenient hours, or in offensively coarse language, or any manner likely to cause annoyance or alarm. Conviction subjects a person to a minimum fine of $500.00 and imprisonment of up to 30 days.

Further, federal law provides fines of up to $500 and imprisonment of up to 6 months for the placement of obscene or harassing interstate or foreign telephone calls. Consumers are advised to call their local service center if they need assistance, but are not encouraged to notify the police.

RESEARCH DESIGN

The research reported here was a self-report study designed to secure qualitative and descriptive data on women's experiences of obscene phone calls. The sample consisted of 58 self-selected respondents who anonymously completed a "Call for Information"; 42 were students at William Paterson College (Wayne, New Jersey), and 16 were contacted through a women's network in Boston. The respondents ranged in age from 18 to 52; 48 were white, 5 black, 1 Hispanic, and 4 unidentified. Most lived in suburban or urban settings, in dormitory, familial, shared, and single housing.

The questionnaire did not attempt to define obscene phone calls. Thus the respondents were encouraged to record their experiences and perceptions as they defined obscene phone calls. Of the 58 respondents, 5 reported never having received an obscene phone call. Of the remaining 53, 23 said they had experienced between 1 and 5 such calls; 21 respondents reported experiencing 6-25 calls; 6 reported experiencing 26-50; and 3 reported experiencing more than 50 obscene calls. All except four of the callers (of whom two were known to the respondents) were male. What is relevant here is not the accuracy of record keeping by the respondents but that more than 90 percent of them reported experiencing several to many obscene phone calls. This frequency is the basis of the perceived commonness of obscene calls.

FINDINGS

Psychological Reactions

The reactions to receiving an obscene telephone call varied, but not considerably. Five reported that the call had no effect and dismissed them as "humorous," "annoying," "pathetic," or "just one of those things women have to put up with." One woman commented, "It's kind of scary but life goes on." Forty-eight of the responses clustered around feelings of "anger," "fear," "disgust," "degradation," and "abuse."

One woman wrote that there is a "curious blank spot" about a number of calls she had received while in college and that she could not articulate her feelings, but she was disturbed by having to recollect the experience. Completing the "Call for Information" made her realize that it is "not a finished episode" in her life. Another respondent commented that it is "about time someone investigated this" and considered obscene phone calls as "assault with intent to harm."

Whether or not the women in this study experienced fear or perceived harm from the telephone calls depended on the time and place of the call (cf. Hanmer & Saunders, 1984, p. 38). Women felt safest when others were present. The two women who received calls at work reported that they found them offensive and annoying but not frightening. One woman reported that several obscene calls were received at a pay phone in her dormitory, and because they seemed not to be directed at anyone in particular, the women felt safe and "laughed it off." Another wrote, "I don't let them affect me unless I'm home alone; then I feel more scared." Four reported that they were frightened only when the call came in the middle of the night, whereas feelings of anger or annoyance characterized receipt of daytime calls.

The level of fear and a perception of harm were also linked to some prior knowledge or experience of male violence. Prior knowledge of racist violence was a factor in the fear of one respondent whose caller told her "I know where you live, and I know that you are black." In another instance, a husband who had witnessed his wife's fright at receiving obscene phone calls later made similar calls to her with a disguised voice, hoping they would make her too afraid to leave him.

Several women described feelings of "paranoia" and said they had to work hard to convince themselves that the callers were anonymous. The intrusion was regarded as less threatening if the caller was unknown to them. Others expressed a fear that although they did not know—or could not readily identify—the caller, he might know them. What frightened them was the concern that the call might not be random, and that the intrusion would not be limited to an obscene phone call, but would escalate to a physical assault. One woman said that she felt "violated, nervous, paranoid" and as if she were being watched. Another wondered "if you know them or not, if you see them every day, and if they are following you or watching what you do." As Hanmer and Saunders (1984, p. 40) point out, knowing or not knowing the aggressor is a complicated issue. The majority of the responses support the findings that women's perceptions of safety are "profoundly shaped by their inability to control interactions with strangers."

Another factor in the assessment of harmfulness was stress. For women whose lives were already stressful, the intrusion of an obscene phone call seemed most devastating. One woman described a time in her life when she began to receive middle-of-the-night obscene phone calls while caring for two terminally ill loved ones. She felt that her ability to cope with the phone calls was greatly diminished by her circumstances. In addition, the calls in and of themselves induce stress. Ten women experienced sleeplessness, were afraid to be home alone, or were reluctant to leave the house. Two women, dependent on the telephone because of work or family responsibilities, reported that the calls were significant stressors and the source of psychological pain and fear.

Hanging Up and Other Responses

Ten respondents said that they hung up "quietly," "silently," on their caller. Two reported a more active response—blowing a whistle into the phone. One woman reported that after receiving several calls and each time hanging up, she worked up the nerve to reply in a sexual manner. When she did, the caller told her that she had a dirty mouth and hung up on her. Two other respondents reported attempting to talk to the caller; each time, the caller hung up after hearing her voice.

In sum, the dynamics of obscene phone calls mirror the social construction of masculinity and femininity. The male caller assumes a traditional masculine role: He is active, the aggressor, the one with a voice. The social construction of femininity includes both silence and passivity.

Reporting Obscene Telephone Calls

Most of the respondents (40) did not report the call to either the police or the telephone company. The 13 who did report were more likely to call the telephone company than the police. The police were cooperative only in those rare instances in which the caller was known. Such calls, however, are not typically regarded as obscene phone calls. Except for the cases in which the caller was known, the police advised the complainant that there was nothing they could do, that the complainant could continue to report the incidents or refer the calls to the telephone company.

One respondent reported that she had contacted the police regarding two incidents, one an unknown male caller and the other a female caller known to the respondent. Although she reported being much more frightened by the unknown caller because he said he knew where she lived and that she was black, the police advised her to have the calls from the female caller traced and to press charges against her. Their advice for dealing with the male caller was to have her telephone number changed.

The eight respondents who reported the calls to the telephone company expressed similar dissatisfaction with the ineffectiveness of the company's response. The responses they received ranged from someone taking the information, to the company offering an appointment 2 weeks later or referring them to the police.

Six respondents had their telephone numbers changed, four immediately and two at a later date. One woman reported that she had had her telephone number changed three times. Many women were adamant about not changing their telephone number. They said that experiencing the call was enough of an intrusion, and changing their telephone number was seen as a tremendous inconvenience that they refused to be forced into. One woman reported that she was afraid to change her telephone number—fearful that whoever was calling her would then come to her home.

CONCLUSIONS

It is clear from these responses that obscene phone calls are a form of sexual intimidation and harassment. Although they do not involve direct physical assault or violence, many women experienced them as terroristic. Except for two heavy breathers, the content of the calls was explicitly sexual. Words such as "cunt" and "bitch" were used frequently, as were references to the sexual acts that the callers would like to do to the women. Four women mentioned that the content of the calls invoked the fear of rape. One wrote, "He was talking about something sexual, you start to think of rape." Another said that the calls "reinforced my feelings of vulnerability, as rapable."

The phenomenon of obscene phone calls appears to reflect a fusion of dominance and sexuality. The content of the calls embodies the patriarchal myths of rape: that women are sexually "bad"—depraved, insatiable, lustful. Therefore, men justify what they do or say to women on the assumption that women deserve it or like it. The reactions of the women who felt physically and psychologically threatened by the calls support Dworkin's (1983) contention that women "fear the language of the rapist" as well as the rapist (p. 202). Although the obscene telephone call does not seem to engender the feelings of guilt, shame, and self-blame common to physically and sexually assaulted women, such calls remind women and girls that they can be intruded upon by known or unknown males at any time or in any place. As Rich (1979) said, "In a world where language and naming are power, silence is oppression, is violence" (p. 204).

REFERENCES

Dworkin, A. (1983). *Right wing women*. New York: G. P. Putnam.
Hanmer, J., & Saunders, S. (1984). *Well-founded fear*. London: Hutchinson.
New Jersey Bell Telephone Directory. 1989.
Rich, A. (1979). *On lies, secrets and silence: Selected prose: 1966-1978*. New York: Norton.
Sheffield, C. J. (1987). Sexual terrorism and the social control of women. In B. Hess & M. Marx Ferree (Eds.), *Analyzing gender* (pp. 177-189). Newbury Park, CA: Sage.
Sheffield, C. J. (1989). Sexual terrorism. In J. Freeman (Ed.), *Women: A feminist perspective* (pp. 3-19). Palo Alto, CA: Mayfield.

Part II

Structural Supports for Violence Against Women

Introduction

The violence and abuse men perpetrate against women and girls is rooted in a tradition of male supremacy that teaches boys and men that females are worth less; are less deserving, and may be treated poorly or worse. Even more profoundly, boys and men learn that females are the "other," that to be male means to be *not* female (Beauvoir, 1970). When groups are considered inferior, it is only "natural" to withhold resources from them. Negative attitudes and stereotypes develop and are institutionalized. Disdain for the inferior group is cultivated. The group is objectified and patterns of exclusion may emerge.

The violence and abuse that men inflict on women is rooted not only in men's belief in women's inferiority but in their hatred of women. "Most men just hate women, Ted Bundy killed them" (Caputi, Chapter 1, this volume). The abuse of women is systematic . . . receiving cultural and structural support. Women's subordination is accomplished and maintained by patterns of interpersonal interaction prescribed by culture and social structures.

Because male supremacy is institutionalized, one does not need to invoke a plot to account for the mistreatment of women. It does not have to do with the individual motivation of individual men consciously trying to harm women, any more than speaking English is a plot by English-speaking parents to coerce their children into speaking English. It is possible for the children to speak French or Spanish as their first language, but only if special effort is made. It is no accident that mothers-in-law are the butt of jokes rather than fathers-in-law, but neither is it a conspiracy.

In her analysis of the sexual politics of Black womanhood, Patricia Hill Collins (Chapter 6) addresses the complex integration of sex, race, and class in maintaining social inequality. The sexual exploitation of Black women from slavery to the present maintains the privilege of White men relative to all women and men of color. Pornography is developed and disseminated, thus reinforcing racial stereotypes. Asians symbolize compliance, Latinas "hot" sexuality, and African Americans are presented as subhuman with animal sexuality. Mind-body dualism characterizes Western thought with women symbolizing the body and nature and thus more animal-like (Griffin, 1980). The roots of inequality among classes, ethnic groups, and races are modeled on the patriarchal characterization of man's superiority to woman.

This section shows that the abuse of women is structurally supported, that is, institutionally reproduced, in religious (Young, Chapter 7) and medical (Warshaw, Chapter 10) institutions, as well as in social organizations (Martin & Hummer, Chapter 8). The chapters by Collins and Caputi (Part I) demonstrate the subordinating effect of pornography, and both Joanne Stato and Caputi present evidence of the role the media plays in this systemic subordination. In any society with very unequal distribution of political and economic power, we expect that dominant groups will have "natural" advantages and privileges in the routine operations of organizations and institutions. The objectification and dehumanization of women as a class is a recurring theme in this section.

Kathleen Young's chapter on Maria Goretti exemplifies the religious value placed on female virginity and the church's idealization of virgin martyrs as role models for girls and women. Death is preferable to defilement, even for children. Girls and women are merely sexual beings, whether symbolized as seducers or madonnas. An unmarried girl who loses her virginity, even in a violent assault, is devalued in the eyes of the community and her family. The Catholic Church used Maria Goretti's victimization to reiterate its patriarchal biases: Girls and women are always responsible for men's sexual sins. Men are stereotypically unable to control sexual urges and women are made culpable by their existence. (Catholics in parochial schools were taught that girls and women were occasions of sin for men.) The violence of stabbing a child to death because she would not yield is buried as Maria, through her forgiveness, becomes an instrument of a man's redemption. Using the victimization of the child to teach chastity to the postwar generation, the church and its male, allegedly celibate leadership, discloses its own fear and loathing of women as "occasions of sin." It taught generations of Catholics to hold victims accountable for men's sexual assaults. A rape survivor was tainted by definition. Young also comments on the pornographic telling of Maria's murder. In forgiving her attacker, the Church's myth supports men's expecting forgiveness from women and children. Although forgiveness is extolled as a Christian virtue, it is also cast as a feminine virtue.

Fraternities as social organizations idealize masculinity and foster the sexual coercion of women—paradigmatically through gang rapes. The fraternities' codes of loyalty, authoritarianism, and secrecy facilitate the exploitation of women, including "Little Sisters" who are used as bait to achieve organizational goals such as recruiting "pledges." Studies show fraternities are overrepresented in rapes on campus. The commodification of women as sexual prey and as an arena for male competitiveness are mainstays of fraternity culture on U.S. campuses (Martin & Hummer). Alcohol use, omnipresent at "frat parties," makes women culpable for the attacks, just as it reduces the accountability of the male assailants.

Fraternities deliberately recruit young men who already embrace highly stereotyped views of masculinity and femininity. Fraternal culture legitimates the sexual abuse of women as a means of men demonstrating their masculinity, that is, heterosexuality, to one another. Women and intramurals are both sport, and the code of secrecy insulates the perpetrators from legal accountability. Ironically, the intramural games may be more consistently regulated to ensure "fair play," as they concern behavior among equals. Fraternities, along with other exclusive male associations, reinforce beliefs about women's inferiority and men's entitlements relative to women.

Fraternal life is a training ground for future corporate men. They have already been socialized into a code of secrecy and male bonding as well as sexism and homophobia. Undeterred by humanistic principles, they are desensitized to the harm done to "outsiders." It is therefore no accident that the practices of dumping toxic products, union busting, discrimination, and general exploitation are not exceptional. Ends justify means. The bottom line justifies whatever it takes.

Turning from gang rape to mass murder, it is noteworthy that the media fail to include gender in their analysis, limiting their accounting of such crimes to individual pathology even when the murderer explicitly states his motivation. Lepine, who killed female engineering students, said he hated feminists, and Bundy, a serial killer, said pornography fueled his behavior. The media's limiting all discussion to psychological explanations excludes the feminist sociocultural analyses. Certainly a man who commits mass murder is deranged, but his choice of victims also reflects the misogyny being supported in the culture. The massacre in Montreal underscores the privileges, such as seats in certain schools, that have been a male entitlement. Until we connect the routine harassment of women who are "firsts" in positions previously monopolized by men to the murders in Montreal, we miss the role that woman hating plays in confining women's activities.

Several chapters in this section identify the social contexts within groups and institutions that support the subordination of women through violent assaults and murder. In Carole Warshaw's analysis of hospital emergency room procedures, the patterns that undermine the treatment of battered women are tied to traditional medical education and practice. The depersonalization of the patient-doctor relationship, in which doctors are trained to address body parts in need of repair, enables them to avoid recognizing battery. They describe wounds clinically without asking how they occurred. This is akin to treating a diabetic without discussing diet.

Yet the settings of busy emergency rooms and the training in the medical model facilitates doctors' limiting their intervention to narrowly prescribed medical problems they can solve. The doctors' reluctance to ask "personal questions" also facilitates ignoring the causes of the injuries. Warshaw points out that such medical encounters confirm the abused woman's belief in the invisibility of her situation. The significant context of her injuries is avoided, leaving her to continue or resolve her abusive relationship. In spite of available protocols to report suspected abuse to the police and refer women to counseling, such recommendations are rarely implemented. Observing the boundary that masquerades as respect for privacy indirectly supports what men do to their partners.

The chapters in this section show how male dominance, once established, is structured into the daily operations of institutions and that ideologies develop to justify the existing arrangements. The civil rights and feminist movements have challenged the privileges of White men with only limited success.

REFERENCES

Beauvoir, S. de. (1970). *The second sex.* New York: Knopf.

Griffin, S. (1980). *Woman and nature: The roaring inside her.* New York: Harper & Row.

6 The Sexual Politics of Black Womanhood

PATRICIA HILL COLLINS
University of Cincinnati

> Even I found it almost impossible to let her say what had happened to her as *she* perceived it. . . . And why? Because once you strip away the lie that rape is pleasant, that children are not permanently damaged by sexual pain, that violence done to them is washed away by fear, silence, and time, you are left with the positive horror of the lives of thousands of children . . . who have been sexually abused and who have never been permitted their own language to tell about it.
>
> —Alice Walker (1988, p. 57)

In *The Color Purple* Alice Walker (1982) creates the character of Celie, a Black adolescent girl who is sexually abused by her stepfather. By writing letters to God and forming supportive relationships with other Black women, Celie finds her own voice, and her voice enables her to transcend the fear and silence of her childhood. By creating Celie and giving her the language to tell of her sexual abuse, Walker adds Celie's voice to muted yet growing discussions of the sexual politics of Black womanhood in Black feminist thought. Black feminists have investigated how rape as a specific form of sexual violence is embedded in a system of interlocking race, gender, and class oppression (Davis, 1978, 1981, 1989; Hall, 1983). Reproductive rights issues such as access to information on sexuality and birth control, the struggles for abortion rights, and patterns of forced sterilization have also garnered attention (Davis, 1981). Black lesbian feminists have vigorously challenged the basic assumptions and mechanisms of control underlying compulsory

Reprinted from *Black Feminist Thought* by Patricia Hill Collins by permission of the publisher, Routledge, Chapman and Hall, Inc.

heterosexuality and have investigated homophobia's impact on African-American women (Clarke, 1983; Lorde, 1984; Shockley, 1983; Smith, 1983).

But when it comes to other important issues concerning the sexual politics of Black womanhood, like Alice Walker, Black feminists have found it almost impossible to say what has happened to Black women. In the flood of scholarly and popular writing about Black heterosexual relationships, analyses of domestic violence against African-American women—especially those that link this form of sexual violence to existing gender ideology concerning Black masculinity and Black femininity—remain rare. Theoretical work explaining patterns of Black women's inclusion in the burgeoning international pornography industry has been similarly neglected. Perhaps the most curious omission has been the virtual silence of the Black feminist community concerning the participation of far too many Black women in prostitution. Ironically, although the image of African-American women as prostitutes has been aggressively challenged, the reality of African-American women who work as prostitutes remains unexplored.

These patterns of inclusion and neglect in Black feminist thought merit investigation. Examining the links between sexuality and power in a system of interlocking race, gender, and class oppression should reveal how important controlling Black women's sexuality has been to the effective operation of domination overall. The words of Angela Davis, Audre Lorde, Barbara Smith, and Alice Walker provide a promising foundation for a comprehensive Black feminist analysis. But Black feminist analyses of sexual politics must go beyond chronicling how sexuality has been used to oppress. Equally important is the need to reconceptualize sexuality with an eye toward empowering African-American women.

A WORKING DEFINITION OF SEXUAL POLITICS

Sexual politics examines the links between sexuality and power. In defining sexuality it is important to distinguish among sexuality and the related terms, *sex* and *gender* (Andersen, 1988; Vance, 1984). Sex is a biological category attached to the body—humans are born female or male. In contrast, gender is socially constructed. The sex/gender system consists of marking the categories of biological sex with socially constructed gender meanings of masculinity and femininity. Just as sex/

gender systems vary from relatively egalitarian systems to sex/gender hierarchies, ideologies of sexuality attached to particular sex/gender systems exhibit similar diversity. Sexuality is socially constructed through the sex/gender system on both the personal level of individual consciousness and interpersonal relationships and the social structural level of social institutions (Foucault, 1980). This multilevel sex/gender system reflects the needs of a given historical moment such that social constructions of sexuality change in tandem with changing social conditions.

African-American women inhabit a sex/gender hierarchy in which inequalities of race and social class have been sexualized. Privileged groups define their alleged sexual practices as the mythical norm and label sexual practices and groups that diverge from this norm as deviant and threatening (Lorde, 1984; Vance, 1984). Maintaining the mythical norm of the financially independent, white, middle-class family organized around a monogamous heterosexual couple requires stigmatizing African-American families as being deviant, and a primary source of this assumed deviancy stems from allegations about Black sexuality. This sex/gender hierarchy not only operates on the social structural level but is potentially replicated within each individual. Differences in sexuality thus take on more meaning than just benign sexual variation. Each individual becomes a powerful conduit for social relations of domination whereby individual anxieties, fears, and doubts about sexuality can be annexed by larger systems of oppression (Foucault, 1980, p. 99; Hoch, 1979).

According to Cheryl Clarke (1983), African-Americans have been profoundly affected by this sex/gender hierarchy:

> Like all Americans, black Americans live in a sexually repressive culture, and we have made all manner of compromise regarding our sexuality in order to live here. We have expended much energy trying to debunk the racist mythology which says our sexuality is depraved: Unfortunately, many of us have overcompensated and assimilated. . . . Like everyone else in America who is ambivalent in these respects, black folk have to live with the contradictions of this limited sexual system by repressing or closeting any other sexual/erotic urges, feelings, or desires. (p. 199)

Embedded in Clarke's statement is the theme of self-censorship inherent when a hierarchy of any kind invades interpersonal relationships among individuals and the actual consciousness of individuals themselves. Sexuality and power as domination become intertwined.

In her ground-breaking essay, "Uses of the Erotic: The Erotic as Power," Black feminist poet Audre Lorde (1984) explores this fundamental link between sexuality and power:

> There are many kinds of power, used and unused, acknowledged or other-wise. The erotic is a resource within each of us that lies in a deeply female and spiritual plane, firmly rooted in the power of our unexpressed or unrecognized feeling. In order to perpetuate itself, every oppression must corrupt or distort those various sources of power within the culture of the oppressed that can provide energy for change. For women, this has meant a suppression of the erotic as a considered source of power and information in our lives. (p. 53)

For Lorde sexuality is a component of the larger construct of the erotic as a source of power in women. Lorde's notion is one of power as energy, as something people possess which must be annexed in order for larger systems of oppression to function.[1]

Sexuality becomes a domain of restriction and repression when this energy is tied to the larger system of race, class, and gender oppression. But Lorde's words also signal the potential for Black women's empow-erment by showing sexuality and the erotic to be a domain of explora-tion, pleasure, and human agency. From a Black feminist standpoint sexuality encompasses the both/and nature of human existence, the potential for a sexuality that simultaneously oppresses and empowers.

One key issue for Black feminist thought is the need to examine the processes by which power as domination on the social structural level—namely, institutional structures of racism, sexism, and social class privi-lege—annexes this basic power of the erotic on the personal level—that is, the construct of power as energy, for its own ends.

BLACK WOMEN AND THE SEX/GENDER HIERARCHY

The social construction of Black women's sexuality is embedded in this larger, overarching sex/gender hierarchy designed to harness power as energy to the exigencies of power as race, gender, and social class domination. The discussion in Chapter 3 [*Black Feminist Thought*] on slave owner attempts to control Black women's fertility, the analysis in Chapter 4 of the significance of the controlling images of Black women in regulating Black women's sexuality and fertility, and the analysis in Chapter 6 of Black motherhood all explore efforts by the dominant group to control and exploit Black women's reproduction. Pornography, prostitution, and rape as a specific tool of sexual violence have also been key to the sexual politics of Black womanhood. Together they form three essential and interrelated components of the sex/gender hierarchy framing Black women's sexuality.

Pornography and Black Women's Bodies

For centuries the black woman has served as the primary pornographic "outlet" for white men in Europe and America. We need only think of the black women used as breeders, raped for the pleasure and profit of their owners. We need only think of the license the "master" of the slave women enjoyed. But, most telling of all, we need only study the old slave societies of the South to note the sadistic treatment—at the hands of white "gentlemen"— of "beautiful young quadroons and octoroons" who became increasingly (and were deliberately bred to become) indistinguishable from white women, and were the more highly prized as slave mistresses because of this. (Walker, 1981, p. 42)

Alice Walker's description of the rape of enslaved African women for the "pleasure and profit of their owners" encapsulates several elements of contemporary pornography. First, Black women were used as sex objects for the pleasure of white men. This objectification of African-American women parallels the portrayal of women in pornography as sex objects whose sexuality is available for men (McNall, 1983). Exploiting Black women as breeders objectified them as less than human because only animals can be bred against their will. In contemporary pornography women are objectified through being portrayed as pieces of meat, as sexual animals awaiting conquest. Second, African-American women were raped, a form of sexual violence. Violence is typically an implicit or explicit theme in pornography. Moreover, the rape of Black women linked sexuality and violence, another characteristic feature of pornography (Eisenstein, 1983). Third, rape and other forms of sexual violence act to strip victims of their will to resist and make them passive and submissive to the will of the rapist. Female passivity, the fact that women have things done to them, is a theme repeated over and over in contemporary pornography (McNall, 1983). Fourth, the profitability of Black women's sexual exploitation for white "gentlemen" parallels pornography's financially lucrative benefits for pornographers (Eisenstein, 1983). Finally, the actual breeding of "quadroons and octoroons" only reinforces the themes of Black women's passivity, objectification, and malleability to male control but reveals pornography's grounding in racism and sexism. The fates of both Black and white women were intertwined in this breeding process. The ideal African-American woman as a pornographic object was indistinguishable from white women and thus approximated the images of beauty, asexuality, and chastity forced on white women. But inside was a highly sexual whore, a "slave mistress" ready to cater to her owner's pleasure.[2]

Contemporary pornography consists of a series of icons or representations that focus the viewer's attention on the relationship between the portrayed individual and the general qualities ascribed to that class of individuals. Pornographic images are iconographic in that they represent realities in a manner determined by the historical position of the observers, their relationship to their own time and to the history of the conventions which they employ (Gilman, 1985). The treatment of Black women's bodies in 19th-century Europe and the United States may be the foundation upon which contemporary pornography as the representation of women's objectification, domination, and control is based. Icons about the sexuality of Black women's bodies emerged in these contexts. Moreover, as race- and gender-specific representations, these icons have implications for the treatment of both African-American and white women in contemporary pornography.

I suggest that African-American women were not included in pornography as an afterthought but instead form a key pillar on which contemporary pornography itself rests. As Alice Walker (1981) points out, "The more ancient roots of modern pornography are to be found in the almost always pornographic treatment of black women who, from the moment they entered slavery . . . were subjected to rape as the 'logical' convergence of sex and violence. Conquest, in short" (p. 42).

One key feature about the treatment of Black women in the 19th century was how their bodies were objects of display. In the antebellum American South white men did not have to look at pornographic pictures of women because they could become voyeurs of Black women on the auction block. A chilling example of this objectification of the Black female body is provided by the exhibition, in early 19th-century Europe, of Sarah Bartmann, the so-called Hottentot Venus. Her display formed one of the original icons for Black female sexuality. An African woman, Sarah Bartmann was often exhibited at fashionable parties in Paris, generally wearing little clothing, to provide entertainment. To her audience she represented deviant sexuality. At the time European audiences thought that Africans had deviant sexual practices and searched for physiological differences, such as enlarged penises and malformed female genitalia, as indications of this deviant sexuality. Sarah Bartmann's exhibition stimulated these racist and sexist beliefs. After her death in 1815, she was dissected. Her genitalia and buttocks remain on display in Paris (Gilman, 1985).

Sander Gilman (1985) explains the impact that Sarah Bartmann's exhibition had on Victorian audiences:

> It is important to note that Sarah Bartmann was exhibited not to show her genitalia—but rather to present another anomaly which the European audience . . . found riveting. This was the steatopygia, or protruding buttocks, the other physical characteristic of the Hottentot female which captured the eye of early European travelers. . . . The figure of Sarah Bartmann was reduced to her sexual parts. The audience which had paid to see her buttocks and had fantasized about the uniqueness of her genitalia when she was alive could, after her death and dissection, examine both. (p. 213)

In this passage Gilman unwittingly describes how Bartmann was used as a pornographic object similar to how women are represented in contemporary pornography. She was reduced to her sexual parts, and these parts came to represent a dominant icon applied to Black women throughout the 19th century. Moreover, the fact that Sarah Bartmann was both African and a woman underscores the importance of gender in maintaining notions of racial purity. In this case Bartmann symbolized Blacks as a "race." Thus the creation of the icon applied to Black women demonstrates that notions or gender, race, and sexuality were linked in overarching structures of political domination and economic exploitation.

The process illustrated by the pornographic treatment of the bodies of enslaved African women and of women like Sarah Bartmann has developed into a full-scale industry encompassing all women objectified differently by racial/ethnic category. Contemporary portrayals of Black women in pornography represent the continuation of the historical treatment of their actual bodies. African-American women are usually depicted in a situation of bondage and slavery, typically in a submissive posture, and often with two white men. As Bell (1987) observes, "This setting reminds us of all the trappings of slavery: chains, whips, neck braces, wrist clasps" (p. 59). White women and women of color have different pornographic images applied to them. The image of Black women in pornography is almost consistently one featuring them breaking from chains. The image of Asian women in pornography is almost consistently one of being tortured (Bell, 1987, p. 161).

The pornographic treatment of Black women's bodies challenges the prevailing feminist assumption that because pornography primarily affects white women, racism has been grafted onto pornography. African-American women's experiences suggest that Black women were not added into a preexisting pornography, but rather that pornography itself must be reconceptualized as an example of the interlocking nature of race, gender, and class oppression. At the heart of both racism and sexism are notions of biological determinism claiming that people of African descent and women possess immutable biological characteristics marking their inferiority to elite white men (Fausto-Sterling, 1989; Gould, 1981; Halpin, 1989). In pornography these racist and sexist beliefs are sexualized. Moreover, for African-American women pornography has not been timeless and universal but was tied to Black women's experiences with the European colonization of Africa and with American slavery. Pornography emerged within a specific system of social class relationships.

This linking of views of the body, social constructions of race and gender, and conceptualizations of sexuality that inform Black women's treatment as pornographic objects promises to have significant implications for how we assess contemporary pornography. Moreover, examining how pornography has been central to the race, gender, and class oppression of African-American women offers new routes for understanding the dynamics of power as domination.

Investigating racial patterns in pornography offers one route for such an analysis. Black women have often claimed that images of white women's sexuality were intertwined with the controlling image of the sexually denigrated Black woman: "In the United States, the fear and fascination of female sexuality was projected onto black women; the passionless lady arose in symbiosis with the primitively sexual slave" (Hall, 1983, p. 333). Comparable linkages exist in pornography (Gardner, 1980). Alice Walker (1981) provides a fictional account of a Black man's growing awareness of the different ways that African-American and white women are objectified in pornography: "What he has refused to see—because to see it would reveal yet another area in which he is unable to protect or defend black women—is that where white women are depicted in pornography as 'objects,' black women are depicted as animals. Where white women are depicted as human bodies if not beings, black women are depicted as shit" (p. 52).

Walker's distinction between "objects" and "animals" is crucial in untangling gender, race, and class dynamics in pornography. Within the mind/body, culture/nature, male/female oppositional dichotomies in Western social thought, objects occupy an uncertain interim position. As objects white women become creations of culture—in this case, the mind of white men—using the materials of nature—in this case, uncontrolled female sexuality. In contrast, as animals Black women receive no such redeeming dose of culture and remain open to the type of exploitation visited on nature overall. Race becomes the distinguishing feature in determining the type of objectification women will encounter. Whiteness as symbolic of both civilization and culture is used to separate objects from animals.

The alleged superiority of men to women is not the only hierarchical relationship that has been linked to the putative superiority of the mind to the body. Certain "races" of people have been defined as being more bodylike, more animal-like, and less godlike than others (Spelman, 1982, p. 52). Race and gender oppression may both revolve around the same axis of disdain for the body; both portray the sexuality of subordinate groups as animalistic and therefore deviant. Biological notions of race and gender prevalent in the early 19th century that fostered the animalistic icon of Black female sexuality were joined by the appearance of a racist biology incorporating the concept of degeneracy (Foucault, 1980). Africans and women were both perceived as embodied entities, and Blacks were seen as degenerate. Fear of and disdain for the body thus formed a key element in both sexist and racist thinking (Spelman, 1982).

Although the sexual and racial dimensions of being treated like an animal are important, the economic foundation underlying this treatment is critical. Animals can be economically exploited, worked, sold, killed, and consumed. As "mules," African-American women become susceptible to such treatment. The political economy of pornography also merits careful attention. Pornography is pivotal in mediating contradictions in changing societies (McNall, 1983). It is no accident that racist biology, religious justifications for slavery and women's subordination, and other explanations for 19th-century racism and sexism arose during a period of profound political and economic change. Symbolic means of domination become particularly important in mediating contradictions in changing political economies. The exhibition of Sarah Bartmann and Black women on the auction block were not benign intellectual exercises—these practices defended real material and political interests. Current transformations in international capitalism require similar ideological justifications. Where does pornography fit in these current transformations? This question awaits a comprehensive Afrocentric feminist analysis.

Publicly exhibiting Black women may have been central to objectifying Black women as animals and to creating the icon of Black women as animals. Yi-Fu Tuan (1984) offers an innovative argument about similarities in efforts to control nature—especially plant life—the domestication of animals, and the domination of certain groups of humans. Tuan suggests that displaying humans alongside animals implies that such humans are more like monkeys and bears than they are like "normal" people. This same juxtaposition leads spectators to view the captive animals in a special way. Animals acquire definitions of being like humans, only more openly carnal and sexual, an aspect of animals that forms a major source of attraction for visitors to modern zoos. In discussing the popularity of monkeys in zoos, Tuan notes: "Some visitors are especially attracted by the easy sexual behavior of the monkeys. Voyeurism is forbidden except when applied to subhumans" (p. 82). Tuan's analysis suggests that the public display of Sarah Bartmann and of the countless enslaved African women on the auction blocks of the antebellum American South—especially in proximity to animals—fostered their image as animalistic.

This linking of Black women and animals is evident in 19th-century scientific literature. The equation of women, Blacks, and animals is revealed in the following description of an African woman published in an 1878 anthropology text:

> She had a way of pouting her lips exactly like what we have observed in the orangutan. Her movements had something abrupt and fantastical about them, reminding one of those of the ape. Her ear was like that of many apes. . . . These are animal characters. I have never seen a human head more like an ape than that of this woman. (Halpin, 1989, p. 287)

In a climate such as this, it is not surprising that one prominent European physician even stated that Black women's "animallike sexual appetite went so far as to lead black women to copulate with apes" (Gilman, 1985, p. 212).

The treatment of all women in contemporary pornography has strong ties to the portrayal of Black women as animals. In pornography women become nonpeople and are often represented as the sum of their fragmented body parts. Scott McNall (1983) observes:

This fragmentation of women relates to the predominance of rear-entry position photographs. . . . All of these kinds of photographs reduce the woman to her reproductive system, and, furthermore, make her open, willing, and available—not in control. . . . The other thing rear-entry position photographs tell us about women is that they are animals. They are animals because they are the same as dogs—bitches in heat who can't control themselves. (pp. 197-198)

This linking of animals and white women within pornography becomes feasible when grounded in the earlier denigration of Black women as animals.

Developing a comprehensive analysis of the race, gender and class dynamics of pornography offers possibilities for change. Those Black feminist intellectuals investigating sexual politics imply that the situation is much more complicated than that advanced by some prominent white feminists (see, e.g., Dworkin, 1981) in which "men oppress women" because they are men. Such approaches implicitly assume biologically deterministic views of sex, gender, and sexuality and offer few possibilities for change. In contrast, Afrocentric feminist analyses routinely provide for human agency and its corresponding empowerment and for the responsiveness of social structures to human action. In the short story "Coming Apart," Alice Walker (1981) describes one Black man's growing realization that his enjoyment of pornography, whether of white women as "objects" or Black women as "animals," degraded him:

He begins to feel sick. For he realizes that he has bought some of the advertisements about women, black and white. And further, inevitably, he has bought the advertisements about himself. In pornography the black man is portrayed as being capable of fucking anything . . . even a piece of shit. He is defined solely by the size, readiness and unselectivity of his cock. (p. 52)

Walker conceptualizes pornography as a race/gender system that entraps everyone. But by exploring an African-American *man's* struggle for a self-defined standpoint on pornography, Walker suggests that a changed consciousness is essential to social change. If a Black man can understand how pornography affects him, then other groups enmeshed in the same system are equally capable of similar shifts in consciousness and action.

Prostitution and the Commodification of Sexuality

In *To Be Young, Gifted and Black,* Lorraine Hansberry (1969) creates three characters: a young domestic worker; a chic professional, middle-aged woman; and a mother in her thirties. Each speaks a variant of the following:

In these streets out there, any little white boy from Long Island or Westchester sees me and leans out of his car and yells—"Hey there, *hot chocolate*! Say there, Jezebel! Hey you—'Hundred Dollar Misunderstanding'! YOU! Bet you know where there's a good time tonight . . ." Follow me sometimes and see if I lie. I can be coming from eight hours on an assembly line or fourteen hours in Mrs. Halsey's kitchen. I can be all filled up that day with three hundred years of rage so that my eyes are flashing and my flesh is trembling—and the white boys in the streets, they look at me and think of sex. They look at me and that's *all* they think. . . . Baby, you could be Jesus in drag—but if you're brown they're sure you're selling! (p. 98)

Like the characters in Hansberry's fiction, all Black women are affected by the widespread controlling image that African-American women are sexually promiscuous, potential prostitutes. The pervasiveness of this image is vividly recounted in Black activist lawyer Pauli Murray's (1987) description of an incident she experienced while defending two women from Spanish Harlem who had been arrested as prostitutes: "The first witness, a white man from New Jersey, testified on the details of the sexual transaction and his payment of money. When asked to identify the woman with whom he had engaged in sexual intercourse, he unhesitatingly pointed directly at me, seated beside my two clients at the defense table!" (p. 274). Murray's clients were still convicted.

The creation of Jezebel, the image of the sexually denigrated Black woman, has been vital in sustaining a system of interlocking race, gender, and class oppression. Exploring how the image of the African-American woman as prostitute has been used by each system of oppression illustrates how sexuality links the three systems. But Black women's treatment also demonstrates how manipulating sexuality has been essential to the political economy of domination within each system and across all three.

Yi-Fu Tuan (1984) suggests that power as domination involves reducing humans to animate nature in order to exploit them economically or to treat them condescendingly as pets. Domination may be either cruel and exploitative with no affection or may be exploitative yet coexist with affection. The former produces the victim—in this case, the Black woman as "mule" whose labor has been exploited. In contrast, the combination of dominance and affection produces the pet, the individual who is subordinate but whose survival depends on the whims of the more powerful. The "beautiful young quadroons and octoroons" described by Alice Walker were bred to be pets—enslaved Black mistresses whose existence required that they retain the affection of their owners. The treatment afforded these women illustrates a process that affects all African-American women: their portrayal as actual or potential victims and pets of elite white males.[3]

African-American women simultaneously embody the coexistence of the victim and the pet, with survival often linked to the ability to be appropriately subordinate as victims or pets. Black women's experiences as unpaid and paid workers demonstrate the harsh lives victims are forced to lead. Although the life of the victim is difficult, pets experience a distinctive form of exploitation. Zora Neale Hurston's 1943 essay, "The 'Pet' Negro System," speaks contemptuously of this ostensibly benign situation that combines domination with affection. Written in a Black oratorical style, Hurston notes, "Brother and Sisters, I take my text this morning from the Book of Dixie. . . . Now it says here, 'And every white man shall be allowed to pet himself a Negro. Yea, he shall take a black man unto himself to pet and cherish, and this same Negro shall be perfect in his sight'" (Walker 1979a, p. 156). Pets are treated as exceptions and live with the constant threat that they will no longer be "perfect in his sight," that their owners will tire of them and relegate them to the unenviable role of victim.

Prostitution represents the fusion of exploitation for an economic purpose—namely, the commodification of Black women's sexuality—with the demeaning treatment afforded pets. Sex becomes commodified not merely in the sense that it can be purchased—the dimension of economic exploitation—but also in the sense that one is dealing with a totally alienated being who is separated from and who does not control her body: the dimension of power as domination (McNall, 1983). Commodified sex can then be appropriated by the powerful. When the "white boys from Long Island" look at Black women and *all* they think about is sex, they believe that they can appropriate Black women's bodies. When they yell, "Bet you know where there's a good time tonight," they expect commodified sex with Black women as "animals" to be better than sex with white women as "objects." Both pornography and prostitution commodify sexuality and imply to the "white boys" that all African-American women can be bought.

Prostitution under European and American capitalism thus exists within a complex web of political and economic relationships whereby sexuality is conceptualized along intersecting axes of race and gender. Gilman's (1985) analysis of the exhibition of Sarah Bartmann as the "Hottentot Venus" suggests another intriguing connection between race, gender, and sexuality in 19th-century Europe—the linking of the icon of the Black woman with the icon of the white prostitute. Whereas the Hottentot woman stood for the essence of Africans as a race, the white prostitute symbolized the sexualized woman. The prostitute represented the embodiment of sexuality and all that European society associated with it: disease as well as passion. As Gilman points out, "It is this uncleanliness, this disease, which forms the final link between two images of women, the black and the prostitute. Just as the genitalia of the Hottentot were perceived as parallel to the diseased genitalia of the prostitute, so too the power of the idea of corruption links both images" (p. 237). These connections between the icons of Black women and white prostitutes demonstrate how race, gender, and the social class structure of the European political economy interlock.

In the American antebellum South both of these images were fused in the forced prostitution of enslaved African women. The prostitution of Black women allowed white women to be the opposite; Black "whores" make white "virgins" possible. This race/gender nexus fostered a situation whereby white men could then differentiate between the sexualized woman-as-body who is dominated and "screwed" and the asexual woman-as-pure-spirit who is idealized and brought home to mother (Hoch, 1979, p. 70). The sexually denigrated woman, whether she was made a victim through her rape or a pet through her seduction, could be used as the yardstick against which the cult of true womanhood was measured. Moreover, this entire situation was profitable.

Rape and Sexual Violence

Force was important in creating African-American women's centrality to American images of the sexualized woman and in shaping their experiences with both pornography and prostitution. Black women did not willingly submit to their exhibition on southern auction blocks— they were forced to do so. Enslaved African women could not choose whether to work—they were beaten and often killed if they refused. Black domestics who resisted the sexual advances of their employers often found themselves looking for work where none was to be found.

Both the reality and the threat of violence have acted as a form of social control for African-American women. Rape has been one fundamental tool of sexual violence directed against African-American women. Challenging the pervasiveness of Black women's rape and sexual extortion by white men has long formed a prominent theme in Black women's writings. Autobiographies such as Maya Angelou's (1970) *I Know Why the Caged Bird Sings* and Harriet Jacobs's (1860/1987) "The Perils of a Slave Woman's Life" from *Incidents in the Life of a Slave Girl* record examples of actual and threatened sexual assault. The effects of rape on African-American women is a prominent theme in Black women's fiction. Gayl Jones's (1975) *Corregidora* and Rosa Guy's (1983) *A Measure of Time* both explore interracial rape of Black women. Toni Morrison's (1970) *The Bluest Eye,* Alice Walker's (1982) *The Color Purple,* and Gloria Naylor's (1980) *The Women of Brewster Place* all examine rape within African-American families and communities. Elizabeth Clark-Lewis's (1985) study of domestic workers found that mothers, aunts, and community othermothers warned young Black women about the threat of rape. One respondent in Clark-Lewis's study, an 87-year-old North Carolina Black domestic worker, remembers, "Nobody was sent out before you was told to be careful of the white man or his sons" (p. 15).

Rape and other acts of overt violence that Black women have experienced, such as physical assault during slavery, domestic abuse, incest, and sexual extortion, accompany Black women's subordination in a system of race, class, and gender oppression. These violent acts are the visible dimensions of a more generalized, routinized system of oppression. Violence against Black women tends to be legitimated and therefore condoned, whereas the same acts visited on other groups may remain nonlegitimated and nonexcusable. Certain forms of violence may garner the backing and control of the state even as others remain uncontrolled (Edwards, 1987). Specific acts of sexual violence visited on African-American women reflect a broader process by which violence is socially constructed in a race- and gender-specific manner. Thus Black women, Black men, and white women experience distinctive forms of sexual violence. As Angela Davis (1981) points out, "It would be a mistake to regard the institutionalized pattern of rape during slavery as an expression of white men's sexual urges. . . . Rape was a weapon of domination, weapon of repression, whose covert goal was to extinguish slave women's will to resist, and in the process, to demoralize their men" (p. 23).

Angela Davis's work (1978, 1981, 1989) illustrates this effort to conceptualize sexual violence against African-American women as part of a system of interlocking race, gender, and class oppression. Davis suggests that sexual violence has been central to the economic and political subordination of African-Americans overall. But although Black men and women were both victims of sexual violence, the specific forms they encountered were gender specific.

Depicting African-American men as sexually charged beasts who desired white women created the myth of the Black rapist.[4] Lynching emerged as the specific form of sexual violence visited on Black men, with the myth of the Black rapist as its ideological justification. The significance of this myth is that it "has been methodically conjured up when recurrent waves of violence and terror against the black community required a convincing explanation" (Davis, 1978, p. 25). Black women experienced a parallel form of race- and gender-specific sexual violence. Treating African-American women as pornographic objects and portraying them as sexualized animals, as prostitutes, created the controlling image of Jezebel. Rape became the specific act of sexual violence forced on Black women, with the myth of the Black prostitute as its ideological justification.

Lynching and rape, two race- and gender-specific forms of sexual violence, merged with their ideological justifications of the rapist and prostitute in order to provide an effective system of social control over African-Americans. Davis (1978) asserts that the controlling image of Black men as rapists has always "strengthened its inseparable companion: the image of the black woman as chronically promiscuous. And with good reason, for once the notion is accepted that black men harbor irresistible, animal-like sexual urges, the entire race is invested with bestiality" (p. 27). A race of "animals" can be treated as such—as victims or pets. "The mythical rapist implies the mythical whore—and a race of rapists and whores deserves punishment and nothing more" (p. 28).

Some suggestive generalizations exist concerning the connection between the social constructions of the rapist and the prostitute and the tenets of racist biology. Tuan (1984) notes that humans practice certain biological procedures on plants and animals to ensure their suitability as pets. For animals the goal of domestication is manageability and control, a state that can be accomplished through selective breeding or, for some male animals, by castration. A similar process may have affected the historical treatment of African-Americans. As dominant groups have generally refrained from trying to breed humans in the same way that they breed animals, the pervasiveness of rape and lynching suggests that these practices may have contributed to mechanisms of population control. Although not widespread, in some slave settings selective breeding and, if that failed, rape were used to produce slaves of a certain genetic heritage. In an 1858 slave narrative, James Roberts recounts the plantation of Maryland planter Calvin Smith, a man who kept 50-60 "head of women" for reproductive purposes. Only whites were permitted access to these women in order to ensure that 20-25 racially mixed children were born annually. Roberts also tells of a second planter who competed with Smith in breeding mulattos, a group that at that time brought higher prices, the "same as men strive to raise the most stock of any kind, cows, sheep, horses, etc." (Weisbord, 1975, p. 27). For Black men, lynching was frequently accompanied by castration. Again, the parallels to techniques used to domesticate animals, or at least serve as a warning to those Black men who remained alive, is striking.

Black women continue to deal with this legacy of the sexual violence visited on African-Americans generally and with our history as collective rape victims. One effect lies in the treatment of rape victims. Such women are twice victimized, first by the actual rape, in this case the collective rape under slavery. But they are victimized again by family members, community residents, and social institutions such as criminal justice systems that somehow believe that rape victims are responsible for their own victimization. Even though current statistics indicate that Black women are more likely to be victimized than white women, Black women are less likely to report their rapes, less likely to have their cases come to trial, less likely to have their trials result in convictions, and, most disturbing, less likely to seek counseling and other support services. Existing evidence suggests that African-American women are aware of their lack of protection and that they resist rapists more than other groups (Bart & O'Brien, 1985).

Another significant effect of this legacy of sexual violence concerns Black women's absence from antirape movements. Angela Davis (1978) argues, "If black women are conspicuously absent from the ranks of the antirape movement today, it is, in large part, their way of protesting the movement's posture of indifference toward the frame-up rape charge as an incitement to racist aggression" (p. 25). But this absence fosters Black women's silence concerning a troubling issue: The fact that most Black women are raped by Black men. Although the historical legacy of the triad of pornography, prostitution, and the

institutionalized rape of Black women may have created the larger
social context within which all African-Americans reside, the unfortunate current reality is that many Black men have internalized the controlling images of the sex/gender hierarchy and condone either Black
women's rape by other Black men or their own behavior as rapists. Far
too many African-American women live with the untenable position of
putting up with abusive Black men in defense of an elusive Black unity.

The historical legacy of Black women's treatment in pornography,
prostitution, and rape forms the institutional backdrop for a range of
interpersonal relationships that Black women currently have with Black
men, whites, and one another. Without principled coalitions with other
groups, African-American women may not be able to effect lasting
change on the social structural level of social institutions. But the first
step to forming such coalitions is examining exactly how these institutions harness power as energy for their own use by invading both
relationships among individuals and individual consciousness itself.
Thus understanding the contemporary dynamics of the sexual politics
of Black womanhood in order to empower African-American women
requires investigating how social structural factors infuse the private
domain of Black women's relationships.

NOTES

1. French philosopher Michel Foucault (1980) makes a similar point: "I believe that
the political significance of the problem of sex is due to the fact that sex is located at the
point of intersection of the discipline of the body and the control of the population"
(p. 125). The erotic is something felt, a power that is embodied. Controlling sexuality
harnesses that power for the needs of larger, hierarchical systems by controlling the body
and hence the population.

2. Offering a similar argument about the relationship between race and masculinity,
Paul Hoch (1979) suggests that the ideal white man is a hero who upholds honor. But
inside lurks a "Black beast" of violence and sexuality, traits that the white hero deflects
onto men of color.

3. Any group can be made into pets. Consider Tuan's (1984) discussion of the role that
young Black boys played as exotic ornaments for wealthy white women in the 1500s to
the early 1800s in England. Unlike other male servants, the boys were favorite attendants
of noble ladies and gained entry into their mistresses' drawing rooms, bedchambers, and
theater boxes. Boys were often given fancy collars with padlocks to wear. "As they did
with their pet dogs and monkeys, the ladies grew genuinely fond of their black boys" (p.
142). In addition, Nancy White's analysis in Chapter 5 of the differences between how
white and Black women are treated by white men uses this victim/pet metaphor (Gwaltney,
1980, p. 148).

4. See Hoch's (1979) discussion of the roots of the white hero, black beast myth in Eurocentric thought. Hoch contends that white masculinity is based on the interracial competition for women. To become a "man," the white, godlike hero must prove himself victorious over the dark "beast" and win possession of the "white goddess." Through numerous examples Hoch suggests that this explanatory myth underlies Western myth, poetry, and literature. One example describing how Black men were depicted during the witch hunts is revealing. Hoch notes, "The Devil was often depicted as a lascivious black male with cloven hoofs, a tail, and a huge penis capable of super-masculine exertion—an archetypal leering 'black beast from below' " (p. 44).

REFERENCES

Andersen, M. (1988). *Thinking about women: Sociological perspectives on sex and gender* (2nd ed.). New York: Macmillan.

Angelou, M. (1969). *I know why the caged bird sings.* New York: Bantam.

Bart, P. B., & O'Brien, P. H. (1985). Ethnicity and rape avoidance: Jews, white Catholics and blacks. In P. D. Bart & P. H. O'Brien (Eds.), *Stopping rape: Successful survival strategies* (pp. 70-92). New York: Pergamon.

Bell, L. (Ed.). (1987). *Good girls/bad girls: Feminists and sex trade workers face to face.* Toronto: Seal.

Clark-Lewis, E. (1985). *"This work had a' end": The transition from live-in to day work. Southern women: The intersection of race, class and gender* (Working Paper No. 2). Memphis: Center for Research on Women, Memphis State University.

Clarke, C. (1983). The failure to transform: Homophobia in the black community. In B. Smith (Ed.), *Home girls: A black feminist anthology* (pp. 197-208). New York: Kitchen Table Press.

Davis, A. Y. (1978). Rape, racism and the capitalist setting. *Black Scholar, 9*(7), 24-30.

Davis, A. Y. (1981). *Women, race and class.* New York: Random House.

Davis, A. Y. (1989). *Women, culture and politics.* New York: Random House.

Dworkin, A. (1981). *Pornography: Men possessing women.* New York: Perigee.

Edwards, A. (1987). Male violence in feminist theory: An analysis of the changing conceptions of sex/gender violence and male dominance. In J. Hanmer & M. Maynard (Eds.), *Women, violence and social control* (pp. 13-29). Atlantic Highlands, NJ: Humanities Press.

Eisenstein, H. (1983). *Contemporary feminist thought.* Boston: G. K. Hall.

Fausto-Sterling, A. (1989). Life in the XY corral. *Women's Studies International Forum, 12*(3), 319-331.

Foucault, M. (1980). *Power/knowledge: Selected interviews and other writings 1972-1977* (C. Gordon, Ed.). New York: Pantheon.

Gilman, S. L. (1985). Black bodies, white bodies: Toward an iconography of female sexuality in late nineteenth-century art, medicine, and literature. *Critical Inquiry, 12*(1), 205-243.

Gould, S. J. (1981). *The mismeasure of man.* New York: Norton.

Guy, R. (1983). *A measure of time.* New York: Bantam.

Hall, J. D. (1983). The mind that burns in each body: Women, rape, and racial violence. In A. Snitow, C. Stansell, & S. Thompson (Eds.), *Powers of desire: The politics of sexuality* (pp. 329-349). New York: Monthly Review Press.

Halpin, Z. T. (1989). Scientific objectivity and the concept of "the other." *Women's Studies International Forum, 12*(3), 285-294.

Hansberry, L. (1969). *To be young, gifted and black.* New York: Signet.

Hoch, P. (1979). *White hero black beast: Racism, sexism and the mask of masculinity.* London: Pluto.

Jacobs, H. (1987). The perils of a slave woman's life. In M. H. Washington (Ed.), *Invented lives: Narratives of black women 1860-1960* (pp. 16-67). Garden City, NY: Anchor.

Jones, G. (1975). *Corregidora.* New York: Bantam.

Lorde, A. (1984). *Sister outsider.* Trumansburg, NY: Crossing.

McNall, S. G. (1983). Pornography: The structure of domination and the mode of reproduction. In S. G. McNall (Ed.), *Current perspectives in social theory* (Vol. 4, pp. 181-203). Greenwich, CT: JAI.

Morrison, T. (1970). *The bluest eye.* New York: Pocket.

Murray, P. (1987). *Song in a weary throat: An American pilgrimage.* New York: Harper & Row.

Naylor, G. (1980). *The women of Brewster Place.* New York: Penguin.

Shockley, A. A. (1974). *Loving her.* Tallahassee, FL: Naiad.

Shockley, A. A. (1983). The black lesbian in American literature: An overview. In B. Smith (Ed.), *Home girls: A black feminist anthology* (pp. 83-93). New York: Kitchen Table Press.

Smith, B. (1983). Introduction. In B. Smith (Ed.), *Home girls: A black feminist anthology* (pp. xix-lvi). New York: Kitchen Table Press.

Spelman, E. V. (1982). Theories of race and gender: The erasure of black women. *Quest, 5*(4), 36-62.

Tuan, Y.-F. (1984). *Dominance and affection: The making of pets.* New Haven, CT: Yale University Press.

Vance, C. S. (1984). Pleasure and danger: Toward a politics of sexuality. In C. S. Vance (Ed.), *Pleasure and danger: Exploring female sexuality* (pp. 1-27). Boston: Routledge & Kegan Paul.

Walker, A. (Ed.). (1979a). *I love myself when I am laughing, and then again when I am looking mean and impressive: A Zora Neale Hurston Reader.* Old Westbury, NY: Feminist Press.

Walker, A. (1979b, August). One child of one's own: A meaningful digression within the work(s). *Ms, 8*(2), 47-50, 72-75.

Walker, A. (1981). Coming apart. In *You can't keep a good woman down* (pp. 41-53). New York: Harcourt Brace Jovanovich.

Walker, A. (1982). *The color purple.* New York: Washington Square.

Walker, A. (1988). *Living by the word.* New York: Harcourt Brace Jovanovich.

Weisbord, R. G. (1975). *Genocide? Birth control and the black American.* Westport, CT: Greenwood.

7 The Imperishable Virginity of Saint Maria Goretti

KATHLEEN Z. YOUNG
Western Washington University

Within Roman Catholicism, many female saints have been virgin martyrs whose lives exemplify a feminine Christian ideal. Young women who "gave" their lives because of a spiritual commitment to the preservation of the hymen are held up as role models. Virginity is viewed as a spiritual commitment more important than the young Catholic woman's life.

The physical fact of virginity indicates spiritual valor. A preserved hymen may not guarantee entrance into heaven, but the inappropriate loss of the hymen diminishes the chances for eternal salvation. For the young Catholic virgin, sexual history and spiritual identity are difficult to separate, and when the Catholic woman "loses" her virginity because of rape, her spiritual life is damaged or diminished. Virgin rape is as devastating as incest in trespassing the boundary between the personal and spiritual self. The suffering that follows rape, especially virgin rape, is not just physical but also metaphysical and spiritual. The spiritual importance placed upon virginity makes Roman Catholic women especially vulnerable following rape or incest.

In this chapter, I examine the legend of the modern virgin martyr Maria Goretti, whose sainthood and idealization are used to regulate Catholic women's lives and condone violence against them. The institutionalization of violence (and male dominance) in the Catholic Church is accomplished through the handing on of stories of virgin martyrs as one facet of the social control of women, their sexuality, and their bodies. Maria Goretti is a modern mythic figure, with many levels of meaning to the myth.

105

THE RAPE OF MARIA GORETTI

In July 1902, Maria Goretti, a 12-year-old Italian girl, was stabbed in a sexual assault and died. Although details of the story have been influenced over the years by constant retelling and adaptation, the basic facts are as follows: Maria Goretti was from a poor rural family. Home one day alone, Maria was attacked by a young man, Alessandro Serenelli. He threatened to kill her if she did not have sex with him. Maria refused, and he stabbed her repeatedly with a knife. She died 24 hours after the attack. Serenelli was caught and tried for murder. He was sentenced to 30 years in prison. When he was released, Serenelli went to live with an order of monks. Reportedly, Maria appeared to him in a vision during his imprisonment. She forgave him, and he repented of his sin. When she was canonized by the Roman Catholic church in 1950, Serenelli was present, along with Maria's mother and her family.

There are discrepancies in almost every account of Maria Goretti. Marina Warner (1983) describes her as an 11-year-old murdered "by a young man from her village, whom she knew" (p. 70). But according to other sources (Delaney, 1980; MacConastair, 1951), Alessandro Serenelli lived in the same house, and Maria cooked and cleaned for him, and waited on him. He was neither consanguineous nor affinal kin, but he was part of the "family." In these accounts, Serenelli is described as the 20-year-old son of Maria's mother's partner in a sharecropping venture, a widower who lived with Assunta Goretti, a widow, and her six children in a barn on the estate of Count Mazzoleni. Serenelli is also sometimes described as a 19-year-old neighbor (Buehrle, 1967, p. 632) and sometimes as the son of her deceased father's partner who lived with the Goretti family (Delaney, 1980, p. 262).

Maria Goretti died in the hospital in the town of Nettuno on the Feast of the Most Precious Blood. The religious celebration brought people from the surrounding countryside into town, and a crowd gathered at the hospital for the deathwatch. Her funeral took place 2 days later. According to a biography of Serenelli, "Mourning thousands from Nettuno, Anzio and even distant places came to the hospital chapel and filed tearfully past Marietta's bier. Though it was a work day, Nettuno's shops closed for the funeral" (DiDonato, 1962, p. 73).

The immediate public acclaim for Maria Goretti was unprecedented. Why were thousands touched by her story? Why did so many go to her funeral? Why did her life and death reach mythic proportions almost immediately? She was known by many of the people of Nettuno (8 miles from her village), as she regularly stood on the street corner selling pigeon eggs. Her extraordinary beauty and obvious poverty made her memorable, according to one account (MacConastair, 1951, p. 89). She was also different from most young women in either her innocence of sexual desire or her determination to protect her virginity. According to his biographer Pietro DiDonato (1962), Serenelli reasoned:

> In every man lurked the possible rapist and killer. If, fearing the shame of the violation being known or to save her life, the girl acquiesces, the sensual man is then not included in the public criminal ranks. Supposing he had been a Mazzoleni or one of the wealthy ruling class? One never or rarely heard of the rich and powerful being punished for an act of passion. . . . If Marietta had submitted he would have made a habit of it. . . . Sooner or later she would have become the mother of his child—a not uncommon happening amongst the peasants and the poor. . . . [H]e would have married Marietta and perhaps developed a sentiment for her also. (p. 107)

But Serenelli's self-portrayal as a potential attractive lover can be questioned. Speaking for Serenelli at his trial, the lawyer Canalintas blamed the pornography industry for inciting Serenelli (DiDonato, 1962, p. 91). Pornography was unlikely to teach a young man how to attract a young woman. Maria may not have been innocent or chaste but repulsed by him. Most biographies recount Serenelli's "attempt to seduce her" (Delaney, 1980, p. 262) and her resistance to his "advances." According to these biographies, his seduction technique consisted of advancing upon her with a weapon while threatening to kill her. The weapon is variously described as a stiletto (Warner, 1983, p. 71), a dagger (Buehrle, 1967, p. 632), a brush hook (DiDonato, 1962, p. 89), or a machete (MacConastair, 1951). Serenelli said he would not have hacked her up if she had submitted to him when he confronted her with the weapon (DiDonato, 1962, p. 94).

Nevertheless, seduction is suggested because they knew each other and because he protested that he would not have stabbed her 14 times if she had submitted (DiDonato, 1962, p. 51). Apparently, she did not "submit," but some sources vary as to whether he raped her as well as murdering her (Rivers, 1973, p. 150). Her clothes were ripped off, and she was stabbed repeatedly, but she was not vaginally penetrated, according to most accounts (Buehrle, 1967; DiDonato, 1962; MacConastair, 1951). The prevailing myth is that she died with her virginity intact.

108   STRUCTURAL SUPPORTS FOR WOMEN

THE SAINTHOOD OF MARIA GORETTI

Maria Goretti is a modern virgin martyr, canonized in 1950. The short amount of time from her death to her canonization, only 48 years, is extraordinary. In the modern era, only two people have been made saints in a similar amount of time: the Italian-American nun "Mother" Frances Cabrini, who was canonized in 1946, and in 1982 the Polish priest Maximilian Kolbe. The canonization process has always been influenced by social and political considerations, as well as moral theology. As a model of chastity, Maria Goretti was preached to a generation of Roman Catholics in parochial schools before Vatican II. According to Debra Campbell (1988), "It was impossible for a girl to attend a parochial or convent school at any time during the six decades prior to Vatican II and not learn about Maria Goretti, who constituted the core curriculum in moral theology for Catholic girls during this period" (p. 668).

Hagiographies often compare Maria Goretti and two saints of an earlier era, Agnes and Agatha, both tortured and killed by spurned "suitors." Saint Agnes was beheaded rather than sacrifice her virginity. Saint Agatha was subjected to various tortures, most notably the tearing off of her breasts. The saint's torture was typically directed to the femaleness of the victim, reflecting the elements of sadism or pornography in the legend. Hagiographies usually record the name of Agatha's attacker (Attwater, 1965; Hoever, 1963), just as most of the compendium biographies refer to a relationship between Maria Goretti and her murderer, Alessandro Serenelli. In these accounts, Goretti, the innocent virgin, is the spiritual principle, and Serenelli, her murderer, the profane. She is beautiful, innocent, and good. He is evil and guilty.

In the hagiography of female virgin martyrs, the symbolic dualism of the male-female dyad established them as a couple reflecting the dichotomy of matter and spirit. It is impossible to imagine any sort of gender-role reversal. There are no popular heroes or male saints who went to their death rather than surrender their virginity. Older women are rarely portrayed as life-threatening rapists or potentially murderous, unless it is within the supernatural realm of witches.

At the canonization of Saint Maria Goretti, Pope Pius XII read a homily that said Serenelli was a "vicious stranger burst upon her" (Second Vatican Ecumenical Council 1975, p. 1525). But the Pope must have known that Serenelli was no stranger. A life-threatening rape is described as "an attractive pleasure" by Pius XII: "From Maria's story carefree children and young people with their zest for life can learn not to be led astray by attractive pleasures which are not only ephemeral and empty but also sinful" (p. 1526). The Pope, a male celibate with the power to define and construct appropriate sexuality, compared the attempted sexual assault to the sexual seduction of a passive young female. The legends and myths of virgin martyrs reinforce passivity and the victimization of Catholic girls and women. In these accounts, the passive female exhibits a potential that is activated by the male. Women are potentially dangerous in themselves for what they might incite men to do. When a man murders a virgin in the course of a sexual assault, he facilitates for her the eternal reward of heaven that is promised to virgin martyrs. But women are responsible for men's actions. When women do not incite but resist, they help men to be good. Thus the virgin martyr is an ideal woman—for men.

THE SYMBOLISM OF MARIA GORETTI

Serenelli's trial placed blame on Maria for struggling and on the Church for inspiring her struggle. A 12-year-old facing a menacing weapon was expected to be reasonable, to submit. The assumption was that by struggling, she precipitated, even if unwittingly, her own victimization. But from the church's perspective, her struggle is what made her a martyr and a saint. July 6 is the feast day of Saint Maria Goretti. The liturgy of her feast day Mass includes the following prayer:

O God, who among the other miracles of your power, have given even to the weaker sex the victory of martyrdom, grant, we beseech You, that we, who are celebrating the heavenly birthday of Blessed Maria, Your Virgin and Martyr, may, by her example draw nearer to You. (Hoever, 1963, p. 261)

These cultural paradigms of virginity and martyrdom have implications for the construction of sexuality, codes of reproduction, gender identity, and life experience for Catholic women.

Anthropologists have often noted the cross-cultural concern for female chastity. Among others, Pitt-Rivers (1954) and Peristany (1966) have discussed the values of honor and shame, particularly in the Mediterranean. According to Jane Collier (1986):

A man's honor was a function of his mother's, sister's, and wife's sexual chastity. A family's reputation depended on the sexual shame of its women and on the readiness of its men to defend, with violence if need be, its women's purity. (p. 101)

Sherry Ortner has stated that all complex agrarian societies have forms of the "virginity complex" (1978). The complex is found in societies in which inheritance is associated with legitimate birth and is the basis of status inequalities. Legitimate inheritance and status or place in society are dependent upon the social perception of female chastity. The appropriate construction of female sexuality is linked to preservation of the social order and legitimate inheritance (Ortner, 1978). A man's honor rests upon the control of his female relatives. The good reputation of his mother is imperative because her recognized virginity at marriage ensures publicly that he is legitimate. The public perception of his wife's "appropriate sexuality" (her good reputation) ensures that his heirs are accepted as legitimate. As Collier (1986) says:

> In such a world, women's bodies appear as gateways to all privileges. But women's bodies are gateways any man may enter. Women's penetrability is their most significant feature. The status and reputation of a family thus rest on the degree to which its women are protected from penetration—by women's own sense of sexual shame, by being locked away, and/or by the courage of family men in repelling seducers. (p. 101)

A man's honor is contingent upon his control of others. A woman's honor is associated with her own sense of sexual shame. How others treat her affects her own personal and internal spiritual life. Sexual transgressions committed against her reflect her own lack of sexual shame even if she did not precipitate the transgression. Sexual transgressions jeopardize her place in the material and spiritual world and are the gateway to her material and spiritual disgrace and that of her family. Religious values portrayed in myths that spiritualize virginity are functional in a society based on the ownership and control of property by men.

The legends of the saints that Roman Catholic women are raised with associate female sexuality with virginity and motherhood. Personal identity and sexual identity, both associated with virginity and motherhood, are conjunctive. *Inviolate* is a synonym for virgin. The virgin has not yet been sexually violated, the mother obviously has been. Sexuality is not the gateway to autonomy for women but instead implies social and spiritual vulnerability and lack of autonomy. The cultic idealization of virginity both reflects and promotes the degradation of women, defining them as actual or potential rape victims. By being identified with the codes of procreation and patrilineal inheritance, women embody sexual shame. The lives of the female saints, primarily virgin martyrs, exemplify this construction of nonvirgins and nonmothers as the embodiment of sexual shame and pollution.

In 1950, as traditional social mores were shaken in the aftermath of the horrors of World War II, the Catholic Church apparently perceived a need for an exemplar like Maria Goretti. According to DiDonato (1962), "The military occupation by enemies and allies alike, tended to profane family life and shamefully deprave the moral fiber of the young. As never before, the spirit of Maria Goretti was needed as a virtuous hope and inspiration towards purity for girls in Italy and all lands" (p. 157).

Maria Goretti not only exemplified the glorification of chastity and the duty of women to uphold family purity, but she had an additional use—to forgive men their sins. Maria Goretti forgave her attacker before she died. Because Maria forgave him, her mother forgave him. Because Maria and her mother could forgive him, Alessandro Serenelli could forgive himself and expect society to do likewise. Thus the rape victim, the sexually abused girl, and the battered wife are given a message by the Catholic Church to take responsibility for their abusers, to forgive them, and by forgiving them, redeem them.

A FEMINIST READING OF MARIA GORETTI

In the Western cultural tradition, women's sexuality makes them physically and spiritually vulnerable. Their vulnerability is a necessary cultural production. A sexually autonomous woman undermines patrilinearity and the legitimacy of children. Christendom and patriarchy, by turning women into the protectors of chastity, dialectically strengthened and encouraged their sexual suffering:

> It is possible that the woman in the pornographic movie . . . is a tired secular relic of this Western tradition of Christendom which links female sexuality with pain and humiliation. The alliance of pain and punishment with women and sex is clearly in line with the sexual disgust that informed Christian emotion. Men have been taught in our culture to take pleasure in the sight of a woman suffering; suffering is seen as a female virtue and it is also, obscurely, seen as sexy. (Armstrong, 1986, p. 210)

Christianity, and Catholicism in particular, emphasizes suffering as redemptive. For women, that suffering has been rooted in sexual shame. Simply by being alive and having a body all people will suffer, but women will especially suffer because of sex. Men may contribute to, but they are not the cause of, women's shame. Women's embodiment of suffering affects not only them but also their family relationships. For example, before she died, Maria Goretti reportedly apologized to her mother for upsetting her by being murdered (DiDonato, 1962). Apparently, she felt guilty for "causing" her mother pain. Her body suffered physically, and her mind suffered mental anguish.

If Maria Goretti had "preferred" to be raped rather than stabbed to death, she would not be a saint today. According to the legend, she preferred to die rather than commit such an "ugly sin" (MacConastair, 1951). The legend emphasizes her choice. Did she prefer death, or was she given no choice? If she did have a choice, what are the implications for Catholicism today? By today's secular standards, the 12-year-old would not be perceived as sinful if she "chose" to be raped and live. But rape is traumatic for a female of any age or religion and is a compounded trauma if the survivor is a virgin, as it robs her of control over the transition into adult sexuality. For Catholic women, there is the additional element of spiritual victimization portrayed in the Maria Goretti myth. Any sex outside of marriage, including rape, is associated with a female's "moral disgrace," and myths of virgin martyrs, like Maria Goretti, are used as a kind of sexual terrorism.

A motif of suffering is feminized in a virginity fetish exemplified by Maria Goretti. The cultural fetishization of female virginity reduces the female's identity to sexuality. The result is the objectification of part of the body separate from the self. Maria Goretti died in order to preserve her hymen; her physical intactness was the only metaphor for her value to her family, her church, her community, and her culture. Any other contribution she might have made did not count.

It would be easy to dismiss virgin martyrs and the valorization of female sexual suffering as a reflection of the masculinist tradition of the Catholic Church. That dismissal ignores the societal, historical, and spiritual function of these myths. When Maria Goretti was made a saint in 1950, World War II had been over for only 5 years, and the process of healing and forgiving and rebuilding Western civilization was still incipient. Women's roles were changing in response to spreading urbanization and increased industrialization. Maria Goretti, as a virgin martyr, became a useful reactionary symbol of patriarchal, religious, and family values.

REFERENCES

Armstrong, K. (1986). *The gospel according to woman.* Garden City, NY: Anchor.

Attwater, D. (1965). *The Avenel dictionary of saints.* New York: Avenel.

Buehrle, M. C. (1967). *New Catholic encyclopedia.* New York: McGraw-Hill.

Campbell, D. (1988). Dorothy Dohen's reclamation of virginity. *The Christian Century, 7*(20), 667-670.

Collier, J. F. (1986). From Mary to modern woman: The material basis of Marianismo and its transformation in a Spanish village. *American Ethnologist, 13,* 100-107.

Delaney, J. L. (1980). *Dictionary of saints.* Garden City, NY: Doubleday.

DiDonato, P. (1962). *The penitent.* New York: Hawthorn.

Hoever, H. (1963). *Lives of the saints.* New York: Catholic Book Publishing.

MacConastair, A. (1951). *Lily of the marshes.* New York: Macmillan.

Ortner, S. (1978). The virgin and the state. *Feminist Studies, 4,* 19-37.

Peristany, J. G. (Ed.). (1966). *Honour and shame: The values of Mediterranean society.* London: Weidenfield & Nicholson.

Pitt-Rivers, J. (1954). *The people of the Sierra.* Chicago: University of Chicago Press.

Rivers, C. (1973). *Aphrodite at mid-century.* Garden City, NY: Doubleday.

Second Vatican Ecumenical Council. (1975). *The liturgy of the hours.* New York: Catholic Book Publishing.

Warner, M. (1983). *Alone of all her sex.* New York: Vintage.

8 Fraternities and Rape on Campus

PATRICIA YANCEY MARTIN
ROBERT A. HUMMER
Florida State University

Rapes are perpetrated on dates, at parties, in chance encounters, and in specially planned circumstances. That group structure and processes, rather than individual values or characteristics, are the impetus for many rape episodes was documented by Blanchard (1959) 30 years ago (also see Geis, 1971), yet sociologists have failed to pursue this theme (for an exception, see Chancer, 1987). A recent review of research (Muehlenhard & Linton, 1987) on sexual violence, or rape, devotes only a few pages to the situational contexts of rape events, and these are conceptualized as potential risk factors for individuals rather than qualities of rape-prone social contexts.

Many rapes—far more than come to the public's attention—occur in fraternity houses on college and university campuses, yet little research has analyzed fraternities at U.S. colleges and universities as rape-prone contexts (cf. Ehrhart & Sandler, 1985). Most of the research on fraternities reports on samples of individual fraternity men. One group of studies compares the values, attitudes, perceptions, family socioeconomic status, psychological traits (aggressiveness, dependence), and so on of fraternity and nonfraternity men (Bohrnstedt, 1969; Fox, Hodge, & Ward, 1987; Kanin, 1967; Lemire, 1979; Miller, 1973). A second group attempts to identify the effects of fraternity membership over

AUTHORS' NOTE: We gratefully thank Meena Harris and Diane Mennella for assisting with data collection. The senior author thanks the graduate students in her fall 1988 graduate research methods seminar for help with developing the initial conceptual framework. Judith Lorber and two anonymous *Gender & Society* referees made numerous suggestions for improving our chapter and we thank them also.

time on the values, attitudes, beliefs, or moral precepts of members (Hughes & Winston, 1987; Marlowe & Auvenshine, 1982; Miller, 1973; Wilder, Hoyt, Doren, Hauck, & Zettle, 1978; Wilder, Hoyt, Surbeck, Wilder, & Carney, 1986). With minor exceptions, little research addresses the group and organizational context of fraternities or the social construction of fraternity life (for exceptions, see Letchworth, 1969; Longino & Kart, 1973; Smith, 1964).

Gary Tash (1988), writing as an alumnus and trial attorney in his fraternity's magazine, claims that over 90 percent of all gang rapes on college campuses involve fraternity men (p. 2). Tash provides no evidence to substantiate this claim, but students of violence against women have been concerned with fraternity men's frequently reported involvement in rape episodes (Adams & Abarbanel, 1988). Ehrhart and Sandler (1985) identify over 50 cases of gang rapes on campus perpetrated by fraternity men, and their analysis points to many of the conditions that we discuss here. Their analysis is unique in focusing on conditions in fraternities that make gang rapes of women by fraternity men both feasible and probable. They identify excessive alcohol use, isolation from external monitoring, treatment of women as prey, use of pornography, approval of violence, and excessive concern with competition as precipitating conditions to gang rape (also see Merton, 1985; Roark, 1987).

The study reported here confirmed and complemented these findings by focusing on both conditions and processes. We examined dynamics associated with the social construction of fraternity life, with a focus on processes that foster the use of coercion, including rape, in fraternity men's relations with women. Our examination of men's social fraternities on college and university campuses as groups and organizations led us to conclude that fraternities are a physical and sociocultural context that encourages the sexual coercion of women. We make no claims that all fraternities are "bad" or that all fraternity men are rapists. Our observations indicated, however, that rape is especially probable in fraternities because of the kinds of organizations they are, the kinds of members they have, the practices their members engage in, and a virtual absence of university or community oversight. Analyses that lay blame for rapes by fraternity men on "peer pressure" are, we feel, overly simplistic (cf. Burkhart, 1989; Walsh, 1989). We suggest, rather, that fraternities create a sociocultural context in which the use of coercion in sexual relations with women is normative and in which the mechanisms to keep this pattern of behavior in check are minimal at best and absent at worst.

We conclude that unless fraternities change in fundamental ways, little improvement can be expected.

METHODOLOGY

Our goal was to analyze the group and organizational practices and conditions that create in fraternities an abusive social context for women. We developed a conceptual framework from an initial case study of an alleged gang rape at Florida State University that involved four fraternity men and an 18-year-old coed. The group rape took place on the third floor of a fraternity house and ended with the "dumping" of the woman in the hallway of a neighboring fraternity house. According to newspaper accounts, the victim's blood-alcohol concentration, when she was discovered, was .349 percent, more than three times the legal limit for automobile driving and an almost lethal amount. One law enforcement officer reported that sexual intercourse occurred during the time the victim was unconscious: "She was in a life-threatening situation" (*Tallahassee Democrat,* 1988b). When the victim was found, she was comatose and had suffered multiple scratches and abrasions. Crude words and a fraternity symbol had been written on her thighs (*Tampa Tribune,* 1988). When law enforcement officials tried to investigate the case, fraternity members refused to cooperate. This led, eventually, to a 5-year ban of the fraternity from campus by the university and by the fraternity's national organization.

In trying to understand how such an event could have occurred, and how a group of over 150 members (exact figures are unknown because the fraternity refused to provide a membership roster) could hold rank, deny knowledge of the event, and allegedly lie to a grand jury, we analyzed newspaper articles about the case and conducted open-ended interviews with a variety of respondents about the case and about fraternities, rapes, alcohol use, gender relations, and sexual activities on campus. Our data included over 100 newspaper articles on the initial gang rape case; open-ended interviews with Greek (social fraternity and sorority) and non-Greek (independent) students (*N*=20); university administrators (*N*=8; 5 men, 3 women); and alumni advisers to Greek organizations (*N*=6). Open-ended interviews were held also with judges, public and private defense attorneys, victim advocates, and state prosecutors regarding the processing of sexual assault cases. Data were analyzed using the grounded theory method (Glaser, 1978; Martin & Turner, 1986). In the following analysis, concepts generated from the data analysis are integrated with the literature on men's social fraternities, sexual coercion, and related issues.

FRATERNITIES AND THE SOCIAL CONSTRUCTION
OF MEN AND MASCULINITY

Our research indicated that fraternities are vitally concerned—more than with anything else—with masculinity (cf. Kanin, 1967). They work hard to create a macho image and context and try to avoid any suggestion of "wimpiness," effeminacy, and homosexuality. Valued members display, or are willing to go along with, a narrow conception of masculinity that stresses competition, athleticism, dominance, winning, conflict, wealth, material possessions, willingness to drink alcohol, and sexual prowess vis-à-vis women.

Valued Qualities of Members

When fraternity members talked about the kind of pledges they prefer, a litany of stereotypical and narrowly masculine attributes and behaviors was recited and feminine or woman-associated qualities and behaviors were expressly denounced (cf. Merton, 1985). Fraternities seek men who are "athletic," "big guys," good in intramural competition, "who can talk college sports." Males "who are willing to drink alcohol," "who drink socially," or "who can hold their liquor" are sought. Alcohol and activities associated with the recreational use of alcohol are cornerstones of fraternity social life. Nondrinkers are viewed with skepticism and rarely selected for membership.[1]

Fraternities try to avoid "geeks," nerds, and men said to give the fraternity a "wimpy" or "gay" reputation. Art, music, and humanities majors, majors in traditional women's fields (nursing, home economics, social work, education), men with long hair, and those whose appearance or dress violate current norms are rejected. Clean-cut, handsome men who dress well (are clean, neat, conforming, fashionable) are preferred. One sorority woman commented that "the top ranking fraternities have the best looking guys."

One fraternity man, a senior, said his fraternity recruited "some big guys, very athletic" over a 2-year period to help overcome its image of wimpiness. His fraternity had won the interfraternity competition for highest grade point average several years running but was looked down on as "wimpy, dancy, even gay." With their bigger, more athletic recruits, "our reputation improved; we're a much more recognized fraternity now." Thus a fraternity's reputation and status depend on members' possession of stereotypically masculine qualities. Good grades, campus leadership, and community service are "nice," but masculinity, dominance —for example, in athletic events, physical size of members, athleticism of members—counts most.

Certain social skills are valued. Men are sought who "have good personalities," are friendly, and "have the ability to relate to girls" (cf. Longino & Kart, 1973). One fraternity man, a junior, said: "We watch a guy [a potential pledge] talk to women . . . we want guys who can relate to girls." Assessing a pledge's ability to talk to women is, in part, a preoccupation with homosexuality and a conscious avoidance of men who seem to have effeminate manners or qualities. If a member is suspected of being gay, he is ostracized and informally drummed out of the fraternity. A fraternity with a reputation as wimpy or tolerant of gays is ridiculed and shunned by other fraternities. Militant heterosexuality is frequently used by men as a strategy to keep each other in line (Kimmel, 1987).

Financial affluence or wealth, a male-associated value in U.S. culture, is highly valued by fraternities. In accounting for why the fraternity involved in the gang rape that precipitated our research project had been recognized recently as "the best fraternity chapter in the United States," a university official said: "They were good-looking, a big fraternity, had lots of BMWs [expensive, German-made automobiles]." After the rape, newspaper stories described the fraternity members' affluence, noting the high number of members who owned expensive cars (*St. Petersburg Times*, 1988).

The Status and Norms of Pledgeship

A pledge (sometimes called an associate member) is a new recruit who occupies a trial membership status for a specific period of time. The pledge period (typically ranging from 10 to 15 weeks) gives fraternity brothers an opportunity to assess and socialize new recruits. Pledges evaluate the fraternity also and decide if they want to become brothers. The socialization experience is structured partly through assignment of a "Big Brother" to each pledge. Big Brothers are expected to teach pledges how to become a brother and to support them as they progress through the trial membership period. Some pledges are repelled by the pledging experience, which can entail physical abuse; harsh discipline; and demands to be subordinate, follow orders, and engage in demeaning routines and activities similar to those used by the military to "make men out of boys" during boot camp.

Characteristics of the pledge experience are rationalized by fraternity members as necessary to help pledges unite into a group, rely on each other, and join together against outsiders. The process is highly masculinist in execution as well as conception. A willingness to submit to authority, follow orders, and do as one is told is viewed as a sign of loyalty, togetherness, and unity. Fraternity pledges who find the pledge process offensive often drop out. Some do this by openly quitting, which can subject them to ridicule by brothers and other pledges, or they may deliberately fail to make the grades necessary for initiation or transfer schools and decline to reaffiliate with the fraternity on the new campus. One fraternity pledge who quit the fraternity he had pledged described an experience during pledgeship as follows:

> This one guy was always picking on me. No matter what I did, I was wrong. One night after dinner, he and two other guys called me and two other pledges into the chapter room. He said, "Here, X, hold this 25 pound bag of ice at arms' length 'til I tell you to stop." I did it even though my arms and hands were killing me. When I asked if I could stop, he grabbed me around the throat and lifted me off the floor. I thought he would choke me to death. He cussed me and called me all kinds of names. He took one of my fingers and twisted it until it nearly broke. . . . I stayed in the fraternity for a few more days, but then I decided to quit. I hated it. Those guys are sick. They like seeing you suffer.

Fraternities' emphasis on toughness, withstanding pain and humiliation, obedience to superiors, and using physical force to obtain compliance contributes to an interpersonal style that deemphasizes caring and sensitivity but fosters intragroup trust and loyalty. If the least macho or most critical pledges drop out, those who remain may be more receptive to, and influenced by, masculinist values and practices that encourage the use of force in sexual relations with women and the covering up of such behavior (cf. Kanin, 1967).

Norms and Dynamics of Brotherhood

Brother is the status occupied by fraternity men to indicate their relations to each other and their membership in a particular fraternity organization or group. Brother is a male-specific status; only males can

120   STRUCTURAL SUPPORTS FOR WOMEN

become brothers, although women can become "Little Sisters," a form
of pseudomembership. "Becoming a brother" is a rite of passage that
follows the consistent and often lengthy display by pledges of appropriately masculine qualities and behaviors. Brothers have a quasi-famil-
ial relationship with each other, are normatively said to share bonds of
closeness and support, and are sharply set off from nonmembers. Brotherhood is a loosely defined term used to represent the bonds that develop
among fraternity members and the obligations and expectations incum-
bent upon them (cf. Marlowe & Auvenshine, 1982, on fraternities' failure to encourage "moral development" in freshman pledges).

Some of our respondents talked about brotherhood in almost rever-
ential terms, viewing it as the most valuable benefit of fraternity membership. One senior, a business major who had been affiliated with a
fairly high-status fraternity through 4 years on campus, said:

> Brotherhood spurs friendship for life, which I consider its best aspect, al-
> though I didn't see it that way when I joined. Brotherhood bonds and unites.
> It instills values of caring about one another, caring about community, caring
> about ourselves. The values and bonds [of brotherhood] continually de-
> velop over the four years [in college] while normal friendships come and go.

Despite this idealization, most aspects of fraternity practice and
conception are more mundane. Brotherhood often plays itself out as an
overriding concern with masculinity, and by extension, femininity. As
a consequence, fraternities comprise collectivities of highly masculinized men with attitudinal qualities and behavioral norms that predispose
them to sexual coercion of women (cf. Kanin, 1967; Merton, 1985;
Rapaport & Burkhart, 1984). The norms of masculinity are complemented by conceptions of women and femininity that are equally distorted and stereotyped and that may enhance the probability of women's
exploitation (cf. Ehrhart & Sandler, 1985; Sanday, 1981, 1986).

Practices of Brotherhood

Practices associated with fraternity brotherhood that contribute to the
sexual coercion of women include a preoccupation with loyalty, group
protection, and secrecy; use of alcohol as a weapon; involvement in violence and physical force; and an emphasis on competition and superiority.

Loyalty, Group Protection, and Secrecy. Loyalty is a fraternity preoccupation. Members are reminded constantly to be loyal to the frater-

nity and to their brothers. Among other ways, loyalty is played out in the practices of group protection and secrecy. The fraternity must be shielded from criticism. Members are admonished to avoid getting the fraternity in trouble and to bring all problems "to the chapter" (local branch of a national social fraternity) rather than to outsiders. Fraternities try to protect themselves from close scrutiny and criticism by the Interfraternity Council (a quasi-governing body composed of representatives from all social fraternities on campus), their fraternity's national office, university officials, law enforcement, the media, and the public. Protection of the fraternity often takes precedence over what is procedurally, ethically, or legally correct. Numerous examples were related to us of fraternity brothers' lying to outsiders to "protect the fraternity."

Group protection was observed in the alleged gang rape case with which we began our study. Except for one brother, a rapist who turned state's evidence, the entire remaining fraternity membership was accused by university and criminal justice officials of lying to protect the fraternity. Members consistently failed to cooperate even though the alleged crimes were felonies and involved only four men (two of whom were not even members of the local chapter), and the victim of the crime nearly died. According to a grand jury's findings, fraternity officers repeatedly broke appointments with law enforcement officials, refused to provide police with a list of members, and refused to cooperate with police and prosecutors investigating the case (*Florida Flambeau*, 1988).

Secrecy is a priority value and practice in fraternities, partly because full-fledged membership is premised on it (for confirmation, see Ehrhart & Sandler, 1985; Longino & Kart, 1973; Roark, 1987). Secrecy is also a boundary-maintaining mechanism, demarcating in-group from out-group, us from them. Secret rituals, handshakes, and mottoes are revealed to pledge brothers as they are initiated into full brotherhood. As only brothers are supposed to know a fraternity's secrets, such knowledge affirms membership in the fraternity and separates a brother from others. Extending secrecy tactics from protection of private knowledge to protection of the fraternity from criticism is a predictable development. Our interviews indicated that individual members knew the difference between right and wrong, but fraternity norms that emphasize loyalty, group protection, and secrecy often overrode standards of ethical correctness.

Alcohol as Weapon. Alcohol use by fraternity men is normative. They use it on weekdays to relax after class and on weekends to "get drunk," "get crazy," and "get laid." The use of alcohol to obtain sex from women is pervasive—in other words, it is used as a weapon against sexual reluctance. According to several fraternity men whom we interviewed, alcohol is the major tool used to gain sexual mastery over women (cf. Adams & Abarbanel, 1988; Ehrhart & Sandler, 1985). One fraternity man, a 21-year-old senior, described alcohol use to gain sex as follows: "There are girls that you know will fuck, then some you have to put some effort into it. . . . You have to buy them drinks or find out if she's drunk enough. . . . "

A similar strategy is used collectively. A fraternity man said that at parties with Little Sisters: "We provide them with 'hunch punch' and things get wild. We get them drunk and most of the guys end up with one." " 'Hunch punch,' " he said, "is a girls' drink made up of overproof alcohol and powdered Kool-Aid, no water or anything, just ice. It's very strong. Two cups will do a number on a female." He had plans in the next academic term to surreptitiously give hunch punch to women in a "prim and proper" sorority because "having sex with prim and proper sorority girls is definitely a goal." These women are a challenge because they "won't openly consume alcohol and won't get openly drunk as hell." Their sororities have "standards committees" that forbid heavy drinking and easy sex.

In the gang rape case, our sources said that many fraternity men on campus believed the victim had a drinking problem and was thus an "easy make." According to newspaper accounts, she had been drinking alcohol on the evening she was raped; the lead assailant is alleged to have given her a bottle of wine after she arrived at his fraternity house. Portions of the rape occurred in a shower, and the victim was reportedly so drunk that her assailants had difficulty holding her in a standing position (*Tallahassee Democrat,* 1988a). While raping her, her assailants repeatedly told her they were members of another fraternity under the apparent belief that she was too drunk to know the difference. Of course, if she was too drunk to know who they were, she was too drunk to consent to sex (cf. Allgeier, 1986; Tash, 1988).

One respondent told us that gang rapes are wrong and can get one expelled, but he seemed to see nothing wrong in sexual coercion one-on-one. He seemed unaware that the use of alcohol to obtain sex from a woman is grounds for a claim that a rape occurred (cf. Tash, 1988). Few women on campus (who also may not know these grounds) report date rapes, however; so the odds of detection and punishment are slim for fraternity men who use alcohol for "seduction" purposes (cf. Byington & Keeter, 1988; Merton, 1985).

Violence and Physical Force. Fraternity men have a history of violence (Ehrhart & Sandler, 1985; Roark, 1987). Their record of hazing, fighting, property destruction, and rape has caused them problems with insurance companies (Bradford, 1986; Pressley, 1987). Two university officials told us that fraternities "are the third riskiest property to insure behind toxic waste dumps and amusement parks." Fraternities are increasingly defendants in legal actions brought by pledges subjected to hazing (Meyer, 1986; Pressley, 1987) and by women who were raped by one or more members. In a recent alleged gang rape incident at another Florida university, prosecutors failed to file charges but the victim filed a civil suit against the fraternity nevertheless (*Tallahassee Democrat*, 1989).

Competition and Superiority. Interfraternity rivalry fosters in-group identification and out-group hostility. Fraternities stress pride of membership and superiority over other fraternities as major goals. Interfraternity rivalries take many forms, including competition for desirable pledges, size of pledge class, size of membership, size and appearance of fraternity house, superiority in intramural sports, highest grade point averages, giving the best parties, gaining the best or most campus leadership roles, and of great importance, attracting and displaying "good-looking women." Rivalry is particularly intense over members, intramural sports, and women (cf. Messner, 1989).

FRATERNITIES' COMMODIFICATION OF WOMEN

In claiming that women are treated by fraternities as commodities, we mean that fraternities knowingly, and intentionally, *use* women for their benefit. Fraternities use women as bait for new members, as servers of brothers' needs, and as sexual prey.

Women as Bait. Fashionably attractive women help a fraternity attract new members. As one fraternity man, a junior, said, "They are good bait." Beautiful, sociable women are believed to impress the right kind of pledges and give the impression that the fraternity can deliver this type of woman to its members. Photographs of shapely, attractive coeds are included in fraternity brochures and videotapes that are distributed and shown to potential pledges. The women pictured are often dressed in bikinis, at the beach, and are pictured hugging the brothers of the fraternity. One university official says such recruitment materials give the message: "Hey, they're here for you, you can have whatever you want," and, "We have the best looking women. Join us and you can have them too." Another commented: "Something's wrong when males join an all-male organization as the best place to meet women. It's so illogical."

Fraternities compete in promising access to beautiful women. One fraternity man, a senior, commented, "The attraction of girls [i.e., a fraternity's success in attracting women] is a big status symbol for fraternities." One university official commented that the use of women as a recruiting tool is so well entrenched that fraternities that might be willing to forgo it say they cannot afford to unless other fraternities do so as well. One fraternity man said, "Look, if we don't have Little Sisters, the fraternities that do will get all the good pledges." Another said, "We won't have as good a rush [the period during which new members are assessed and selected] if we don't have these women around."

In displaying good-looking, attractive, skimpily dressed, nubile women to potential members, fraternities implicitly, and sometimes explicitly, promise sexual access to women. One fraternity man commented, "Part of what being in a fraternity is all about is the sex" and explained how his fraternity uses Little Sisters to recruit new members:

> We'll tell the sweetheart [the fraternity's term for Little Sister], "You're gorgeous; you can get him." We'll tell her to fake a scam and she'll go hang all over him during a rush party, kiss him, and he thinks he's done wonderful and wants to join. The girls think it's great too. It's flattering for them.

Women as Servers. The use of women as servers is exemplified in the Little Sister program. Little Sisters are undergraduate women who are rushed and selected in a manner parallel to the recruitment of fraternity men. They are affiliated with the fraternity in a formal but unofficial way and are able, indeed required, to wear the fraternity's Greek letters. Little Sisters are not full-fledged fraternity members, however; and fraternity national offices and most universities do not register or regulate them. Each fraternity has an officer called Little Sister chairman who oversees their organization and activities. The Little Sisters elect officers among themselves, pay monthly dues to the fraternity, and have well-defined roles. Their dues are used to pay for the fraternity's social events, and Little Sisters are expected to attend and hostess fraternity parties and hang around the house to make it a "nice place to be." One fraternity man, a senior, described Little Sisters this way: "They are very social girls, willing to join in, be affiliated with the group, devoted to the fraternity." Another member, a sophomore, said: "Their sole purpose is social—attend parties, attract new members, and 'take care' of the guys."

Our observations and interviews suggested that women selected by fraternities as Little Sisters are physically attractive, possess good social skills, and are willing to devote time and energy to the fraternity and its members. One undergraduate woman gave the following job description for Little Sisters to a campus newspaper:

> It's not just making appearances at all the parties but entails many more responsibilities. You're going to be expected to go to all the intramural games to cheer the brothers on, support and encourage the pledges, and just be around to bring some extra life to the house. [As a Little Sister] you have to agree to take on a new responsibility other than studying to maintain your grades and managing to keep your checkbook from bouncing. You have to make time to be a part of the fraternity and support the brothers in all they do. (*The Tomahawk*, 1988)

The title of Little Sister reflects women's subordinate status; fraternity men in a parallel role are called Big Brothers. Big Brothers assist a sorority primarily with the physical work of sorority rushes, which, compared to fraternity rushes, are more formal, structured, and intensive. Sorority rushes take place in the daytime and fraternity rushes at night so fraternity men are free to help. According to one fraternity member, Little Sister status is a benefit to women because it gives them a social outlet and "the protection of the brothers." The gender-stereotypic conceptions and obligations of these Little Sister and Big Brother statuses indicate that fraternities and sororities promote a gender hierarchy on campus that fosters subordination and dependence in women, thus encouraging sexual exploitation and the belief that it is acceptable.

Women as Sexual Prey. Little Sisters are a sexual utility. Many Little Sisters do not belong to sororities and lack peer support for refraining from unwanted sexual relations. One fraternity man (whose fraternity has 65 members and 85 Little Sisters) told us they had recruited "wholesale" in the prior year to "get lots of new women." The structural access to women that the Little Sister program provides and the absence of normative supports for refusing fraternity members' sexual advances may make women in this program particularly susceptible to coerced sexual encounters with fraternity men.

Access to women for sexual gratification is a presumed benefit of fraternity membership, promised in recruitment materials and strategies and through brothers' conversations with new recruits. One fraternity man said: "We always tell the guys that you get sex all the time, there's always new girls. . . . After I became a Greek, I found out I could be with females at will." A university official told us that, based on his observations, "No one [i.e., fraternity men] on this campus wants to have 'relationships.' They just want to have fun [i.e., sex]." Fraternity men plan and execute strategies aimed at obtaining sexual gratification, and this occurs at both individual and collective levels.

Individual strategies include getting a woman drunk and spending a great deal of money on her. As for collective strategies, most of our undergraduate interviewees agreed that fraternity parties often culminate in sex and that this outcome is planned. One fraternity man said fraternity parties often involve sex and nudity and can "turn into orgies." Orgies may be planned in advance, such as the Bowery Ball party held by one fraternity. A former fraternity member said of this party:

> The entire idea behind this is sex. Both men and women come to the party wearing little or nothing. There are pornographic pinups on the walls and usually porno movies playing on the TV. The music carries sexual overtones . . . . They just get schnockered [drunk], and in most cases, they also get laid.

When asked about the women who come to such a party, he said: "Some Little Sisters just won't go. . . . The girls who do are looking for a good time, girls who don't know what it is, things like that."

Other respondents denied that fraternity parties are orgies but said that sex is always talked about among the brothers and they all know "who each other is doing it with." One member said that most of the time, guys have sex with their girlfriends "but with socials, girlfriends aren't allowed to come and it's their [members'] big chance [to have sex with other women]." The use of alcohol to help them get women into bed is a routine strategy at fraternity parties.

CONCLUSIONS

In general, our research indicated that the organization and membership of fraternities contribute heavily to coercive and often violent sex. Fraternity houses are occupied by same-sex (all men) and same-age (late teens, early twenties) peers whose maturity and judgment is often less than ideal. Yet fraternity houses are private dwellings that are mostly off-limits to, and away from scrutiny of, university and community representatives, with the result that fraternity house events seldom come to the attention of outsiders. Practices associated with the social construction of fraternity brotherhood emphasize a macho conception of men and masculinity, a narrow, stereotyped conception of women and femininity, and the treatment of women as commodities. Other practices contributing to coercive sexual relations and the cover-up of rapes include excessive alcohol use, competitiveness, and normative support for deviance and secrecy (cf. Bogal-Allbritten & Allbritten, 1985; Kanin, 1967).

Some fraternity practices exacerbate others. Brotherhood norms require "sticking together" regardless of right or wrong; thus rape episodes are unlikely to be stopped or reported to outsiders, even when witnesses disapprove. The ability to use alcohol without scrutiny by authorities and alcohol's frequent association with violence, including sexual coercion, facilitates rape in fraternity houses. Fraternity norms that emphasize the value of maleness and masculinity over femaleness and femininity and that elevate the status of men and lower the status of women in members' eyes undermine perceptions and treatment of women as persons who deserve consideration and care (cf. Ehrhart & Sandler, 1985; Merton, 1985).

Androgynous men and men with a broad range of interests and attributes are lost to fraternities through their recruitment practices. Masculinity of a narrow and stereotypical type helps create attitudes, norms, and practices that predispose fraternity men to coerce women sexually, both individually and collectively (Allgeier, 1986; Hood, 1989; Sanday, 1981, 1986). Male athletes on campus may be similarly disposed for the same reasons (Kirshenbaum, 1989; Telander & Sullivan, 1989).

Research into the social contexts in which rape crimes occur and the social constructions associated with these contexts illumine rape dynamics on campus. Blanchard (1959) found that group rapes almost always have a leader who pushes others into the crime. He also found that the leader's latent homosexuality, desire to show off to his peers, or fear of failing to prove himself a man are frequently an impetus. Fraternity norms and practices contribute to the approval and use of sexual coercion as an accepted tactic in relations with women. Alcohol-induced compliance is normative, whereas, presumably, use of a knife, gun, or threat of bodily harm would not be, because the woman who "drinks too much" is viewed as "causing her own rape" (cf. Ehrhart & Sandler, 1985).

Our research led us to conclude that fraternity norms and practices influence members to view the sexual coercion of women, which is a felony crime, as sport, a contest, or a game (cf. Sato, 1988). This sport is played not between men and women but between men and men. Women are the pawns or prey in the interfraternity rivalry game; they prove that a fraternity is successful or prestigious. The use of women in this way encourages fraternity men to see women as objects and sexual coercion as sport. Today's societal norms support young women's right to engage in sex at their discretion, and coercion is unnecessary in a mutually desired encounter. But nubile young women say they prefer to be "in a relationship" to have sex whereas young men say they prefer to "get laid" without a commitment (Muehlenhard & Linton, 1987). These differences may reflect, in part, U.S. puritanism and men's fears of sexual intimacy or perhaps intimacy of any kind. In a fraternity context, getting sex without giving emotionally demonstrates "cool" masculinity. More important, it poses no threat to the bonding and loyalty of the fraternity brotherhood (cf. Farr, 1988). Drinking large quantities of alcohol before having sex suggests that "scoring" rather than intrinsic sexual pleasure is a primary concern of fraternity men.

Unless fraternities' composition, goals, structures, and practices change in fundamental ways, women on campus will continue to be sexual prey for fraternity men. As all-male enclaves dedicated to opposing faculty and administration and to cementing in-group ties, fraternity members eschew any hint of homosexuality. Their version of masculinity transforms women, and men with womanly characteristics, into the out-group. "Womanly men" are ostracized; feminine women are used to demonstrate members' masculinity. Encouraging renewed emphasis on their founding values (Longino & Kart, 1973), service orientation and activities (Lemire, 1979), or members' moral development (Marlowe & Auvenshine, 1982) will have little effect on fraternities' treatment of women. A case for or against fraternities cannot be made by studying individual members. The fraternity qua group and organization is at issue. Located on campus along with many vulnerable women, embedded in a sexist society, and caught up in masculinist goals, practices, and values, fraternities' violation of women—including forcible rape—should come as no surprise.

NOTE

1. Recent bans by some universities on open-keg parties at fraternity houses have resulted in heavy drinking before coming to a party and an increase in drunkenness among those who attend. This may aggravate, rather than improve, the treatment of women by fraternity men at parties.

REFERENCES

Allgeier, E. (1986, August). *Coercive versus consensual sexual interactions.* G. Stanley Hall Lecture to American Psychological Association Annual Meeting, Washington, DC.

Adams, A., & Abarbanel, G. (1988). *Sexual assault on campus: What colleges can do.* Santa Monica, CA: Rape Treatment Center.

Blanchard, W. H. (1959). The group process in gang rape. *Journal of Social Psychology, 49,* 259-266.

Bogal-Allbritten, R. B., & Allbritten, W. L. (1985). The hidden victims: Courtship violence among college students. *Journal of College Student Personnel, 43,* 201-204.

Bohrnstedt, G. W. (1969). Conservatism, authoritarianism and religiosity of fraternity pledges. *Journal of College Student Personnel, 27,* 36-43.

Bradford, M. (1986, March 2). Tight market dries up nightlife at university. *Business Insurance,* pp. 2, 6.

Burkhart, B. (1989, February 2). [Comments in seminar on acquaintance/date rape prevention]. A National Video Teleconference.

Burkhart, B. R., & Stanton, A. L. (1985). Sexual aggression in acquaintance relationships. In G. Russell (Ed.), *Violence in intimate relationships* (pp. 43-65). Englewood Cliffs, NJ: Spectrum.

Byington, D. B., & Keeter, K. W. (1988). Assessing needs of sexual assault victims on a university campus. In *Student services: Responding to issues and challenges* (pp. 23-31). Chapel Hill: University of North Carolina Press.

Chancer, L. S. (1987). New Bedford, Massachusetts, March 6, 1983-March 22, 1984: The 'before and after' of a group rape. *Gender & Society, 1,* 239-260.

Ehrhart, J. K., & Sandler, B. R. (1985). *Campus gang rape: Party games?* Washington, DC: Association of American Colleges.

Farr, K. A. (1988). Dominance bonding through the good old boys sociability network. *Sex Roles, 18,* 259-277.

Florida Flambeau. (1988, May 19). Pike members indicted in rape. pp. 1, 5.

Fox, E., Hodge, C., & Ward, W. (1987). A comparison of attitudes held by black and white fraternity members. *Journal of Negro Education, 56,* 521-534.

Geis, G. (1971). Group sexual assaults. *Medical Aspects of Human Sexuality, 5*, 101-113.

Glaser, B. G. (1978). *Theoretical sensitivity: Advances in the methodology of grounded theory.* Mill Valley, CA: Sociology Press.

Hood, J. (1989, May 16). Why our society is rape-prone. *New York Times.*

Hughes, M. J., & Winston, R. B., Jr. (1987). Effects of fraternity membership on interpersonal values. *Journal of College Student Personnel, 45*, 405-411.

Kanin, E. J. (1967). Reference groups and sex conduct norm violations. *Sociological Quarterly, 8*, 495-504.

Kimmel, M. (Ed.). (1987). *Changing men: New directions in research on men and masculinity.* Newbury Park, CA: Sage.

Kirshenbaum, J. (1989, February 27). Special report. An American disgrace: A violent and unprecedented lawlessness has arisen among college athletes in all parts of the country. *Sports Illustrated,* pp. 16-19.

Lemire, D. (1979). One investigation of the stereotypes associated with fraternities and sororities. *Journal of College Student Personnel, 37*, 54-57.

Letchworth, G. E. (1969). Fraternities now and in the future. *Journal of College Student Personnel, 10*, 118-122.

Longino, C. F., Jr., & Kart, C. S. (1973). The college fraternity: An assessment of theory and research. *Journal of College Student Personnel, 31*, 118-125.

Marlowe, A. F., & Auvenshine, D. C. (1982). Greek membership: Its impact on the moral development of college freshmen. *Journal of College Student Personnel, 40*, 53-57.

Martin, P. Y., & Turner, B. A. (1986). Grounded theory and organizational research. *Journal of Applied Behavioral Science, 22*, 141-157.

Merton, A. (1985, September). On competition and class: Return to brotherhood. *Ms.,* pp. 60-65, 121-122.

Messner, M. (1989). Masculinities and athletic careers. *Gender & Society, 3*, 71-88.

Meyer, T. J. (1986, March 12). Fight against hazing rituals rages on campuses. *Chronicle of Higher Education,* pp. 34-36.

Miller, L. D. (1973). Distinctive characteristics of fraternity members. *Journal of College Student Personnel, 31*, 126-128.

Muehlenhard, C. L., & Linton, M. A. (1987). Date rape and sexual aggression in dating situations: Incidence and risk factors. *Journal of Counseling Psychology, 34*, 186-196.

Pressley, S. A. (1987, August 11). Fraternity hell night still endures. *Washington Post,* p. B1.

Rapaport, K., & Burkhart, B. R. (1984). Personality and attitudinal characteristics of sexually coercive college males. *Journal of Abnormal Psychology, 93*, 216-221.

Roark, M. L. (1987). Preventing violence on college campuses. *Journal of Counseling and Development, 65*, 367-370.

Sanday, P. R. (1981). The socio-cultural context of rape: A cross-cultural study. *Journal of Social Issues, 37*, 5-27.

Sanday, P. R. (1986). Rape and the silencing of the feminine. In S. Tomaselli & R. Porter (Eds.), *Rape* (pp. 84-101). Oxford, UK: Basil Blackwell.

St. Petersburg Times. (1988, May 29). A Greek tragedy. Pp. 1F, 6F.

Sato, I. (1988). Play theory of delinquency: Toward a general theory of "action." *Symbolic Interaction, 11*, 191-212.

Smith, T. (1964). Emergence and maintenance of fraternal solidarity. *Pacific Sociological Review, 7*, 29-37.

Tallahassee Democrat. (1988a, April 27). FSU fraternity brothers charged. Pp. 1A, 12A.

Tallahassee Democrat. (1988b, April 24). FSU interviewing students about alleged rape. P. 1D.

Tallahassee Democrat. (1989, March 19). Woman sues Stetson in alleged rape. P. 3B.

Tampa Tribune. (1988, April 27). Fraternity brothers charged in sexual assault of FSU coed. P. 6B.

Tash, G. B. (1988). Date rape. *The Emerald of Sigma Pi Fraternity, 75*(4), 1-2.

Telander, R., & Sullivan, R. (1989, February 27). Special report: You reap what you sow. *Sports Illustrated,* pp. 20-34.

The Tomahawk. (1988, April/May). A look back at rush: A mixture of hard work and fun. P. 3D.

Walsh, C. (1989, February 2). [Comments in seminar on acquaintance/date rape prevention]. A National Video Teleconference.

Wilder, D. H., Hoyt, A. E., Doren, D. M., Hauck, W. E., & Zettle, R. D. (1978). The impact of fraternity and sorority membership on value and attitudes. *Journal of College Student Personnel, 36,* 445-449.

Wilder, D. H., Hoyt, A. E., Surbeck, B. S., Wilder, J. C., & Carney, P. I. (1986). Greek affiliation and attitude change in college students. *Journal of College Student Personnel, 44,* 510-519.

9 Montreal Gynocide

JOANNE STATO

Fourteen women were slain in their classroom at the engineering school at the University of Montreal by a 25-year-old male with a hunting rifle on Wednesday evening, December 6 (1989). The killer, Marc Lepine, later shot himself, leaving a three-page statement, which police said blamed feminists for his problems, and which listed 15 prominent feminists, none of whom was among the victims. Police have not released further information on the statement. The murders vaulted the issue of violence against women into the mainstream press because the admission by Lepine that his intent was to kill feminists stymied the usual tendency of the media to portray violence against women as the isolated acts of maniacs and focused attention on the pervasive phenomenon of woman hating in our society. "The incident will do for the issue of violence against women what the *Webster* decision has done for reproductive rights," said San Francisco feminist writer Koré Archer. Archer was one of many women all over Canada and the United States who participated in spontaneous candlelight vigils to pay respect to the murdered women. One such vigil, held in Montreal by members of Concordia University's Women's Collective, and other women and men, suffered from sexist interference by some participating men, according to Martin Dufresne, a member of Montreal Men Against Sexism. "[Concordia Women's Center] organize[d] a demonstration on the day after the shooting at the University of Montreal, but male student leaders from the University of Montreal practically took over the demonstration . . . , defined everything, and physically kept women from

From *off our backs*, *18*(8), p. 12, 1988. Reprinted with permission of the author and *off our backs*, a woman's news journal, Washington, DC.

speaking. The women tried to counter that, but it created a situation that the media then exploited, [i.e.] that males were being shouted down [by women]." Montreal Men Against Sexism, a "pro-feminist men's group," has been working to "try and counter the general denial that this was a gender issue," said Dufresne. "There have been a lot of people, males, in the media denying that this was a social problem, that it was a gender issue. The dead women were very often spoken of in the masculine. [Editor's Note: We think Dufresne was referring to gender specific word endings in the French language.] Having people speak of the dead in the feminine was already a struggle, and there's just this general denial and so everybody was looking for someone to scapegoat on this issue. And there's a lot of pressure on feminists because the killer made his gesture a political act by stating that feminists had wasted his life and that's why he was going there to kill as many women as he could. So we've been trying to get the media to speak to feminists and to not deny that this was a gender issue." Dufresne's remarks echoed those of numerous feminists who spoke to radio commentators and newspaper reporters, including Molly Yard of NOW, who said, "There is something wrong with a society that doesn't really deal with these problems. We bring up young men in a sexist society . . . that is what they learn. Society doesn't do anything serious to correct it, so they think it is OK to be anti-female."

10 Limitations of the Medical Model in the Care of Battered Women

CAROLE WARSHAW
Cook County Hospital, Chicago

Many investigators have documented the discrepancy between the large number of women who come to health care settings with symptoms related to living in abusive relationships and the low rate of detection and intervention by medical staff (Hilberman [now Carmen], 1980; McLeer, 1989; Stark, Flitcraft, & Frazier, 1979). Up to 64 percent of hospitalized female psychiatric patients have histories of being physically abused as adults (Carmen, Rieker, & Mills, 1984; Jacobsen & Richardson, 1987; Post et al., 1990; Walker, 1979), and 23 percent of obstetric patients (across class, race, and educational lines) are at risk for abuse during pregnancy (Helton, Anderson, & McFarlane, 1987). Studies that have focused on emergency room visits have found that 22 to 35 percent of women presenting with any complaint are there because of symptoms related to ongoing abuse, whether secondary to an injury or as a manifestation of the stress of living under abusive conditions (Appleton, 1980; Goldberg & Tomlanovich, 1984; McLeer & Anwar, 1987, 1989; Stark et al. 1979, 1981).

AUTHOR'S NOTE: This research was supported by NIMH Clinical Research Grant PHS 5 T32 MH14668-13. I am indebted to Judith Cook for her invaluable assistance and suggestions; to Sue Fisher, Pauline Bart, and Andy Boxer for their support and readings of this chapter; to Pat Kelleher for assistance with the initial data collection; to Sharon Southe and Pat Kelleher, who collaborated on the pilot study; and to Barbara Engel for sharing her vast knowledge and experience working with battered women. I thank Judith Lorber, Betsy Stanko, and an anonymous reviewer for their extensive editorial comments.

In this study, I examined the medical records of encounters between medical staff (nurses and physicians) and women whose injuries were highly indicative of having been caused by abuse. I analyzed the use of language as a reflection of the nurses' and physicians' thinking about battered women, the impact of the medical model on the care of these patients, and how women who have been victims of interpersonal violence respond to these medical encounters. I found that the structural constraints of a busy urban emergency room in a training institution led not only to nondetection and nonintervention, but more important, to a lack of receptiveness and response by health care providers to the issues that a battered woman struggles with—issues that are vital to her life and well-being.

RESEARCH DESIGN

The study was conducted at a large public hospital that serves a low-income, predominantly African American and Latino population. There are an average of 214,000 patient visits each year to the emergency room, which functions both as a major trauma center and as the only source of pri- mary medical care for the city's poor. Patients must frequently wait more than 8 hours to be seen.

All emergency room charts generated for women patients during the 2-week period from August 21, 1987, to September 4, 1987, were reviewed for indications of abuse. Criteria for selection were the following: explicit mention of having been injured by a significant other; evidence of having been injured by an unnamed other; injuries described as accidental, self-inflicted, or undefined; mention of marital difficulties; vague psychosomatic complaints; abortion, miscarriage, or premature labor; substance abuse; suicide attempts; depression; anxiety; psychosis; panic disorder; and posttraumatic stress disorder. For this study, I analyzed only cases in which the women were deliberately injured by another person, that is, the most obvious cases (N=52). Eighty-five percent presented with an injury that was moderately severe (husband twisted her ankle causing a fracture) or severe (gunshot wound to the abdomen). Life-threatening injuries were present in 8.3 percent. Analysis focused on how information was recorded by the triage nurse and the physician who saw the woman, characteristics of the woman and of the physician, and outcomes of their interaction.

The mean age of the women was 27.6 years and the range was 16 to 54 years. The racial distribution was 84.6 percent African American,

7.7 percent white, 5.8 percent Latino, and 1.9 percent other, a distribution consistent with the demographics of the hospital.

The physician sample consisted of a group of 15 MDs, 4 of whom saw the majority of cases. Three were women. There were 8 surgeons, 5 internists, 1 obstetrician-gynecologist, and 1 anesthesiologist. Five of the 15 physicians were born outside the United States: 1 was Latino, 2 were East Indian, 1 was Middle Eastern, and 1 was Chinese. None of the physicians was African American.

In order to see what characteristics of the patient, physician, and medical situation influenced whether abuse was attended to, the following independent variables were used: patient's age, physician's ethnicity (foreign-born and white native-born), physician's specialty (surgeon and other), and severity of injury (a score ranging from 0 to 4, no injury to life-threatening injury).

Dependent variables were derived from three places in the charts where information about abuse would potentially be recorded: triage nurse's recording of the woman's presenting complaint, physician's recording of patient's history, and discharge diagnosis. On each chart, these three data points were coded for explicitness, ambiguity, or absence of information regarding abuse. Within each of these categories, statements were rated according to degree of disembodiment (hit by thing versus by a body part versus by a person), and instrumentality (something happened to her versus someone did something to her).

Although there are many reasons medical staff do not address abuse in a busy emergency room (Kurz, 1987) and do not record all pertinent information (Garfinkel, 1967), I hypothesized that the way statements were recorded on the chart would reflect how the triage nurse and the physician organized their perceptions about the patient. If this were true, the records in which statements were the most consistent with the biomedical model, the most decontextualized (Rieker & Carmen, 1986), would also be the charts with the least appropriate outcomes, that is, failure to acknowledge abuse and to refer.

FINDINGS

In the majority of cases, the women gave very strong clues about being at risk for abuse and these clues were recorded, but were rarely expanded upon. They were addressed directly in only one case, and for the most part, were specifically avoided. The lack of attention to these clues occurred in an emergency room that has a formal protocol for recognizing and caring for women at risk for abuse.

There were no major differences between the nurses and doctors in their recording of explicit information of abuse. The nurse was explicit in 12 percent and the physician in 15 percent of the cases; the nurse was ambiguous in 73 percent and the physician in 65 percent of the cases; and the nurse recorded no information about abuse in 15 percent of cases and the physician in 21 percent.

The physicians tended to obscure information already recorded by the nurse (41.7 percent) rather than to elaborate (31.1 percent), as would be expected in a full history. Foreign-born doctors were more likely to elaborate on information provided by the triage nurse than white native-born physicians (38 versus 29 percent; $r=.24$, $p<.05$). They were not, however, more likely to initiate recognition of abuse, nor were they more likely to integrate information into the discharge diagnosis.

Surgeons were significantly less likely than physicians in other specialties to elaborate on information recorded by the nurse (23 versus 86 percent; $r=.40$, $p<.01$), were less likely to have their discharge diagnosis reflect the highest level of information available (2 versus 29 percent; $r=23$, $p<.10$), and were less likely to record explicit information about abuse (14 versus 29 percent; $r=18$, $p<.10$). These findings are consistent with the more action-oriented (as contrasted with investigational) surgical framework. Although nonsurgeons took fuller histories, the majority still did not integrate the information about abuse into their final diagnoses or discharge plans.

For younger women (mean age=23), the discharge diagnosis was more likely to reflect the highest level of information available on the chart ($r= -.21$, $p<.10$). These women had the majority of gunshot and stab wounds, almost necessitating their falling into the abuse category (cf. McLeer & Anwar, 1989). In general, the mean age (27) for women whose discharge diagnosis did reflect abuse was younger than the mean age of the sample (27.6) and younger than the likely average age of physicians at this level of training. Perhaps young physicians in the emergency room felt more identified with and protective toward women closer to their own age and were less willing to intervene in what they perceived as personal matters in the case of women who were older.

It is at the time the physician takes the patient's history that more detailed information can be obtained and that the patient's story should be elicited. Physicians, however, probed in less than one third of the cases. Furthermore, although in every case there was either explicit information about abuse or very strong clues recorded by the nurse or by the physician, in 92 percent of the cases, the discharge diagnosis did not reflect these presenting symptoms.

The physician records the discharge diagnosis at the time he or she is conceptualizing the case, pulling together what is seen as important both for this visit and for those who see the patient in follow-up. It is the basis on which a disposition and treatment plan are formulated. In all but one of these cases, the most serious and potentially life-threatening risk for the patient, that of ongoing domestic violence, was not reflected in the discharge diagnosis or in the disposition, despite its blatant presence on the chart and in the patient's life. Physicians in other clinical situations would not discharge a patient from the emergency room with a potentially life-threatening condition.

The formal protocol for handling abuse also calls for a psychiatric consultation in identified cases of domestic violence. A social work consultation is also recommended to make referrals to shelters and provide information about other necessary services. At the very least, the protocol calls for the nurse or physician to make a referral list of shelters and legal and counseling services available to the woman before she leaves, even if she does not wish to see a psychiatrist or social worker. Despite this clear protocol, there was no psychiatry consult in 96 percent of the 52 cases reviewed, no social work consult in 92 percent, and no shelter information or referral sheet given in 98 percent of the cases.

Police reports were filed by triage nurses in less than half the cases (46.2 percent). Whether or not a report was filed did not significantly correlate with any of the dependent variables. All the injuries in this sample were inflicted by another person, thus constituting assault and battery. Yet less than half were reported to the police. At the same time, there were twice as many police reports filed as there were charts explicitly recording abuse. Thus the triage nurses were aware of abuse but were reluctant to take on the protocol that calls for a primary nurse to be a patient advocate. If she did, one of the nurses would have had to make sure that the battered woman's care was sensitive and expeditious: that she saw a psychiatrist or social worker if she wished; was given a referral sheet and booklet on abuse with information about shelters, counseling, legal aid, and so on; had a safe place to go; and received appropriate follow-up. This process was initiated in only six cases during the 2-week period studied. In short, triage nurses shifted the problem to another institutional sector rather than to another overburdened nurse.

Physicians were more likely to give medication (68 percent) when signs of abuse were present but not elaborated on or reflected in the diagnosis. Thus physicians would medicate but not face the implications of what or why they were medicating. Most of these medications were given for pain (74 percent), some in combination with antibiotics. Very few psychoactive medications were given, as that would have dictated a psychiatry consult.

THE MEDICAL CONSTRUCTION OF ABUSE

The 52 medical records were also analyzed as the text of what a physician narrator recorded of the discourse between him- or herself and a woman at risk for abuse (Gogel & Terry, 1987; Good & Good, 1981; Ricoeur, 1971/1979; Stark et al., 1979; Steele, 1979). The following questions were addressed: (a) How is the battered woman's experience reconstructed in the medical setting by what is and is not attended to and deemed significant? (b) What do the records reflect about how physicians perceive information in general; what do they deem important and how do they integrate information? (c) How does their use of language reflect their perceptions and relationship to patients? (d) How does the use of standard medical descriptive format shape physicians' ability to see?

Analysis of the records makes it evident that even when a woman had clearly been injured by another person, often her spouse, she would rarely be asked any questions that would indicate an awareness on the part of the physician that he or she was interacting with a woman at risk for abuse. In over 90 percent of the cases, the physician failed to obtain a psychosocial history, failed to ask about sexual abuse or a past history of physical abuse, failed to ask about the woman's living arrangements, and neglected to address the woman's safety. In 78 percent of the cases, the physician failed to identify the relationship of the assailant to the victim. By not asking these questions, he or she not only lost the opportunity to identify abuse when it was less clear but also was unable to address the underlying etiology of the patient's "medical" condition, could not engage in any preventive measures, and could not address the most serious threat to her life and well-being.

More significant, physicians did not open up the possibility for the battered woman to discuss what may have been her most important reason for seeking help. They did not respond to the distress that her physical symptoms reflected or to clues offered about her situation. They chose

to medicalize her chief complaint and address only the physical symptoms, thus reinforcing whatever feelings of helplessness, isolation, and
futility at not being seen or responded to the woman may have already
felt. They missed the animate connection between her injury and how
it happened, who did it, what her relationship to the perpetrator was,
what its impact was, and what the implications and meanings were for
the woman and her life outside the emergency room. Other researchers
have found that the "disconfirmation" (Rieker & Carmen, 1986) of abusive
experience by care givers is an important factor in the development of
subsequent psychopathology (Hamilton, 1989; Miller, 1984).

The abused woman's ongoing need to distort her sense of reality in
order to survive the pain of abuse is, as can be seen in these records,
reinforced by the demands of the medical encounter. By reducing the
battered woman's lived experience to medical facts and not acknowledging the feelings they avoid by doing so, medical staff inadvertently
recreate the abusive dynamic between themselves and their patients.

Physicians frequently used disembodied language to describe a traumatic event such as "was beaten to face and head with fist" "blow to
head by stick with nail in it," "hit on left wrist by a jackhammer." What
they recorded was the mechanism of injury, how the blow impacted on
the body, not on the person. The entire battering event was reduced to
an interaction between a fist and an eye.

The following is a verbatim transcript of a typical emergency room
record:

NURSE TRIAGE NOTE: Was hit on upper lip. teeth loose and c̄ dislocation. Happened
    last night.
MD RECORD: Patient 25y/o BF c/o [complained of] swelling and pain on the mouth
    after was hit by a fist about 5 hours ago. No LOC [loss of consciousness], no visual
    symptoms, no vomiting, no nausea.
PHYSICAL EXAM: Afebrile, hydrated, conscious, oriented x 3 [time, place, person].
    HEENT [head, eyes, ears, nose, throat]: has swelling in the upper lip and loose teeth.
    No evidence of Fx [fracture].
XRAY: No Fracture
DISCHARGE DIAGNOSIS: Blunt Trauma Face
DISPOSITION: Ice Packs, Oral Surgery Clinic appt, Motrin

What is missing? The nurse's note does not mention who hit her, what
her relationship to this person was, what the circumstances of the attack
were, or why she waited 5 hours to seek medical help. We also see that

there is no subject in this statement and that the woman is already out of the picture—only her lip and teeth are there.

Using the standard medical shorthand, which is an important shaper of how physicians learn to organize their thinking, we see how the subject becomes a mere descriptor. What are foregrounded are the symptoms: swelling and pain on the mouth. The physician's note uses the passive voice and focuses on the physical trauma. Even the additional statement, "hit by a fist," is structured to give information relevant to the mechanism of injury and what damage might have been done to the body. It removes the fist from the person attached to it. In doing so, the physician, although perhaps not consciously, makes a choice that obscures both the etiology and meaning of the woman's symptoms. Here, too, the passive voice slides over the real action.

What is so disturbing about this case, particularly from the perspective of a battered woman who enters the health care system to seek help, is the way in which the framework and language of the biomedical model obscure and discount the lived reality of the person it attempts to serve. She essentially says: "Someone hit me." Instead of asking: Who hit you? How did this come about? What is your relationship to this person? How do you feel about this? Has this happened before? Have you thought about what you can do? Is it safe for you to go home or do you need another place to stay? Instead of expanding and deepening, picking up on what she does reveal, however indirectly, the physician moves in the other direction and focuses solely on the pathophysiological endpoint. She says she was hit, clearly implying that a person hit her. Her statement is still open; it leaves room for the possibility of going further. He closes off that possibility by actively concretizing the disembodiment, the lack of relevance of the person or relationship involved in the attack. He specifies that the fist to the lip is all that is relevant. Although both are offered, the physician selectively attends to the "medical facts" rather than the "facts of the lifeworld" (Anspach, 1987; Kleinman, 1988; Mishler, 1981, 1984; Schutz & Luckmann, 1973; Williamson, Beitman, & Katon, 1981).

Merely expanding the medical model to include the pathological category of "battered woman" is not a solution (Kurz, 1987; Stark et al., 1979). What is of greater concern is the nature of the relationship between the woman and the doctor—a woman who is understandably circumspect about revealing abuse and a doctor who is reluctant to know. This relationship, however, is formed in a context that is largely physician controlled. The patient would have to struggle actively to have her concerns recognized (Beckman & Frankel, 1984; Fisher, 1986; Mishler, 1984; Waitzkin, 1984; West, 1984). If the woman's initial overtures are not responded to, it is unlikely that she will want to reveal more or feel that it would be appropriate or helpful to do so. Together, the doctor, nurse, and patient construct a "medical history" that is, in fact, ahistorical— one that extracts an event from its context, even from its status as an event, something that has happened in time and space. The dynamics of an abusive relationship are recreated in an encounter in which the subjectivity and needs of the woman are reduced to categories that meet the needs of another, not her own, a relationship in which she as a person is neither seen nor heard.

What happens when we intervene in this process? A resident once asked me to see a woman who had pain and redness under her right ear. He could not figure out what might have caused these physical findings. I came into the room, introduced myself, looked at her, and said, "Did someone hit you?" She hesitated only for a moment and said, "Yes." I asked her, "Who did it? Was it your boyfriend?" Again, she said, "Yes." I then asked her why she had not told the other doctor, and she said, "He didn't ask." I looked at him questioningly, and he said, "I did ask. I asked if there had been any trauma." The three of us discussed this, and she added that she had not wanted to initiate talking about being hit; she felt ashamed, afraid, and felt that it would be telling on her boyfriend. She later said that this was the first time he had hit her and that he treated her much better than anyone else she had ever been involved with and that he protected her.

In discussing this case later, the resident said that he had not felt it was his place to ask such sensitive intrusive questions about her personal life and that it was the way it was asked (not a way he would have known or felt comfortable with) that had elicited the patient's responses. Conversely, the resident's model of what was appropriate to the medical encounter and his use of technical language protected him from having to face the discomfort of asking direct personal questions.

CONCLUSIONS

In this study of the records of 52 cases of women with clear symptoms indicative of abuse, I found that neither nurses nor doctors were willing or able to take on what would be entailed in directly addressing the issues a battered woman brings to the emergency room. Although there appeared to be some awareness of abuse by doctors and nurses, this information was rarely elaborated or integrated into the diagnosis or disposition of the case. In most of the cases it was obscured. Both nurses and doctors did, however, use indirect means to deal with battered women. Nurses reported cases to the police, satisfying their legal obligations; and physicians prescribed pain medications, satisfying their "medical" obligations. Very few of the medical staff were able to ask the direct questions that would have led to more appropriate and comprehensive interventions. Although gender has been found to play a greater role than professional category in attitudes toward battered women (Rose & Saunders, 1986), overwork and understaffing for both nurses and doctors may have overridden what would be expected differences in responsiveness. For nurses, the difficulty of taking on the multiple role responsibilities and extra work involved in becoming an advocate may have prevented identification of battered women and initiation of the prescribed protocol. The conflict between fulfilling a more nurturant nursing role and the technical demands of a busy emergency room was perhaps greater for the nurses than for the physicians, for whom the medical model and medical training reinforce a detachment that protects against emotional involvement (cf. Anspach, 1987, 1988). In addition, nurses have a less autonomous role in the emergency room, where they have to work more directly with physicians, than in inpatient units. For both, the psychosocial aspects of abuse were defined as outside the framework of medical intervention. In this setting, where large numbers of patients must be seen expeditiously, it is the medical model that predominates.

In an underfunded, understaffed urban public hospital, it is harder to create the kind of sterile, high-tech environment that controls and transforms life-world issues into medical problems. The street impinges to a far greater extent there, putting an even greater burden on individual staff to maintain the "medical framework."

The medical model, in fact, can only "medicalize," reduce things to categories it can handle and control. The need to control and reduce is inherent in its scientific and epistemological base (Harding, 1986; Keller, 1995; MacKinnon, 1987; Smith, 1987; Yllö, 1988). The analysis of language in these records reveals how the model works at an interactional level and how it limits what can happen between patients and doctors. The issue of battered women is a subversive one. In order to take it on fully, medical staff risk losing control in ways that the model normally protects them from; having to deal with unpleasant, potentially overwhelming feelings that are often evoked by actually listening empathically to a patient; and having to deal with agencies and institutions (i.e., battered women's networks) that are outside the control of medicine and that often have a critical perspective on the delivery of health care. Most important, they risk having to change the doctor-patient relationship itself, a relationship in which the unacknowledged need to maintain control and power reproduces an abusive dynamic antithetical to the care a battered woman most needs. By deconstructing the use of language in these medical records, we see how medicine's epistemological model of care recreates abusive relationships through a medical encounter in which what is most significant is not seen. The issues battered women bring to the medical setting radically challenge this model of care.

REFERENCES

Anspach, R. R. (1987). Prognostic conflict in life-and-death decisions: The organization as an ecology of knowledge. *Journal of Health and Social Behavior, 28,* 215-231.

Anspach, R. R. (1988). The sociology of medical discourse: The language of case presentation. *Journal of Health and Social Behavior, 29,* 357-375.

Appleton, W. (1980). The battered woman syndrome. *Annals of Emergency Medicine, 9,* 84-91.

Beckman, H. B., & Frankel, R. M. (1984). The effect of physician behavior on the collection of data. *Annals of Internal Medicine, 101,* 692-696.

Carmen, E., Rieker, P., & Mills, T. (1984). Victims of violence and psychiatric illness. *American Journal of Psychiatry, 141,* 378-383.

Fisher, S. (1986). *In the patient's best interest: Women and the politics of medical decisions.* New Brunswick, NJ: Rutgers University Press.

Garfinkel, H. (1967). Good organizational reasons for bad clinic records. In *Studies in Ethnomethodology* (pp. 186-207). Englewood Cliffs, NJ: Prentice-Hall.

Gogel, E. L., & Terry, J. S. (1987). Medicine as interpretation: The uses of literary metaphors and methods. *Journal of Medicine and Philosophy, 12,* 205-217.

Goldberg, W. G., & Tomlanovich, M. C. (1984). Domestic violence victims in the emergency department: New findings. *Journal of Medicine and Philosophy, 12,* 205-217.

Good, B. J., & Good, M.-J. D. (1981). The meaning of symptoms: A cultural hermeneutic model for clinical practice. In L. Eisenberg & A. Kleinman (Eds.), *The relevance of social science for medicine* (pp. 165-196). Dordrecht, Holland: Reidel.

Hamilton, J. A. (1989). Emotional consequences of victimization and discrimination in special populations of women. *Psychiatric Clinics of North America, 12,* 35-51.

Harding, S. (1986). *The science question in feminism.* Ithaca, NY: Cornell University Press.

Helton, A. S., Anderson, E., & McFarlane, J. (1987). Battered and pregnant: A prevalence study with intervention measures. *American Journal of Public Health, 77,* 1337-1339.

Hilberman, E. (1980). Overview: The wife-beater's wife reconsidered. *American Journal of Psychiatry, 137,* 1336-1347.

Jacobsen, A., & Richardson, B. (1987). Assault experiences of 100 psychiatric inpatients: Evidence of the need for routine inquiry. *American Journal of Psychiatry, 144,* 908-913.

Keller, E. F. (1985). *Reflections on gender and science.* New Haven, CT: Yale University Press.

Kleinman, A. (1988). *The illness narratives: Suffering, healing, and the human condition.* New York: Basic Books.

Kurz, D. (1987). Emergency department response to battered women: A case of resistance. *Social Problems, 34,* 501-513.

MacKinnon, C. A. (1987). *Feminism unmodified: Discourses on life and law.* Cambridge, MA: Harvard University Press.

McLeer, S. V. (1989). Education is not enough: A systems failure in protecting battered women. *Annals of Emergency Medicine, 18,* 651-653.

McLeer, S. V., & Anwar, R. (1987). The role of the emergency physician in the prevention of domestic violence. *Annals of Emergency Medicine, 16,* 1155-1161.

McLeer, S. V., & Anwar, R. (1989). A study of battered women presenting in an emergency department. *American Journal of Public Health, 79,* 65-66.

Miller, A. (1984). *Thou shalt not be aware: Society's betrayal of the child.* New York: Farrar, Straus & Giroux.

Mishler, E. (1981). Viewpoint: Critical perspectives on the biomedical model. In E. Mishler (Ed.), *Social contexts of health, illness and patient care* (pp. 1-19). Cambridge, MA: Cambridge University Press.

Mishler, E. (1984). *The discourse of medicine: Dialectics of medical interviews.* Norwood, NJ: Ablex.

Post, R. D., Willet, A. B., Franks, R. D., House, R. M., Beck, S., & Weissberg, M. P. (1980). A preliminary report on the prevalence of domestic violence among psychiatric inpatients. *American Journal of Psychiatry, 137,* 974-975.

Ricoeur, P. (1979). The model of the text: Meaningful action considered as a text. In P. Rabinow & W. M. Sullivan (Eds.), *An interpretive social science reader* (pp. 73-101). Berkeley: University of California Press. (Original work published 1971)

Rieker, P. P., & Carmen, E. (Hilberman). (1986). The victim-to-patient process: The disconfirmation and transformation of abuse. *American Journal of Orthopsychiatry, 56,* 360-370.

Rose, K., & Saunders, D. G. (1986). Nurses' and physicians' attitudes about women abuse: The effects of gender and professional role. *Health Care for Women International, 7,* 427-438.

Schutz, A., & Luckmann, T. (1973). *The structures of the life-world.* Evanston, IL: Northwestern University Press.

Smith, D. E. (1987). *The everyday world as problematic: A feminist sociology.* Boston: Northeastern University Press.

Stark, E., Flitcraft, A., & Frazier, W. (1979). Medicine and patriarchal violence: The social construction of a private event. *International Journal of Health Services, 9,* 461-492.

Stark, E., Flitcrast, A., Zuckerman, D., Grey, A., Robison, J., & Frazier, W. (1981). *Wife abuse in the medical setting: An introduction for health per- sonnel* (Monograph no. 7). Washington, DC: Office of Domestic Violence.

Steele, R. S. (1979). Psychoanalysis and hermeneutics. *International Revue of Psychoanalysis, 6,* 389-411.

Waitzkin, H. (1984). Doctor-patient communication: Clinical implications of social scientific research. *Journal of the American Medical Association, 252,* 2441-2446.

Walker, L. E. (1979). *The battered woman.* New York: Harper & Row.

West, C. (1984). *Routine complications: Troubles with talk between doctors and patients.* Bloomington: Indiana University Press.

Williamson, P., Beitman, B. D., & Katon, W. (1981). Beliefs that foster physician avoidance of psychosocial aspects of health care. *Journal of Family Practice, 13,* 999-1003.

Yllö, K. (1988). Political and methodological debates in wife abuse research. In K. Yllö & M. Bograd (Eds.), *Feminist perspectives on wife abuse* (pp. 28-50). Newbury Park, CA: Sage.

Part III

The Politics of Institutional Responses to Violence Against Women

Introduction

The first half of this volume covered the continuum of assaults and threats that permeate women's experiences and identified the structural supports for violence against women. In this section, the institutional responses to feminist claims will be examined. How is the violation of women woven into the fabric of everyday life? How have feminists responded? Then we will ask what have been the consequences of accepting government funding and of the reform process itself. Finally we will move beyond reform to ask what is learned about male dominance and violence from more radical feminist critics, such as Catharine MacKinnon and Andrea Dworkin, who address the eroticization of violence.

VIOLENCE IS EVERYWHERE

Over the past 25 years feminists have developed organizations that have successfully challenged social institutions for failing to protect women. Thus, battered women's advocates have publicized their criticisms of police departments, courts, and the law and have forced legislatures and the criminal justice system to respond. Similarly, laws have been passed or "reformed" in response to feminist advocates on a number of fronts, such as rape, battery, and sexual harassment. In this section, some of these institutional responses are scrutinized, with particular emphasis on the inherent limits of piecemeal reforms in a society in which gender inequity persists and is endemic.

In television and movies violence against women—rape, murder, incest, and battery—is prominently and regularly featured; and in spite of attempts to advocate for the victim, victimizing women is still considered titillating and erotic.

Twenty-five years ago, women's political, social, and economic inequality was an accepted fact of life, immutable; that is no longer quite so true. As feminists organized politically, our analyses uncovered the patterns that keep us in our place, both at home and on the job. The political, social, and economic privileges that men generally enjoy, relative to women, enable them to continue to control women. Male dominance is supported by a continuum of force, which includes murder, rape, battery, and harassment, as well as the ability to impose economic sanctions. Linking the continuum of assaults and intimidation women experience both amplifies and clarifies the social and political impact of men's abuse.

The feminist movement examined and politicized all aspects of women's lives. For women as a class, access to employment, education, reproductive choice, health care, and physical safety were regulated by men. Feminists developed organizations and constituencies committed to ending sex and gender discrimination and assaults on women, thereby institutionalizing these claims on behalf of women's rights. Some of these organizations focused on protecting women, that is, on ensuring safety, at home, at work, and on the street. Feminists made the abuse of women and girls a public issue rather than a private or personal problem.

We know that sexual danger is an everyday reality for women. It structures our lives (Gordon & Riger, 1988; Stanko, 1990), yet it is so interwoven into our identities as women that we hardly notice it. Women routinely assume that they must always be on their guard against assaults from men. As Stanko persuasively argues, women's fear of crime is fear of men.

Women's lives are circumscribed and controlled by violence. The man who does not want his wife, sister, or daughter to go out alone because he fears for her safety may benefit from the limits on her activities. Why hasn't men's concern for women's safety been institutionalized to *thwart* assaults? The law and its administration reflect men's preference for insulating women from the assaults of strangers by confinement rather than by making public space safe.

Yet home is not a safe haven for women. Police officers advise curfews for women for their protection, just as men suggest the solution to male violence is to keep women out of public places. Yet Israel's Golda Meir stated that curfews to prevent sexual assault should be applied to men, as they were the perpetrators of rape. Men benefit from the confinement of women, which reinforces men's control of the lives of women in their family and in the society at large, as well as the social supports for male dominance, in which victims are made responsible for the perpetrators' abusive behavior. Male bias has so permeated the social contract that some routinely ask victims of incest, harassment, rape, or battery what they did to provoke the assaults. We internalize all the precautions girls and women are expected to take to assure our safety. Yet we are confronted by the futility of such activity, subtly aware that we are being made culpable in the process, responsible for men's violence. The incest victim is removed from her home and the battered woman is asked why she didn't leave.

Most of us cope with this tension by denying the constant risk. Men contribute to this denial by believing that the risk of assault is not from them, the "average Joe," but from a smaller number of deviants. As Elizabeth Stanko reports in Chapter 11, adults who were sexually assaulted as children routinely report that they were abused by family members as well as other trustworthy adults known to their family. Yet, public images continue to portray perpetrators as deranged men or immature boys. Class and racial biases conspire to depict the molester as the "other," with the result that precautions offered to women and children are dangerously inappropriate. Women and children's safety are secondary. Greater value is placed on the "average Joe's" ability to emotionally distance himself from the "normal man's" abuse of the power he has over women and children. We know better.

THE LIMITS OF REFORM

Over the last 15 years the movements that emerged to combat the abuse of women have themselves been institutionalized in rape crisis centers, hotlines, battered women's shelters, programs for incest survivors, antipornography programs, and the like. Networks of professional and volunteer service providers lobby for legal reforms to better protect women. The institutionalization of services to victims tended to separate these organizations from their feminist roots, reducing their impact on the analysis of violence and thus on survivors and on the society at large, as they applied single-issue strategies to safeguard their budgets or implement reforms.

Battered women's advocates demanded that the law treat assaults between partners as seriously as assaults by strangers. Ferraro's analysis (Chapter 12) of police and court responses to women victims emphasizes the limits of these criminal justice reforms. She compares violent assaults between partners or intimates to assaults by strangers and finds, contrary to expectation, that violent assaults by strangers are also poorly prosecuted. Her analysis of a Southwestern community finds class, racial, and ethnic barriers operate to thwart the legal protection of poor and non-White victims of assault.

So patriarchy has proven its resilience, its ability to absorb reforms and accommodate social movements without dramatically altering the balance of power between men and women or between adults and children. Class and race are important variables in shaping how much protection victims are afforded. These issues are echoed by Ferraro and Matthews (Chapter 13). Fearing legal liability, police departments secured funding to train officers to deal with wife battery, redefined as domestic violence. In some states, mandatory arrest policies were implemented, with both partners being arrested to avoid accusations of police discrimination against men. MacKinnon (1983) asks why we so quickly marshall resources to protect our institutions from the critical analysis of feminists. Although the criminal justice system has been shown to afford women and children little protection, Ferraro highlights the very large expenditure on research and training of police and experimenting with court procedures. Ironically, spending on low-income housing—which enables women to leave violent men—would prevent more abuse of women and children than huge expenditures tinkering with a very biased criminal justice system. Matthews's research on crisis services for poor minority women and children demonstrates how their options are so intertwined with class and race that serving them effectively requires a broader focus, one that addresses their additional concrete needs.

Although feminist analyses and political organizing have increased the practical services to survivors of rape and battery, their effectiveness is seriously undermined by the persistence of patriarchal biases in the social service and criminal justice systems. Chapter 14 (Boria et al.), depicting a typical day in the life of service providers, illustrates the dilemma of trying to change systems to make them more responsive to victims while simultaneously advising individual women about protecting themselves and their children. In these crisis services staff burnout is clearly tied to their firsthand knowledge of how limited many women's options are and how unequal their access to legal remedies continues to be. Feminists have indeed been ambivalent about how much to rely on institutions to provide redress or relief to abused women. The battered women's and the antirape movements targeted the criminal justice system to redress the abuse of women. In general the legal system ignored "family fights" and child abuse. A number of states, including "progressive" New York, until 1973, required a woman to have a witness other than herself or the perpetrator to press charges for rape. Some states still find it impossible for a woman to be raped by her husband (Russell, 1982). To remedy these evils feminists lobbied to change legislation to facilitate the prosecution of battery, rape, and other sexual assaults and to provide support services to victims. In many communities publicly funded services to victims became available, including 24-hour hotlines for victims of battery and sexual assault.

The first services provided to victims were often delivered by volunteer feminists who had developed either community- or campus-based services. When these first voluntary services sprang up feminists worked simultaneously for reproductive rights and an end to pornography, sexual assaults, and battery. The links between various forms of male dominance, from unequal pay to rape, were made explicit. With funding came considerable debate about "selling out," because of the restrictions that government and foundation support required. With targeted, specialized funding came bureaucratic, that is, hierarchical, accountability that eroded the alternative organizations feminists had built (Michels, 1967; Weber, 1973). Ultimately, the more radical feminists threatened establishment funding sources just as institutionalization threatened the feminist thrust of services.[1]

Yet the value of increased services that public funding provided to both battered women and victims of sexual assault should not be underestimated. It succeeded in making such abuse a public issue for which the community and the whole society should be held accountable. For survivors it increased the possibility of their receiving services and having contact with others who have been abused.

Although some activists have been critical of services staffed by credentialed social workers, they have not intruded upon the all-important peer support. As Matthews points out, even traditionally trained social workers are changed when they work with abused women. Those providing services to battered women and survivors of sexual assault find their work spills over and alters their personal lives, especially their relationships with husbands, lovers, and children. The radicalizing experience of working with victims occurs even within the more conservative state-funded community-based agencies. Matthews also finds that staff are forced to confront the limits being set by the funding source and the inappropriateness of the mandated record keeping. Those who provide services in poor communities are compelled to address issues beyond that of the sexual assault per se. As publicly funded service providers they must document statistically who they serve and the appropriateness of their services. Over time, narrow definitions have been applied to determine a woman's eligibility for help. Does the marital rape victim qualify to enter the battered women's shelter or is she limited to the services for victims of rape? Are rape crisis services trained to address marital rape (Russell, 1982)?

What appears to be operating here is not only the consequence of bureaucratization itself, but another organizational factor. If there are far more women eligible for the service than facilities, service providers can choose to admit the least troublesome clientele, those seeking service Monday through Friday during business hours.

The changes in these organizations that have been wrought by their dependence on public and foundation support are politically important. A measure of their success is that survivors of rape and battery are accepted as worthy of public and charitable support. But as these services are accepted by mainstream society, the connection between the continuum of violence and gender inequality is less and less clear. Increasingly, psychological labels, rather than social analyses, are used to explain the behavior of violent men. More disturbing, more feminist analyses are abandoned. Nonetheless, even the cranked-out TV movies-of-the-week, as a sample of cultural change, tell millions of men and women that men, not women, should be held responsible for rape and battery.

BEYOND REFORM

The analyses by MacKinnon (Chapter 15) and Hill Collins (Chapter 6) affirm the inherent limitations of attempts at reform. MacKinnon's theory explains why the courts and police, and social institutions in general, are unable to respond fairly to women's charges of harassment or assault. "The law sees and treats women the way men see and treat them" (MacKinnon, Chapter 15). MacKinnon thus shows that the law is inherently male. For example, in the case of rape, the law cannot acknowledge that what women experience as rape, men experience as sex, and men's definitions, in court, as in life, dominate. Since "normal men" are considered or believed incapable of such assaults, demonstrating a man's normality may be sufficient defense.

"The law seeks objectivity in rape . . . as if truth is there to be discovered, not that she said rape and he said it's sex. How can neutrality be the norm in law, when neutrality is nonexistent." Instead, the law substantiates the radical feminist claim that because male dominance is eroticized, the difference between assault and ordinary heterosexual dominance is submerged. Similarly, in deciding whether an act is harassment or flirtation, his definition persists. The reaction of the U.S. Senate Judiciary Committee to Professor Anita Hill's charges of sexual harassment against the Supreme Court nominee Clarence Thomas exemplify the masculinist cultural bias that affirms men's control of women's sexuality. The law will never protect women from unwelcome sexual advances because the right to make such advances is what makes men believe they are men.

The notoriety of the Thomas hearings and several recent rape trials—and the fans' response to the heavyweight boxer Mike Tyson's conviction—again show the responsibility for men's sexual misconduct placed on the victim. Some of this extra burden imposed on women reflects the unspoken truth that we all know—but seldom acknowledge: Women are always unsafe, and therefore to let down our guard, with a few drinks, or by trusting acquaintances from work, school, or neighborhood, makes us culpable. Not insignificantly, the persistence of rape myths in the media, and in the culture generally, conspires to make women fear the unknown stranger and to feel relatively safe with men they know. Men want to believe that assaults against women are deviant behavior, committed by the deranged or the stranger. Normal men may engage in "rough sex," but that is not to be confused with rape and murder. The reports of rape survivors parallel that of the child molested by a shopkeeper who, because of his respectability, was considered trustworthy (Stanko).

But in viewing the incidence of campus rapes, where privileged young men conspire to gang-rape women, using spiked drinks and the like, what are our expectations of men? Men victimized by their allegedly uncontrollable sex drive that once aroused can only be healed by penetrating a female orifice are therefore popularly seen as just regular guys engaged in legitimate assaults on women who are defined as "fair game."

What is their view of women? The differences in analyses of the Professor Hill-Justice Thomas hearings led to feminists' claims that men "just don't get it." That is, men fail to appreciate or understand the daily, routine sexual violations experienced by women. To admit the truth of what these women say undermines men's perception of themselves.

The segmenting of services by funding sources with mandates to serve specific categories of victims, the Equal Employment Opportunity Commission (EEOC) for harassment, the rape crisis center for sexual assault, and so forth, also undermines the most significant contribution of feminists—*establishing the connections among these violations against women.* Professionals specializing in treating one type of victim evade the more important questions, reifying men's definitions of women's experiences. MacKinnon identifies what is fundamental about the social construction of sex inequality, an inequality for which violence is paradigmatic. MacKinnon, along with the other authors in this section, calls for a more radical agenda. The final section of this book will address these research implications and policy concerns.

NOTE

1. Bart reports resigning from the board of the Chicago Sexual Assault Network over antifeminist political and organizational compromises the network made to assure its funding and community acceptability.

REFERENCES

Gerth, H. H., & Mills, C. W. (1973). *From Max Weber: Essays in sociology.* New York: Oxford University Press.
Gordon, M., & Riger, S. (1989). *The female fear.* New York: Free Press.
MacKinnon, C. (1983, Summer). Feminism, Marxism, method, and the state: Toward feminist jurisprudence. *Signs, 8*(4), 635-658.
Michels, R. (1967). *Political parties.* New York: Free Press.
Russell, D.E.H. (1982). *Rape in marriage.* New York: Macmillan.
Stanko, E. A. (1990). *Everyday violence.* London: Pandora.

11 Ordinary Fear:
Women, Violence, and Personal Safety

ELIZABETH ANNE STANKO
Brunel University

"I'm just tired of being afraid," stated one university student. Only a few days before, one of her classmates had been raped as she returned from the library. A wave of anxiety seemed to grip the whole campus, but women felt it most, reporting loss of sleep, inability to concentrate, acute anxiety about their safety within university housing, and nervousness about attending classes. Some who had been previously abused experienced flashbacks.

Faced with a growing awareness about women's concern about their sexual safety, university officials are more willing to issue advice to women students about how to minimize the possibility of attack. As students returned to campuses throughout England in fall 1990, for example, they met with such advice. At Leicester Polytechnic, police visited residence halls, lecturing to women about safety, advising students to "never walk out alone at night" and to take self-defense classes. Liverpool University, Nottingham University, and others issued rape alarms to women students.[1] These measures are meant to reassure women and provide tips for avoiding possible criminal victimization. They also remind women that they are targets for men's sexual violence.

But university policy is most curious if it is seriously meant to address women's safety. All the evidence suggests that women's greatest danger is faced *indoors,* usually within the confines of their own social networks and particularly their own homes, from men who are familiar and familial. Yet the bulk of advice to women continues to speak of the potential threat and harm from those strangers who lurk *outside,* which masks the far greater danger facing university students: their male classmates. The reality is that women's encounters with *any* man could be dangerous. Of course, not all men are rapists. But the dilemma for women, not only university students but all women, is to be able to sort out the dangerous from the safe men. Rape alarms, self-defense classes, and police lectures will not provide the information women need to do that.

FEAR OF CRIME: THE CONCEPT

Generally, fear of crime is taken to represent individuals' diffuse sense of danger about being physically harmed by criminal violence (Maxfield, 1984; Skogan & Maxfield, 1981). It is associated with concern about being outside the home, probably in an urban area, alone and potentially vulnerable to personal harm. Typically, the classic fear of crime question appearing on victimization surveys is: How safe do you feel walking alone in your neighborhood [in this area] alone after dark [or at night]? (Hough & Mayhew, 1983, 1985).[2] Individuals may also be asked to assess their probability of encountering, say, a burglary, robbery, or rape within the next 12 months. This line of questioning is used to analyze respondents' evaluation of their risk of victimization. Then, information is collected about "actual" victimization (that is, reported to the researchers).

Although there have been a number of criticisms about how the concept of fear of crime is constructed (e.g., Crawford, Jones, Woodhouse, & Young, 1990; Gibbs, Coyle, & Hanrahan, 1987; Shapland & Vagg, 1988), the concept itself and what it is presumed to represent, citizen anxiety about crime and disorder, is now treated as a social problem in its own right. This is precisely because those segments of the population who are found to be most fearful, women and the elderly, do not report significant levels of this sort of criminal victimization, at least on large-scale crime surveys. Young men, who admit feeling safest, reveal the greatest proportion of personally violent victimizations.

Women's and men's *reported* risk of violent criminal victimization and their fear of falling victim to such violence do not match. Women report fear at levels that are three times those of men, yet their recorded risk of personal violence, especially assault, is, by all official sources, lower than men's. Beyond any doubt, the gender differential is the most consistent finding in the literature on fear of crime (Crawford et al., 1990; Gordon & Riger, 1988; Hindelang, Gottfredson, & Garofalo, 1978; La Grange & Ferraro, 1989; Lewis & Maxfield, 1980; Maxfield, 1984, 1985; Riger & Gordon, 1981; Skogan & Maxfield, 1981; Stanko, 1987, 1990; Warr, 1984, 1985).

Gender, if addressed by researchers as an issue at all (e.g., Gordon & Riger, 1988; Hanmer & Stanko, 1985; La Grange & Ferraro, 1989; Ortega & Myles, 1987; Stanko, 1987, 1990; Warr, 1984, 1985) is linked with how individuals report fear: Men mask fear because the image and language of masculinity does not include acknowledging it (Clemente & Kleiman, 1977); women easily disclose fear in recognition of greater social and physical vulnerability (Maxfield, 1984; Skogan & Maxfield, 1981). The gender differential led to the quest for alternative explanations for why individuals fear being victimized by crime they do not seem to encounter. The hypothesis of the victimization perspective—that victims fear crime more than nonvictims—does not account for the worry and concern from those who surveys indicate are "nonvictims": women. Few attempt to explain why women's fear of crime is higher than men's. Skogan and Maxfield (1981) suggest that women's fear of crime is fostered by greater physical and social vulnerability; and so, when victimized, women feel more frightened than men.

Women's fear, some have suggested, is rooted in their anxiety about the consequences of rape. Maxfield (1984), analyzing the 1982 British Crime Survey, finds some evidence to suggest it is women's fear of sexual assault that "reduces feelings of safety among young women" (1984, p. 14). Warr (1984) argues, "It may well be that [for women]. . . fear of crime *is* fear of rape." Gordon and Riger (1988) go farther by naming women's fear of rape as "the female fear."

If women's fear of crime is related to women's fear of *rape,* how are we to explain such widespread fear in the context of the low number of recorded rapes? The answer lies in taking seriously the impact of the pervading atmosphere of sexual threat to women. Criminologists ignore the ordinary situations in women's lives, such as receiving sexual comments, because these annoyances are assumed to be minor, innocuous events, not real crime. All crime against women, most criminologists now agree, is seriously underreported and underrecorded. The findings of oft-cited government-conducted crime surveys have no way of estimating a "dark figure" of women's victimization (Stanko, 1988). What conventional criminologists generally agree is that women *feel* at risk of rape, but that this concern is not founded in *actual* experience. This perspective has prompted me to challenge conventional criminology (Stanko, 1987) and to suggest that women's fear of crime is in many respects women's fear of men.

FEMINIST RESEARCH:
WOMEN'S EXPERIENCE OF MALE VIOLENCE

The problem of women's fear of crime is not an enigma to feminist researchers, especially those studying men's violence against women (Kelly, 1988; Hanmer & Saunders, 1984; McNeill, 1987; Radford, 1987; Russell, 1982, 1984, 1985; Stanko, 1985, 1990). As part of the feminist strategy of naming sexual violence as a form of oppression, feminist researchers documented women's experiences of sexual and physical violence. More important, these researchers included a wide range of women's experiences of men's violence that are rarely classified as criminal offenses: obscene phone calls, being followed on the street, being touched on public transport, and sexual harassment on the street. These studies also uncovered significant incidence of serious sexual violence among adult women. Russell's (1982) detailed study of 930 California women reports that 44 percent of the women interviewed had experienced rape or attempted rape in their lifetime, with one in seven women reporting a rape by her husband. Warshaw's (1988) analysis of Mary Koss' 1984-1985 *Ms. Report* on date and acquaintance rape found one in four college women reported a rape or attempted rape. Over 84 percent of those raped knew their attacker; 57 percent of the rapes occurred on dates.

What feminist studies indicate is that the reality of sexual violence is a core component of being female and is experienced through a wide range of everyday, mundane situations. What women define as sexually violating and threatening, moreover, is not confined to what is statutorily defined as rape (see also Warshaw, 1988). As Bart and O'Brien (1986) show, even some women who were "legally" raped define their experience as attempted rape. Limiting the explanation of women's fear to the fear of rape, as some criminologists have, directs and narrows our attention to the worst scenario of sexual violence, the violent invasion of rape.

Yet, as Gardner (1980, 1988, 1990) illustrated so clearly, women's everyday lives are permeated by intrusions by men. She interviewed women in a small southwestern city and asked them about their understanding of what to do in case of street crime and whether they ever had put these beliefs into practice in public places (1990, p. 313). Women, she shows, actively construct "presentational strategies" in public to protect themselves from *men's* potential violence. She states: "The felt obligation to behave in a crime-conscious manner can undermine, subtly or not so subtly, women's trust in the majority of quite innocent men whom women observe or with whom they come into contact in public places" (1990, p. 325). She did not question women about their interactions with known men, but other research documents the commonness of men's physical and sexual intimidation of women (Stanko, 1985).

KEEPING SAFE: MANAGING DANGER AND VIOLENCE

Women gather information about potential personal danger and violence throughout their lifetime (Stanko, 1990). Direct involvement with violence; the "but-nothing-happened" encounters; observation of other women's degradation; the impact of the media and cultural images of women; and shared knowledge of family, friends, peers, acquaintances, and co-workers all contribute to assessments of risk and strategies for safety.

By and large, women take more precautions for safety in their everyday lives than do men (Gordon & Riger, 1988; Stanko, 1990) and are likely to limit their movements in public or isolate themselves in private to avoid danger (Crawford et al., 1990). Maria states:

I don't go out at night unless it's with someone. If I'm going out with friends, they will always pick me up at my door. When I come back, they'll walk me to my apartment and make sure everything is OK.

Jane, too, reports that:

When I get into the car, I always check the back seat, to make sure that there is no one lurking around. I always have my keys in my hand, so that when I get to the car, I can stick the key into the door. . . . And I lock the doors right away.

Linda, who was raped in her own home by an unknown man who crawled into her upper-story bedroom, fortified her new home to build in additional reassurance:

We built this house because I had been raped. . . . I think everybody thinks we're crazy. . . . Our doors are really good. We have grates on the basement windows, that sort of thing. Very small windows at the top.

Women's precautionary behavior occurs in both public and private space, aimed to minimize violence from strangers as well as loved ones. Some women learn to cope with so-called trusted men's potential violence and sexual danger during their childhood. Bea, threatened by her first husband and sexually abused by her father, warned her second husband before she married him that she would leave if he was violent. He was not violent to her, but she felt the need to be prepared. Margaret, a 63-year-old, middle-class professional, coped with two trusted men's sexual assaults. In the following excerpt, she describes two events that happened to her before she was 8, events she recalled only after I asked her about situations in her childhood that frightened her.[3]

> I was living on the farm and it [the abuser] happened to be a relative. We were in the horse barn, and he opened his trousers and tried to pull me down in the hay. I do not have a great sense of being threatened, but I was upset about it and ran to tell my mother. She went out. I was probably seven years old.

The second incident she had to manage on her own.

> We must have been very young, seven or eight. It was a candy store. We were visiting my aunt. It was up in town, the town I lived in and it was a soda shop. I remember one of the owners trying to put his hand on my breast. That upset me and I never told anyone about it until later years. I guess I was upset that this older man did that. Whereas I guess I wasn't as upset with this relative who was the hired hand who was younger, and I knew that he had been in trouble. But I think an older man who had respect really bothered me a great deal.

When women are asked about their experiences of physical and sexual intrusion as children and as adults, they reveal a range of sexually frightening incidents, experienced at the hands of uncles, fathers, neighbors, family friends, school companions, colleagues, lovers, husbands, authority figures such as lawyers, and of course, strangers. For a number of reasons—embarrassment, humiliation, self-blame, or self-denial—the women rarely told anyone else about what had happened. Few shared each and every experience of danger, and many made choices about which incidents to report and which ones to keep to themselves. Margaret, for instance, told her mother about the attack in the barn. But when her mother died shortly thereafter, she did not share the later frightening event of the abusive shopkeeper with her aunt or her father. Margaret's solution to the abuse was to avoid the shop.

Only a few of the frightening or abusive events involved the police or social workers. Margaret's mother sent away her distant cousin, but without reporting the incident to the police (Margaret's father was the local sheriff). Bea eventually called police about her father's physically and sexually threatening behavior, but not until she was 15, years after he began tormenting the entire family (the mother never called the police, embarrassed about involving others in "family matters"). The police "spoke" to her father, and he stopped his overtly abusive behavior. Sylvia, who shared her predicament with close friends, used to bring a girlfriend home with her after school until her aunt returned to keep her uncle from making sexual advances. She never told her aunt or any other adult. Nor did she ever directly challenge her uncle about his sexual overtures. It seems that we expect children to handle sexual abuse on their own. We even have programs in school to teach them to say no. But it is clear from these data that children already say no, and they already take on the responsibility for their own safety.

In most of the situations described, moreover, decisions were made to keep the matter "private." It may be that "criminal behavior" is perceived as harm committed by strangers. Sexual assault by those who are respectable or familiar may cause fear, anxiety, and real harm. It is rarely treated as "criminal," as would be that same behavior committed by a stranger. Bea's father was never arrested. Nor was Bea interviewed by the police in an effort to investigate a reported "crime." Even when children tell someone about abuse, as they are now encouraged to do, their harm is unlikely to be considered "criminal" harm. Strategies for keeping safe are, however, necessary, even with so-called trustworthy adults. Regardless of how successful women are in maintaining safety, the concrete knowledge that sexual danger can and does occur carries strong memories of anxiety and vulnerability (Caignon & Groves, 1987).

Indeed, women's lives rest upon a continuum of danger (Kelly, 1988; Stanko, 1990). This does not mean that all women occupy the same position in relation to safety and violence. Many other features of their lives, such as class, race, sexual orientation, physical abilities, or direct experience with serious violence, will mean that their circumstances differ. Not only do many women feel vulnerable because they are female, but being Afro-Caribbean, Asian, Hispanic, or Jewish *and* female, they may also experience racism or anti-Semitism in their everyday life. Though, somehow, as all women reach adulthood, they share a common awareness of their particular *sexual* vulnerability. Learning the strategies for maintaining sexual integrity is a continuous lesson about what it means to be female.

ORDINARY FEAR

Women's wariness of men is not just a "problem" for women in public space. For the most part, women find that they must constantly negotiate their safety with men they know, those with whom they live, work, and socialize. Women often bargain for safety from a disadvantageous physical or economic position. As men are likely to be women's intimate companions and their colleagues and bosses at work, the very people women turn to for protection are the ones who pose the greatest danger.

Despite all the best strategies, the growing body of feminist research indicates that women's actual experiences of sexual assault and perceived sexual danger are widespread and endemic (Kelly, 1988; Russell, 1984; Stanko, 1990). Consequently, women's precautions do not guarantee protection. Avoidance of the street due to potential danger, the advice issued by police and Home Office alike, places women at risk of danger from known men. The limited evidence from police statistics and Home Office research (Davidoff & Dowds, 1989; Smith, 1989a, 1989b) suggests that it is heterosexual intimacies and friendships that lead to physical and sexual assault of women. As Eileen, a 23-year-old Englishwoman, found, her common sense about safety did not help her.

> If I went out to a pub or disco, wherever, at night, I drove back and didn't drink. Or I arranged that I could get there and back or knew I was with people I could get home with or get back to their place and stay [there overnight]. I have never been [in the situation] where I have been out and not known I could get home. I took all the general precautions, like not opening the door, always knowing who was on the other side of the door before opening it, especially at night when there's no people around. All those precautions I took. I didn't expect that somebody I had met two or three times would . . . who had been in my home, who had been invited into my home, would do this [rape me], after having known him.

Women's safety is therefore not just a matter of avoiding the potentially dangerous stranger. Their relationships with known men should be grounds for even greater precaution. The evidence increasingly shows that women understand safety to mean sexual and physical safety. Threatening events do not always fit into existing legal categories. If, as the data indicate, women's experiences of violence are primarily at the hands of known men, and at the same time, women are warned of their vulnerability as women in the public sector, then the concept "fear of crime," interwoven with women's private understanding and experiences of men's violence, ignores the contribution of private violence to women's anxiety about sexual violence. As a result, fear reduction and crime prevention programs aimed at reassuring and advising women about their safety in public are flawed. Women's anxiety about the possibility of violence and their concern about devising the "correct" strategy persists, unabated by crime prevention advice.

NOTES

1. This strategy to reassure women is, however, problematic. Preliminary tests of such alarms by the Consumer Association *Which?* magazine in November 1990 report that no one comes to the aid of a woman setting off such alarms.

2. In responding, interviewees are assumed to be thinking of their personal safety vis-à-vis criminal violence. See Garofalo (1979, 1981) for a discussion of the logic of the methodology and measurement of the concept of fear of crime.

3. Forgetting threatening encounters is common among women. See Kelly (1988) for a discussion of forgetting and remembering.

REFERENCES

Bart, P., & O'Brien, P. (1986). *Stopping rape.* New York: Pergamon.

Caignon, D., & Groves, G. (1987). *Her wits about her: Self-defense success stories by women.* New York: Harper & Row.

Clemente, F., & Kleiman, M. (1977). Fear of crime in the United States: A multivariate analysis. *Social Forces, 56,* 519-531.

Crawford, A., Jones, T., Woodhouse, T., & Young, J. (1990). *The second Islington crime survey.* Middlesex Polytechnic.

Davidoff, L., & Dowds, L. (1989). Recent trends in crimes of violence against the person in England and Wales. *Research Bulletin,* no. 27, 11-17.

Gardner, C. B. (1980). Passing by: Street remarks, address rights and the urban female. *Sociological Inquiry, 50,* 328-356.

Gardner, C. B. (1988). Access information: Private lines and public peril. *Social Problems, 35,* 384-397.

Gardner, C. B. (1990). Safe conduct: Women, crime and self in public places. *Social Problems, 37*(4), 311-328.

Garofalo, J. (1979). Victimization and fear of crime. *Journal of Research in Crime and Delinquency, 16,* 80-97.

Garofalo, J. (1981). The fear of crime: Causes and consequences. *Journal of Criminal Law and Criminology, 72*(2), 839-857.

Gibbs, J., Coyle, E. J., & Hanrahan, K. J. (1987, November). *Fear of crime: A concept in need of clarification*. Paper presented to the American Society of Criminology conference.

Gordon, M., & Riger, S. (1988). *The female fear*. New York: Free Press.

Hanmer, J., & Saunders, S. (1984). *Well-founded fear*. London: Hutchinson.

Hanmer, J., & Stanko, E. A. (1985). Stripping away the rhetoric of protection: Violence to women, law and the state in Britain and the USA. *International Journal of the Sociology of Law, 13,* 357-374.

Hindelang, M., Gottfredson, M., & Garofalo, J. (1978). *The victims of personal crime*. Cambridge, MA: Ballinger.

Hough, M., & Mayhew, P. (1983). *The British Crime Survey*. London: HMSO.

Hough, M., & Mayhew, P. (1985). *Taking account of crime*. London: HMSO.

Kelly, L. (1988). *Surviving sexual violence*. Oxford, UK: Polity.

LaGrange, R. L., & Ferraro, K. F. (1989). Assessing age and gender differences in perceived risk and fear of crime. *Criminology, 27*(4), 697-720.

Lewis, D., & Maxfield, M. (1980). Fear in the neighborhoods: An investigation of the impact of crime. *Journal of Research in Crime and Delinquency, 17,* 160-189.

McNeill, S. (1987). Flashing: Its effects on women. In J. Hanmer & M. Maynard (Eds.), *Women, violence and social control* (pp. 93-109). London: Macmillan.

Maxfield, M. (1984). *Fear of crime in England and Wales*. London: HMSO.

Ortega, S. T., & Myles, J. L. (1987). Race and gender effects on fear of crime: An interactive model with age. *Criminology, 25,* 133-152.

Radford, J. (1987). Policing male violence—Policing women. In J. Hanmer and M. Maynard (Eds.), *Women, violence and social control* (pp. 30-45). London: Macmillan.

Riger, S., Gordon, M., & Lebailly, R. (1978). Women's fear of crime: From blaming to restricting the victim. *Victimology, 3*(3-4), 274-284.

Riger, S., & Gordon, M. (1981). The fear of rape: A study in social control. *Journal of Social Issues, 37*(4), 71-92.

Russell, D.E.H. (1982). *Rape in marriage*. New York: Macmillan.

Russell, D.E.H. (1984). *Sexual exploitation*. Beverly Hills, CA: Sage.

Russell, D.E.H. (1985). *The secret trauma*. New York: Free Press.

Shapland, J., & Vagg, J. (1988). *Policing by the public*. London: Routledge.

Skogan, W., & Maxfield, M. (1981). *Coping with crime*. Beverly Hills, CA: Sage.

Smith, L.J.F. (1989a). *Concerns about rape*. London: HMSO.

Smith, L.J.F. (1989b). *Domestic violence*. London: HMSO.

Stanko, E. A. (1985). *Intimate intrusions*. London: Unwin Hyman.

Stanko, E. A. (1987). Typical violence, normal precaution: Men, women, and interpersonal violence in England, Wales, Scotland and the USA. In J. Hanmer & M. Maynard (Eds.), *Women, violence and social control* (pp. 122-134). London: Macmillan.

Stanko, E. A. (1988). Hidden violence against women. In M. Maguire & J. Pointing (Eds.), *Victims: A new deal?* Milton Keynes, UK: Open University Press.

Stanko, E. A. (1990). *Everyday violence: How women and men experience physical and sexual danger*. London: Pandora.

Warr, M. (1984). Fear of victimization: Why are women and the elderly more afraid? *Social Science Quarterly, 65,* 681-702.

Warr, M. (1985). Fear of rape among urban women. *Social Problems, 32*(3), 238-250.

Warshaw, R. (1988). *I never called it rape*. New York: Harper & Row.

12 Cops, Courts, and Woman Battering

KATHLEEN J. FERRARO
Arizona State University

A feminist perspective on woman battering views male violence as an expression of class, race, gender, and heterosexual privilege. It is a problem rooted primarily in the structure of the social order, rather than the pathological psyches of individual men. The criminal justice system is designed to protect and reinforce the social order through punishment of individual deviants. It is, therefore, fundamentally at odds with a structural, gendered analysis of woman battering.

Prohibitions and sanctions against interpersonal violence have always been imbued with class, race, and gender biases. Violence is condemned most often when it violates existing power and institutional hierarchies. Violence inflicted by dominant groups, such as white, male property owners, against their subordinates, such as slaves, wives, and children, has been accepted as socially necessary and morally just. Historically, the criminal justice system, including the police, prosecutors, and judges, has not enforced assault and battery laws when the victim-offender relationship reflected prevailing social norms of status hierarchies. Violence by husbands against wives represented a form of social control legitimated by conventional law and morality, and thus beyond the purview of criminal justice agents (Dobash & Dobash, 1979; Martin, 1976).

Battered women and their advocates have often criticized the lack of protection afforded by the criminal justice system (Cobbe, 1878; Gordon, 1988; Stone, 1879). Although statutes prohibited wife beating have existed in the United States since 1641, their enforcement was almost nonexistent (Pleck, 1987, p. 21). When the battered women's movement of the

AUTHOR'S NOTE: Thank you to M.A. Bortner for commenting on this manuscript.

1970s began, the criminal justice system became one focus of activism. Since that time, considerable change has occurred in laws, policies, and training regarding intervention in battering (Ferraro, 1989a, 1989b; Dobash & Dobash, 1991). The purpose of this chapter is to describe and assess these changes in three areas: the police, the criminal courts, and the civil courts. The focus for analysis of police is arrest practices; for criminal courts, it is prosecution and sentencing; and for the civil courts, it is effectiveness of restraining orders or orders of protection (TROs).

POLICING BATTERING

The traditional response of police to battering was to tell women, "There's nothing we can do; this is a civil matter," or to make one party leave the home (Martin, 1976, pp. 2-3). One early study of police ineffectiveness indicated that in 80 percent of domestic homicides, police had been called to the home at least once. In 50 percent, they had been called more than five times prior to the homicide (Police Foundation, 1977). These data demonstrated that calls to the police had little or no impact on eliminating woman battering. The battered women's movement challenged this response through legislative changes and lawsuits. The 1976 *Bruno v. Codd* (New York) and *Scott v. Hart* (Oakland, California) class action suits charged police departments with failure to protect. Both cases were settled out of court, but they established the responsibility of police to provide protection to battered women. Pressure created by these civil suits and grass-roots activists resulted in state-by-state changes in legislation that shifted the burden of evidence required for officers to make arrests (see Woods, 1986, for a summary of civil cases). Now most states have legislation that expands police power to arrest in "domestic violence" misdemeanor assault cases without witnessing the assault (Lerman & Livingston, 1983).

After 1980, three factors coalesced to pressure police departments to treat "domestic violence" as a crime. These were: (a) federal pressure via the U.S. Attorney General's Office and the National Institute of Justice (NIJ), (b) social science research, and (c) a major civil liability suit (*Thurman v. Torrington,* 1984). The U.S. Attorney General's Task Force on Family Violence published its report (Hart et al., 1984) recommending that "Family violence should be recognized and responded to as a criminal activity" (p. 10). Second, Lawrence Sherman and Richard Berk (1984) published the findings of their study of the Minneapolis police in the *American Sociological Review,* the most prestigious sociological journal. Sherman and Berk presented their research as an experiment and their findings as scientific evidence that arrest was significantly more effective in deterring future violence in battering situations than either separation or mediation. The original experiment is being replicated in six sites. The National Institute of Justice funded each site with $541,000 to $682,000, investing approximately $3.6 million, or nearly half of the sum allocated by the federal Family Violence Prevention and Services Act to states for direct services. Results from Omaha, Nebraska, have shown no difference in recidivism after one year between cases resulting in arrest, separation, or mediation (Dunford, 1990). Results from the other five sites have not yet been reported.

In 1985, Tracy Thurman won a settlement of $1.9 million from the City of Torrington, Connecticut, police department for its negligence in failing to provide protection to her. Thurman was assaulted and permanently disabled by her husband in the presence of police officers. The large settlement caused insurance companies to request police departments to revamp their arrest policies for domestic violence. The political, academic, and financial pressures to alter police practices led to changes in training, policies, and legislation throughout the country. By the end of 1985, 47 cities with populations over 100,000 had police policies of mandatory or presumptive arrests for "family fights," and 6 states had laws that required arrest under certain circumstances (Crime Control Institute, 1986).

There is general agreement among activists for battered women that a shift from the definition of battering as a "domestic problem" to a criminal activity has taken place, and that this shift is beneficial to battered women. But the implementation of the "get tough" stance has not been without problems and contradictions. Most important, police do not generally share a gendered analysis of battering. Feminists define battering within the context of patriarchy, focusing on male domination within all major social institutions. Criminal justice personnel, including police, view battering in gender-neutral terms as a problem of pathological family interaction. This difference in perspective results in conceptual conflicts in feminist and police definitions of woman battering. Most significant, police standards of harm, responsibility, and victimization exclude an appreciation of women's subordinate status within the family and the economy. Police officers are generally unsympathetic toward women who express ambivalence about their relationships and pressing criminal charges. Although the intent of policies and laws mandating arrest is to reduce the impact of discretionary decision making among police, it is not possible to accomplish this goal entirely through rules imposed on street-level officers by administrators or legislators.

A second major problem with efforts to enhance policing is the historical police repression of people of color, poor people, lesbians and gays, and political activists. Gender is not the only hierarchical theme reinforced by traditional criminal justice policies. Rates of arrest are much higher for low-income and racial and ethnic minority groups, and pressure to increase arrests may exacerbate the use of police force against these groups. Battering in gay and lesbian couples may continue to be ignored due to homophobic police reactions. Research in Duluth, Minnesota, has found a proportionate *decrease* in arrests of minority men, from 32 percent to 8.5 percent of the total, one year after the introduction of mandatory arrest (Dobash & Dobash, 1991). But these percentages are based on small numbers (22 and 175, respectively), and Duluth is unique in the overall success of its intervention project.

Despite efforts to standardize arrest as the most appropriate response to woman battering, wide variations in police practice persist. The Phoenix, Arizona, police department adopted a presumptive arrest policy in May 1984, after Chief Ruben Ortega returned from serving on the U.S. Attorney General's Task Force. The policy stated that:

> Officers should arrest domestic violence violators even if the victim does not desire prosecution. When probable cause exists, an arrest should be made even if a misdemeanor offense did not occur in the officer's presence. (Ortega, 1984, p. 1)

In a study of the implementation of this presumptive arrest policy, it was found that in 69 cases of family fight calls to police, only 9 (18 percent) resulted in arrests (Ferraro, 1989a, 1989b). This low arrest rate reflects the difficulty of mandating police decision making.

Police move within a complex, ever-changing array of considerations that cannot be simplified or held constant by administrators. Legal considerations may appear straightforward from an outsider's perspective: If you get a family fight call, you make an arrest. In practice, the construction of an arrest involves an evaluation of the presence of probable cause [for arrest] and of fault in which an officer interprets the events observed. Witnesses, injuries, property destruction, and weapons all help an officer determine probable cause, but the interpretation of these factors depends on the officer's beliefs and the particular situation. In the Phoenix study, for example, the researcher observed a case in which smashed doors, plants, knickknacks, and plates and a cut to a woman's face did not establish probable cause for an officer who said, "There's no offense here." Similar facts led to arrests in other cases. This particular officer believed the male abuser held the prerogative to damage "his" property if he wanted to, and viewed the woman's injury as too minor to constitute a crime. If the officer does not perceive probable cause, the call does not fit the policy and does not lead to arrest. The discretion inherent in evaluating probable cause may be limited through more explicit training and instruction, but can- not be eliminated.

At the same time, fault is a negotiable decision. When officers arrive at a "family fight," they decide who is most to blame for the problem. If they view each partner as equally liable, both parties will be arrested (Chaudhuri & Daly, 1992; Dobash & Dobash, 1991). Interviews with 17 women who had called the police for help revealed that 2 of these women were arrested and incarcerated overnight (Ferraro, 1989a). In one case, the arrest facilitated the husband's efforts to obtain an order of protection and move the woman out of the house. The neutrality of legal language provides the context for police to view woman battering as "mutual combat" and the arrest of women as appropriate. The ungendered, "mutual combat" perspective is problematic because when women do use violence against their male partners, it is almost always in self-defense and involves the least severe forms of violence (Saunders, 1988). When police arrest women for defending themselves against battering, the abusers are provided social support for initiating and justifying violence.

Determination of probable cause and fault are influenced by the background assumptions officers hold about women and racial and ethnic groups. Officers tend to view the world as divided into distinct categories of normal citizens and deviants. Those falling into the deviant category are considered voluntary participants in a life-style that includes violence. Officers express the opinion that violence is a way of life for deviants, so that police intervention in these battering cases is relatively meaningless. Black's research on policing patterns shows that police are more likely to arrest a low-income, minority person for offenses committed against a wealthy white, and are less likely to arrest the same person for an offense committed against a person of the same race and economic status (Black, 1976). Because most battering occurs against women of the same racial and economic categories as their abusers, arrest goes against the typical pattern of policing.

Police also hold stereotypes of battered women that work against an arrest policy. The most common stereotype of battered women is that they will not follow through with prosecution. In our observations of policing, every officer relayed stories about cases in which police had expended extraordinary resources or endangered themselves, only to have the woman recant her story in front of a judge (Ferraro, 1989a). The difficulties of prosecuting batterers will be discussed in the following section. In terms of the police response, however, the prospects of victim cooperation are not a legally relevant consideration for arrest decisions, particularly when presumptive arrest policies are in effect. The police officer's job is to determine probable cause, not to weigh the likelihood of victim cooperation. All the same, police expectations of victims do influence arrest decisions in woman-battering incidents.

The police are the first line of response to battering. Progress has occurred regarding the official policies of policing and the view of battering as a legitimate arena for police intervention. But the problems outlined above continue to limit the effectiveness of the police as a resource for battered women.

PROSECUTION OF BATTERING

There have been few empirical studies of the prosecutorial component of the criminal justice response. This reflects the priority given to the immediate safety function of the police. Also, the proportion of battering cases involved in the criminal justice system diminishes with each step in the process. Research on the prosecution of these cases is difficult because in most jurisdictions, cases are categorized by offense rather than victim-offender relationship.

One assumption about the prosecution of battering that has been shared by activists and academics is that stranger assault is more likely to result in conviction and sentencing than intimate assault or battering. This assumption reflects the knowledge that very few battering cases result in prison sentences. The assumption that woman battering is treated less seriously than stranger assault makes intuitive sense, but there is little published research on this issue.

Ferraro and Boychuk (1992) compared the processing of intimate and nonintimate violent offenses from the filing to the sentencing stage. Most significant, there were few differences between cases involving intimate partners and those involving strangers. In both types of violent offenses, most cases resulted in dismissal. Those that were prosecuted usually resulted in a sentence of probation. Interpersonal violence very rarely led to significant criminal sanctions. Quarm and Schwartz (1984) found similar results for a misdemeanor court in Ohio. Only 4 percent of their sample spent time in jail, and less than 1 percent served at least 3 months.

In prosecutors' records in Maricopa County, Arizona, for 1987 and 1988, the reasons given for not prosecuting violent offenses were very similar for nonintimate and intimate cases (Ferraro & Boychuk, 1992). Cases were most often rejected because they were not considered serious enough to be tried in superior court and were sent to appropriate lower courts to be tried as misdemeanors. Of cases filed for prosecution, a sample of 104 intimate violent offenses and 100 nonintimate violent offenses was selected (see Ferraro & Boychuk, 1992, for a full discussion). Although all original charges were felony offenses involving serious or permanent injury or the use of lethal weapons, most were bargained to lesser offenses. The nine offenses examined were: murder, kidnap, sexual assault, arson, aggravated assault, resisting arrest, criminal damage, interfering with judicial proceedings, and disorderly conduct. The "intimate" category included victim-offender relationships of current or prior marriage, cohabitation, ongoing sexual relationship, or between immediate family members. Of the intimate victims, 97 individuals (90 percent) were women. Only seven (10 percent) were male intimate partners or family members.

Only 11 percent of defendants in the entire sample received prison sentences, and the relationship between victim and offender was not significantly related to the sentence. The modal category for years in prison was 1.5 years. All but six offenders received 7.5 years or less and almost a third (32 percent) of the cases were dismissed. There was a significant difference between intimate and nonintimate cases on dismissal, with nonintimate cases *more* likely to be dismissed. Of the entire sample, 43 percent received probation sentences from 1 to 70 months. Very few offenders paid restitution to victims (18 percent) or fines (12 percent). In other words, only a small fraction of arrests result in superior court filings, and only a small fraction of filings result in incarceration. The relationship between victim and offender is not a significant variable in predicting prison sentences.

We also examined victims' participation in the prosecution process. Intimate victims were less likely to follow through with prosecution than strangers, but victim cooperation was only one of the factors determining case outcome.

Of all intimate victims, 39 percent wanted charges dropped, whereas only 6 percent of nonintimate victims made this request. But other responses to prosecution diminish differences in cooperation between the two groups: Over one quarter (27 percent) of nonintimate victims were missing at the time of trial, whereas only 7 percent of intimate victims were missing. Another 16 percent of intimate victims cooperated with the prosecution, but specifically stated that they desired help for their abusers rather than prison. This response was entirely absent in the nonintimate group. Of the cases where women victims of intimate assault requested that charges be dropped, 65 percent resulted in guilty pleas. So, even if women do not want to follow through with prosecution, it is likely that there is enough evidence to obtain a plea of guilt if the case is serious enough to warrant felony prosecution. At the same time, 16 percent of cases where victims fully cooperated with and desired prosecution resulted in dismissals. The prevalent belief that prosecuting battering is a waste of time because of victim noncooperation overlooks the importance of other legal and extralegal factors in case dismissal.

There are many factors that influence a woman's request to drop charges against an abuser. Many women are dependent on men's economic contributions for support of children. Imprisonment eliminates current employment and endangers future opportunities. Several months usually pass between the violent incident and court hearings. Most offenders are released from custody during this period and find ways to intimidate and manipulate women into dropping charges against them. Some battered women have other legal problems, such as immigration status or outstanding traffic warrants, which lead them to be wary of involvement with the courts. Women who ask for help for their abusers rather than incarceration may believe that prison will lead to an increase in violence upon the abuser's release.

Most large cities now have victim witness assistance programs to provide advocacy services to victims of crime. Those programs that assist battered women with the prosecution process have had dramatic success in improving victim cooperation. Programs in Santa Barbara, California; Los Angeles; and Philadelphia increased victim cooperation to 80 to 92 percent of all complaints filed (Lerman, 1983). When battered women are provided with information about the legal process and support for testifying, successful prosecution is the norm.

Some jurisdictions have adopted policies of mandating victim witness cooperation by charging women who fail to testify with contempt of court. Women are not given the choice of dropping charges or failing to appear, and may be incarcerated for refusing to testify (Dobash & Dobash, 1991). These policies are an attempt to increase penalties for woman battering, but fail to recognize the diverse needs and experiences of battered women. One study of prosecution found that the only factor that significantly diminishes recidivism among batterers is allowing women to drop charges (Ford & Regolie, 1992). This finding substantiates the feminist principle that women are the best experts on their own lives.

COURT ORDERS OF PROTECTION

A statutory change that accompanied most state laws to enhance police power involved the creation of temporary orders of protection or temporary restraining orders (TROs) designed to protect women from future abuse based on prior experiences. These are court orders that establish the limits of men's access to women and may prohibit a man's presence near a woman, her place of employment, her children, their school, and anyplace else that can be defined as her sphere of activity. Violation of the orders is a civil or criminal offense that can result in immediate arrest. Although these orders were originally limited to married or formerly married people, most states now have provisions for cohabitees and former cohabitees.

The few studies that have examined TROs have found that their effectiveness in controlling male violence depends on the circumstances and history of the men (Chaudhuri & Daly, 1992; Grau, Fagan, & Wexler, 1984). Grau et al. (1984) found that TROs did not reduce verbal and emotional abuse, but did reduce violence in cases where the original violence was not severe. Women who had been severely battered were not effectively protected from future violence by TROs (p. 23).

Chaudhuri and Daly (1992, p. 245) found that TROs generally increased police responsiveness to calls from battered women. But police were *not* more likely to arrest men for violating TROs than for committing battering, unless the men were also involved in other offenses. Future battering was prevented by TROs against employed men with no prior criminal histories, no drug or alcohol abuse, and low levels of initial violence. Men who did not share these characteristics were not deterred by the TROs. Chaudhuri and Daly (1992) note that 1 woman in 10 in their study was beaten *because* she had obtained a TRO (p. 245). In Ferraro's (1989a) police study, 3 of 17 women said that the TRO did not help at all (p. 178). Two women believed that *nothing* could change their husbands.

Yet, TROs may have other positive benefits for women (Chaudhuri & Daly, 1992). The process of obtaining a TRO requires women to talk to attorneys or judges about the battering, and a sympathetic response from these outsiders may help women reinforce the definition of battering as unacceptable (Ferraro & Johnson, 1983). Men responding to petitions for TROs are forced to admit their violence before the court, publicly disclosing what is often privately denied. The majority of abusers, however, do not appear for these hearings or these benefits.

CONCLUSION

The criminal justice approach to woman battering focuses on the control of specific incidents without attention to the complex social and economic problems of women. The isolation of battering from the larger context of women's lives produces absurd contradictions. Women are told that police will arrest, that TROs will keep abusers away, and that judges will send them to prison if the women will only be consistent and cooperative with prosecutors. In the majority of cases, women do not experience these outcomes and continue to be abused, harassed, and threatened. Although frustration accrues from lack of responsiveness to their requests, no assistance with housing, child care, transportation, or employment is available. When battered women "stay with abusers," it is most often a case of their being unable to force the man to leave them alone or to establish an independent economic base.

Defining woman battering as a crime problem radically distorts women's needs and experiences and the larger feminist agenda of the empowerment and emancipation of women. Arrest and incarceration of men who batter women has no direct relationship to enhancing women's economic status, improving and expanding health and reproductive options, softening the rigors of child care and waged labor, or building community. In some cases, the criminal justice system directly opposes these important goals, as when women are incarcerated for hiding their children from sexually abusive fathers (*off our backs*, 1988).

The androcentric, positivistic worldview embodied in legal practices is antithetical to a feminist account of battering. The facts of each case are recorded in legal terms of probable cause, fault, and harm. From this perspective, women become responsible for clearly and consistently demonstrating to police, attorneys and judges that they have been severely injured, have not fought back with greater violence than they received, and do want their abusers arrested and prosecuted. These requirements often exclude women from the system, minimizing their fear and suffering and evoking disdain for the ambivalence and confusion that are a common response to battering.

The data on implementing mandatory arrest suggest that it is difficult to change police responses to woman battering and to eliminate discretion. Data on prosecution of assaults indicates that most interpersonal violence, whether between strangers or intimates, is treated leniently by the courts. The obstacles to increasing protection for women through the criminal justice system are formidable and demand continuous monitoring and involvement from feminists. The projects that have been most successful, such as the Domestic Abuse Intervention Program in Duluth, Minnesota, are located in small communities where a committed group of activists has coordinated the components of the system and insisted on adherence to feminist values (Pence & Shepard, 1988). In large urban centers with entrenched politics, it is much more difficult to hold the criminal justice system accountable to battered women.

This pessimistic overview is not intended as a plea to abandon the criminal justice system as a locus of work against male violence. As stated above, it is often the only option available to women in immediate danger. But it is important to recognize the inherent limitations of the police and courts and the failures of previous efforts. The experience of the past 10 years has demonstrated the ease with which feminist concerns are coopted and transformed by mainstream institutions. It is vital that battering not be viewed only as a crime but also as a manifestation of structured gender inequality.

REFERENCES

Black, D. (1976). *The behavior of law.* New York: Academic Press.

Chaudhuri, M., & Daly, K. (forthcoming). Do restraining orders help? Battered women's experience with male violence and legal process. In E. Buzawa (Ed.), *Domestic violence: The changing criminal justice response* (pp. 227-252). Westport, CT: Greenwood.

Cobbe, F. P. (1878, April). Wife torture in England. *Contemporary Review*, pp. 55-87.

Crime Control Institute. (1986). Police domestic violence policy change. *Response, 9*(2), 16.

Dobash, R. E., & Dobash, R. (1979). *Violence against wives.* New York: Free Press.

Dobash, R. E., & Dobash, R. (1991). *Women, violence and social change.* London: Routledge.

Dunford, F. W. (1990). *Long term recidivism in the Omaha domestic violence experiments.* Paper presented at the annual meeting of the American Society of Criminology, Baltimore, MD.

Ferraro, K. J. (1989a). The legal response to battering in the United States. In J. Hanmer, J. Radford, & E. A. Stanko (Eds.), *Women, policing, and male violence.* London: Routledge.

Ferraro, K. J. (1989b). Policing woman battering. *Social Problems, 36,* 61-74.

Ferraro, K. J., & Boychuk, T. (forthcoming). The court's response to interpersonal violence: A comparison of intimate and nonintimate assault. In E. Buzawa (Ed.), *Domestic violence: The changing criminal justice response* (pp. 209-225). Westport, CT: Greenwood.

Ferraro, K. J., & Johnson, J. M. (1983). How women experience battering. *Social Problems, 30*(3), 325-339.

Ford, D., & Regolie, M. J. (1992). The preventive impacts of policies for prosecuting wife batterers. In E. S. Buzawa & C. G. Buzawa (Eds.), *Domestic violence: The changing criminal justices response* (pp. 181-208). Westport, CT: Auburn House.

Gordon, L. (1988). *Heroes of their own lives.* New York: Viking.

Grau, J., Fagan, J., & Wexler, S. (1984). Restraining orders for battered women: Issues of access and efficacy. *Women and Politics, 4,* 13-28.

Hart, W., Ashcroft, J., Burgess, A., Flanagan, N., Meese, C., Milton, C., Narramore, C., Ortega, R., & Seward, F. (1984). *Attorney general's task force on family violence.* Washington, DC: Department of Justice.

Lerman, L. (1983). *The prosecution of spouse abuse.* Washington, DC: Department of Justice.

Lerman, L., & Livingston, F. (1983). State legislation on domestic violence. *Response, 6,* 1-28.

Martin, D. (1976). *Battered wives.* San Francisco, CA: Glide.

off our backs. (1988). Mississippi project to stop child sexual abuse. *off our backs, 18*(8), 12.

Ortega, R. *Operations Digest, 84-85,* 1-2

Pence, E., & Shepard, M. (1988). Integrating feminist theory and practice. In K. Yllöo & M. Bograd (Eds.), *Feminist perspectives on wife abuse* (pp. 282-298). Newbury Park, CA.: Sage.

Pleck, E. (1987). *Domestic tyranny.* New York: Oxford.

Police Foundation. (1977). *Domestic violence and the police.* Washington, DC: Police Foundation.

Quarm, D., & Schwartz, M. (1984). Domestic violence in criminal court: An examination of new legislation in Ohio. *Women and Politics, 4*(3), 29-46.

Saunders, D. G. (1988). Wife abuse, husband abuse, or mutual combat? In K. Yllö & M. Bograd (Eds.), *Feminist perspectives on wife abuse* (pp. 90-113). Newbury Park, CA: Sage.

Scott v. Hart. (1986). C76-2395 WWS National Center for Women & Family Law Resource List: Battered Women, Litigation, Item #24, Laurie Woods.

Sherman, L. W., & Berk, R. A. (1984). The specific deterrent effects of arrest for domestic assault. *American Sociological Review, 49,* 261-272.

Stone, L. (1879, January 11 and 18). [Untitled news article]. *Women's Journal.*

Woods, L. (1986). *Resource list: Battered women: Litigation.* New York: National Center on Women and Family Law.

13 Surmounting a Legacy: The Expansion of Racial Diversity in a Local Anti-Rape Movement

NANCY A. MATTHEWS
American Bar Foundation

The anti-rape movement in Los Angeles originated from collectivist feminism and feminist social work networks. Between 1973 and 1980, five grass roots rape crisis organizations were started, including the Los Angeles Commission on Assaults Against Women (LACAAW), the Pasadena YWCA Rape Crisis Center and Hotline, the East Los Angeles Rape Hotline (ELA), the Center for the Pacific-Asian Family, and the San Fernando Valley Rape Crisis Service. Although the bilingual, Latina-run East Los Angeles hotline and the multilingual Pacific-Asian hotline brought some women of color into the movement, very few Black women were involved, and the predominantly Black areas of the county (South Central Los Angeles) were virtually unserved. Since 1980, when the California Office of Criminal Justice Planning began funding rape crisis services, the state has promoted a relatively conservative, social service approach to this work. Yet ironically, during these years, state money also furthered one of the more progressive goals of the U.S. anti-rape movement: to become multiracial and multicultural and to expand services to all women.

AUTHOR'S NOTE: This chapter originated as a presentation at the 1988 annual meeting of the American Sociological Association. I want to thank William G. Roy, Karen Brodkin Sacks, Sondra Hale, Ayofemi Folayan, Lise Vogel, and Gail Dubrow for their comments at various stages in its development. I also appreciate the helpful suggestions of the reviewers, Pauline Bart and Elizabeth Stanko.

In this chapter, I examine the problem of racial and ethnic diversity in the Los Angeles anti-rape movement, show how racial diversity in the local movement was facilitated by the state's involvement in establishing two new Black rape crisis centers in the mid-1980s, and explore the consequences for race relations in the anti-rape movement in the United States.

FEMINISM, RACE, AND RAPE

Developing in tandem with the male-dominated new left of the 1960s, collectivist feminism had roots in the civil rights movement (Echols, 1989), but like the new left, the women's liberation movement remained dominated by Whites (Ferree & Hess, 1985). Evans (1979) attributes this narrowness to the historic conjunction of the birth of feminism within the new left just when the Black movement was becoming separatist.

Many Black women who were interested in feminism in the early 1970s agreed with Black Panther Kathleen Cleaver that Black and White women would have to work in separate organizations, coming together in coalitions, because the problems each group of women faced were different enough that they could not be solved in the same organizations (Giddings, 1984, p. 311). Thus the early anti-rape movement in the United States arose in a context of the beginnings of Black feminism and the distrust Black women felt of white feminism. This legacy, combined with the general level of racism in U.S. society, has made multiracial organizing, feminist or otherwise, difficult.

Long before the anti-rape movement, the issues of race and rape were linked in the United States. From the 1880s through the 1950s, lynchings of Black men were justified on the basis of the threat the men posed to White women's virtue. Although Ida B. Wells investigated over 700 lynchings and found that accusations of rape had been made in less than one third, the myth of Black men's proclivity for rape became ingrained in our culture (Davis, 1981; Giddings, 1984; Hooks, 1981) and was manipulated to keep both Black men and White women in their places. Lynching, rather than rape, became the focus of Black women's activism against violence.

Incidents that linked race and rape caused further disjuncture between White feminists and Blacks in the current feminist movement in the United States. First, as the nationalist phase of the Black movement crested, several male leaders, most notably Eldridge Cleaver in *Soul on*

Ice (1968), called for the raping of White women as a political act. Second, Susan Brownmiller, in her eagerness to prove the seriousness of rape, echoed the racist justification of lynching in her path-breaking book *Against Our Will* (1975), perpetuating the "myth of the Black rapist" (Davis, 1981). Rather than confront the issue of rape, even when Black women were raped by Black men, a special issue of *Ebony* magazine on Black-on-Black crime omitted rape (Bart & O'Brien, 1985, p. 90).

In 1973, Roz Pulitzer, a Black member of the Manhattan (New York) Women's Political Caucus, which was lobbying on rape issues, said she did not expect Black women to get very involved in the issue. Like Kathleen Cleaver, she felt that "the split between the concerns of White women and our concerns was so great that strategically we had to have a Black organization to give the women's movement credibility in our own communities. Every group must go through its period of self-identity" (New York Radical Feminists, 1974, p. 243). But Pulitzer, who had been instrumental in forming the Mayor's Task Force on Rape in New York City in 1973, hoped that Black women would take what White women had learned and use it to set up rape counseling and public education in the Black community.

In Los Angeles, it took more than 10 years to happen, and when it did, the impetus came not from grass-roots Black feminist groups, but from Black community organizations responding to the state's call for proposals. This study of the expansion of racial diversity in the Los Angeles anti-rape movement is based primarily on oral history interviews with participants from its beginning in the early 1970s through 1988 and with officials in the California Office of Criminal Justice Planning (OCJP). I conducted 35 interviews between 1987 and 1989 with women who were known as leaders, formal and informal. The interviews took 1 to 3 hours and covered the participant's experience in rape crisis work, her account and perceptions of historical events, and explanations of how the organizations worked. Movement documents, in particular the minutes of the Southern California Rape Hotline Alliance's monthly meetings from 1979 to 1988, supplemented the oral accounts.

WOMEN OF COLOR AND THE LOS ANGELES
ANTI-RAPE MOVEMENT

The early 1980s were a period of increasing awareness of racial and ethnic issues in the U.S. anti-rape movement. Although there were relatively few women of color in the movement in California, the formation of the

Southern California Rape Hotline Alliance ("the Alliance") and the statewide Coalition of Rape Crisis Centers ("the Coalition") brought the women of color together and provided the forum in which to raise issues about doing rape crisis work among Black, Latina and Chicana, Asian, and Native American women. The Coalition's Women of Color Caucus brought together women of color in southern California.

The East Los Angeles Rape Hotline, founded in 1976, was the earliest, and one of the few anti-rape organizations that was not predominantly White. It was founded by Latina women concerned about providing bilingual and culturally appropriate services in the largely Latino, Chicano, and Mexicano area of east Los Angeles county. As one of the few bilingual hotlines of any kind, it was kept busy with all kinds of community services, not just rape crisis work. Its connection to the other local anti-rape organizations waxed and waned over the years until 1979, when the Alliance grew and the statewide Coalition provided a forum for women of color in the movement.

Another ethnically based rape hotline also existed by the late 1970s, although it was less connected to the Los Angeles anti-rape movement. In 1978, Nilda Rimonte started a project to provide rape crisis services to Pacific and Asian immigrant women in Los Angeles. Although Rimonte participated in the Alliance regularly, the Center for the Pacific-Asian Family, as the hotline she founded was called, was not a grass roots organization to the same extent as other hotlines. Because it was set up to serve many language groups (Vietnamese, Korean, Laotian, Cambodian, Filipino, and others), counselors were generally staff members. They also ran a battered women's shelter, so the rape hotline was only one project of the organization. Nevertheless, Rimonte was a central figure in raising ethnic and racial issues in the California anti-rape movement.

By 1982, racism had become a central issue in the movement and in groups' disputes with the state funding agency. Santa Cruz Women Against Rape was defunded (Mackle, Pernell, Shirchild, Baratta, and Groves, 1982) and later that year, the East Los Angeles Rape Hotline was audited by the OCJP. Although the organization was told that the OCJP planned "to very carefully scrutinize all rape crisis centers receiving funds" (Alliance minutes, June 12, 1982), the fact that it was singled out seemed to carry racist overtones. Hotlines had also begun to treat racism as a serious topic in counselor training and the Women of Color Caucus had begun meeting regularly.

The National Coalition Against Sexual Assault (NCASA) had also begun to pay attention to racial diversity. Beverly Smith, a nationally known Black feminist, was a keynote speaker at its 1984 conference and tried to transform the historic connection between lynching and rape into an instructive one by comparing the two crimes rather than setting them in opposition to each other. She made the analogy, "Lynching is to racism as rape is to sexism," suggesting that the cultural context makes such acts possible (Roth & Baslow, 1984, p. 56).

By 1983, the Women of Color Caucus had made a connection between OCJP funding criteria and problems of rape crisis centers serving Third World people. According to Alliance minutes of January 15, 1983, Emilia Bellone and Teresa Contreras noted that state allocations were based primarily on the number of victims served by particular programs. In addition, the state allocated funds for "new and innovative" programs, encouraging new grant proposals, although money was most needed for basic services, community education, and outreach. An Alliance committee prepared a position paper asking the OCJP to revise its funding allocation criteria. The central criticism was that using the number of victims served as the key criterion caused "inequities in the distribution of funds, which especially handicaps ethnic minority rape crisis centers":

> One concern stems from the fact that in order to provide rape crisis services in ethnic minority communities, a great deal of time and effort has to go into doing strong outreach and community education. Although in recent years there has been a marked increase in awareness and information about sexual assault for the general public, much of this has not permeated ethnic minority communities. Many factors affect this—language barriers, racism, distrust of educators and the media, etc. (*Alliance Position Paper,* 1983, p. 1)

The paper goes on to point out several related problems: traditional coping strategies among some cultures that discourage going outside the family for help, the need for materials to be translated to reach nonassimilated people, and the extra hours of work required both for outreach in ethnic communities and to provide adequate services to individual survivors. The Alliance committee linked class issues with those of race and ethnicity:

> Typically, more time must be spent with a survivor who has fewer personal resources. These survivors tend to be ethnic minority women. Often, a

non-assimilated ethnic minority survivor requires translating and interpreting, transportation, overnight shelter for herself and possibly children, and counseling to significant others in addition to the usual counseling and advocacy services. So, if a rape crisis center serves a predominantly ethnic minority population, the "average" number of hours of service provided to each survivor is much higher than for a center that serves a predominantly white population. (*Alliance Position Paper*, 1983, p. 2)

Grant proposals for "innovative" programs had been the only strategy centers had to increase funding for special outreach. A major issue for the East Los Angeles Rape Hotline was how to include families, especially the men, in their services, which was essential in order to gain legitimacy in the Latino community. In 1983, through a grant for innovative projects from the OCJP, they produced a *fotonovela* about a family in which a teenage girl has been sexually assaulted by her uncle. The story line upholds the cultural value placed on the family, but modifies it so that the young girl's integrity is not sacrificed. They also had an innovative theater program for education in rape prevention. These programs were successful for reaching their community, but were costly to the organization in the time spent creating new programs without solving the problem of obtaining more money for basic services.

Although the Alliance committee that wrote the position paper did not get a direct response, Marilyn Peterson, the branch manager of the Sexual Assault Program at the OCJP, began pursuing avenues of additional money for "high crime" and "minority" areas. The OCJP studied the rates of rape reported by police agencies and rape crisis centers in communities across the state, assuming that the rate of underreporting was consistent. It then surveyed the availability of services in the community by district attorneys' offices, law enforcement, hospitals, family service agencies, and so on. In addition to a high crime rate, the poverty rate was factored in, because areas with few resources tend to have fewer social services. According to Peterson, the survey was a necessary formality—a bureaucratic justification for what she already knew was needed. Target money was awarded to some of the existing rape crisis centers in Los Angeles, but the most significant effect in the county was the establishment of two new programs located in predominantly Black areas, South Central Los Angeles and Compton. Women in these areas could theoretically use one of the existing hotlines, but geographical distance made providing in-person services such as hospital accompaniment more difficult. The primarily White hotlines did sparse outreach to the Black community. Furthermore, women of color in the anti-rape movement were developing a theory of service provision that recognized that women in crisis were most likely to feel comfortable and use services if they were provided by someone like themselves (Dubrow et al., 1986; Kanuha, 1987; Lum, 1988; Rimonte, 1985). This notion reflects the influence of the peer counseling roots of rape crisis work as well as increasing awareness of cultural issues. For outreach to succeed, it was important for services like rape crisis to be *of* the community, which the White hotlines were not. Thus homogeneous organizations of different ethnic groups were more effective.

CONSEQUENCES OF FUNDING: A DIFFERENT APPROACH

The first of the new hotlines, the Rosa Parks Sexual Assault Crisis Center, began in late 1984, in anticipation of the target funding. Avis Ridley-Thomas, who was instrumental in its founding, was at the nexus of several networks that led to the founding of Rosa Parks. She had been working for the new Victim Witness Assistance Program out of the city attorney's office since 1980. Because of her work there, she had been recommended by Assemblywoman Maxine Waters to be on the State Sexual Assault Services Advisory Committee (SAC), which advised the OCJP on funding for rape crisis services, training for prosecutors, and funding for research. Ridley-Thomas became chair of the committee, which at first had very little money to give out. Hers was another voice, in addition to those of the Alliance members, raising the issue of underfunding of minority areas. It was clear from her knowledge of South Central Los Angeles that this area had the highest rate of reported sexual assault in the state and no community-provided services.

A longtime activist in the Black community, she tried to organize women's groups to take on rape crisis services as a project, but none of the women she approached felt they could do that in addition to their other work. She and her husband, Mark Ridley-Thomas, who was the director of the local branch of the Southern Christian Leadership Conference (SCLC), applied for and received an OCJP grant to start a rape crisis service. Thus Avis Ridley-Thomas's position in the funding agency, her involvement in service provision to victims, and her relationship to SCLC converged to create a place for the new service.

The Compton YWCA was the second new organization to start a rape crisis program in a predominantly Black community. When the OCJP called for proposals for target funding, the city's police chief encouraged the YWCA director, Elaine Harris, to apply for it. Compton, one of the small cities that compose Los Angeles county, is located south of South Central Los Angeles. Although the rate of home ownership is high, so are the poverty and crime rates. As in many of the economically abandoned areas of the county, gangs are an important source of social identity for young people, which, combined with their involvement in drug dealing, has created a violent environment. The Compton YWCA has struggled to be a community resource in this context. In addition to traditional programs ranging from fitness to music, it offers a minority women's employment program, a job board, a support group for single parents, a food program for needy families, drug diversion counseling, and a support group for families of incarcerated people. With crime and violence a major social and political issue in the community, the organization had a cooperative relationship with the police, which led to the application for target funding. The YWCA had numerous resources, including experience with writing grant proposals, that could be enlisted in starting the Sexual Assault Crisis Program.

How these two new rape crisis programs were started differed markedly from the existing anti-rape organizations, which had consequences for the nature of the movement and relationships between the new organizations and the older ones in the Alliance and the Coalition. All of the older organizations had been founded out of some kind of grassroots process and with some connection to the wider feminist movement of the 1970s. Stands on feminism differed among the older organizations, but because they were founded in the midst of vibrant feminist activism, they associated what they were doing with the women's movement at some level. The Rosa Parks and Compton programs, by contrast, were founded with substantial state funding and without strong links to contemporary feminism.

Their parent organizations were not simply social service agencies. Both SCLC and the YWCA were progressive organizations with grassroots origins, but had long since become established and "becalmed" (Zald & Ash, 1966), with hierarchical leadership and bureaucratic structures. The women who were hired to direct the sexual assault programs were social service administrators, not activists. Nevertheless, many of the women who worked in the new organizations were drawn by the opportunity to work with Black women. As Joan Crear, a staff member at Rosa Parks, said:

Personally, I got involved because I was very much interested in women's issues, in particular Black women, and I didn't feel that there was a forum in my community for them. I know there was resistance to the whole notion of violence, women's issues, feminism, and I wanted to work in an environment that advocated on behalf of Black women. As for the Rosa Parks Center, it seemed like a good place to start, and I envisioned the center as a place where eventually, while we're funded to deal with sexual assault, that it's very difficult to separate sexual assault from just what it means to be a woman in the universe, so it gave me an avenue to do that kind of work. (Interview, January 21, 1988)

Similarly, Monica Williams, director of the Compton YWCA program, said:

I had a genuine concern for women's issues and rights and moreover, I think I had a real concern for living, since I live in this community [Compton] now, a real concern for Black women. I think our image has always been of strong and persevering and you can take it all, and it doesn't make a difference, and I started to notice that most of the women who were assaulted, that it wasn't a priority for them, that they couldn't see that they were hurting, too. And that usually their first concern was their children, or their home or their husband, or how'm I going to make ends meet, so for me it's just, it's a challenge. (Interview, February 24, 1988)

Drawn by their interest in combining working with Black women and working for the Black community, and influenced by the articulated feminism of the women they met through the Alliance, these women began to see themselves as feminists, but the primary interpretive framework in their organizations was community service.

The community action framework, very much a part of the mission of both parent organizations, provided a rationale within which to fit rape crisis services, which replaced the feminist impetus of the older groups. SCLC linked the rape crisis service to its philosophy of nonviolence. The YWCA had a long history of programs to help women and girls in crisis, and many Ys around the country sponsored rape crisis services. Additionally, the emphasis of the target grants on racial and ethnic inequity in service and funding resonated with the national YWCA imperative adopted in 1970 and used in much of its literature: "to thrust our collective power as a women's movement toward the elimination of racism wherever it exists and by any means necessary."

Despite these ideological frames, the new centers were more influenced by the OCJP's definition of rape crisis work than the older anti-rape organizations. Founded with OCJP grants, they had not gone through the grass roots stage of scraping together precious resources from their communities and therefore did not have independent community roots. As a consequence of their dependence on the OCJP, they were more bureaucratized from the beginning and less suspicious of the OCJP, in contrast to the contentious history that members of the Alliance had with the agency, but similar to the feelings of many less radical rape crisis people around the state. (See Rodriguez, 1988, and Schecter, 1982, for accounts of similar splits in the battered women's shelter movement between those who resisted conventional bureaucratic organization and those who accepted it.)

Nevertheless, the community context in which the new services were provided posed contradictions with the state's bureaucratic concerns and practices. The special grants that led to the founding of Rosa Parks and Compton were intended to adjust for problems in the delivery of services, such as "hazardous working conditions, an absence of complementary service providers or agencies, high cost of providing services, lack of alternative funding sources, geographical and/or economic conditions, and unmet need for culturally and/or ethnically appropriate services" (OCJP, 1987, p. 33). These new organizations were therefore encouraged to design programs that met the basic guidelines *and* the specific needs of their communities. The sponsoring organizations, the YWCA and SCLC, were both practiced at responding to their communities and developed rape crisis programs with emphases that differed from other anti-rape programs. For example, the Rosa Parks staff set up support groups to deal with the intertwined problems of incest and alcoholism.

The ways the Compton women served their community despite standardized guidelines was an even sharper contrast. There, rape crisis workers confronted the reality of gangs on a daily basis as part of the context of the community they served. For example, to avoid confrontations among participants, they had to monitor what colors the young women wore to educational and support group meetings. Some of the women they counseled were survivors of gang-related rapes. Because basic survival was often the presenting problem of the women served, they evolved a broader approach to support and counseling. As the director said:

> A woman may come in or call in for various reasons. She has no place to
> go, she has no job, she has no support, she has no money, she has no food,
> she's been beaten, and after you finish meeting all those needs, or try to

meet all those needs, then she may say, by the way, during all this, I was being raped. So the immediate needs have to be met. So that makes our community different than other communities. A person wants their basic needs first. It's a lot easier to discuss things when you're full. So that we see people who, when they come in with their children, and their children are running around and the person is on edge, we may find out that she just hasn't eaten in a few days. And we may have to pool together money and give her everybody's lunch, or take them to lunch, and days later, maybe months later, the person will say, by the way, I did come in because I was raped, but since you brought up . . . the other things, I do need a place to stay, and I do need a job, and I can't go to the police. So . . . needs are different. (Interview, February 24, 1988)

Approaching rape crisis work in such a holistic way did not conform to the requirements of the bureaucracy that provided the funding. In spite of this director's positive view of the OCJP, she also expressed frustration that very labor-intensive work was often not counted toward funding:

A lot of what we do cannot be documented. That there's no place on that form for this woman [who has] called and she's standing outside with three kids and she don't have no place to go. [Because the form asks about] rape! So you know you just, it's almost like you end up having this group that's so concerned that it's very difficult for us when a woman calls and says she's battered, not to tell her to come here for counseling, even though that's not what we're supposed to do. When she says, but I'm right up the street I don't want to go to the shelter, I just want to talk to somebody, and a staff person like Irma or Roslyn will spend hours with this person and afterwards come in and say, god she's feeling better and I think this, and I'm going to take her over to the shelter, and . . . it fits no place. It's just something you did. It was an "information and referral." (Interview, February 24, 1988)

These "special service delivery problems," as the OCJP *Guidelines* (1987) puts it, are also different from the kind of issues other rape crisis centers face, largely because of this center's location in a relatively impoverished community in which services are scarce.

NEED FOR INNOVATIVE OUTREACH

The challenge of successful outreach to ethnically and racially diverse communities was one of the issues that prompted the Alliance position paper. Getting clients was more than a simple issue of publicity;

it involved changing the cultural ethic about seeking help. The ELA and Pacific-Asian rape hotlines had faced this problem for years, and women at the hotlines in the Black communities tackled it anew. Despite the high rates of sexual assault in these communities, there was no mobilized citizens' group demanding services. Once the services were funded, women from both Rosa Parks and Compton had to work on legitimizing the idea of seeking a support group or therapy from the outside, a relatively new idea in the Black community. Joan Crear of Rosa Parks explained:

> In our community, confidentiality, whether it's rape or anything else, is really the key; a community where things don't go outside your family; you know, have a history of family taking care, says don't tell. . . . [I]n terms of picking up and using a hotline, when we're doing education, it's not just about rape, it's about . . . you can call us, we won't tell anybody, we'll keep your secrets. Also in a community where you talk about gang violence, you have people that are afraid. It's really difficult when I talk to a teenager and she's been raped by a gang member. I don't want to . . . tell her to tell the police necessarily, 'cause she's scared for her brother, you know, and she's scared for her family. (Interview, January 21, 1988)

Ethnographic studies of Black communities have illuminated the extent of informal networks that provide both material and emotional support among members of even the poorest communities (e.g., Liebow, 1967; Stack, 1974), but the pursuit of more formal support through counseling is new. Avis Ridley-Thomas, founder of Rosa Parks, talked about the pressure to "strain up"—be tough and take the hard knocks—that militates against seeking outside help with emotional or psychological problems. Williams, director of the Compton YWCA program, elaborated:

> I think we work on empowerment a lot more because of the community we serve. That it's difficult for a person to sit in a group and talk about their rape and the rapist and go through all of the psychological changes without first understanding that they have some other problems too. So that what's been helpful is for Black women to see other Black women, to say I understand what it's like, to have to worry about the kids and him. . . . [T]he former sources of support are gone. That now you see more of us putting children in child care and day care, whereas before we had mothers and sisters and aunts, and you know, the extended family. So that now, we're kind of [little rueful laugh] socialized a little more, so that we're running into the same things that other people are running into. We say we're stressed. Before we just said life was tough. (Interview, February 24, 1988)

The emergence of an ethic to protect victims' rights was a bridge by which rape crisis services came to Black communities. Competition between the Sexual Assault and Victim Witness Programs within OCJP led Marilyn Peterson to look for creative ways to increase rape crisis funding, and the target grants were one such strategy that succeeded. Despite this internal competition, victims' rights were a significant factor in Black communities' receptivity to rape crisis services. The movement for victims' rights helped legitimize the culture of therapy. Because people of color are more likely to be victims of violent crime in the United States, much of the outreach by the newly established victim witness programs in the early 1980s was to Blacks, according to Avis Ridley-Thomas. Seeking help for emotional traumas became more acceptable, not only in state supported services, but also in grass roots victims' groups. Although these groups are only loosely connected to the rape crisis organizations, they contributed to a climate in which reaching and helping sexual assault victims was less alien than it might have been earlier.

RACISM, HOMOPHOBIA, AND FEMINISM

The dynamics of interpersonal racism in the Los Angeles anti-rape movement are intertwined in a complex way with differences of political perspective and homophobia. Although the anti-rape movement had become more diverse, the dominant subculture within the local movement is white feminism, strongly influenced by a lesbian perspective. The combination of feminist jargon and political viewpoints and the high number of lesbians in leadership positions creates an alienating environment for many of the Black women in the anti-rape movement. Although White activists are ideologically predisposed to accept women of color because they believe it is right, their theory about what women of color should be—that is, they should be radical because they are oppressed—does not always fit with reality. Black women hired to work in rape crisis centers have tended to identify with the social service orientation, the more conservative side of the movement, which creates tension with the more politically radical women who have dominated the Alliance.

Racial and political differences are compounded by homophobia. Homosexuality is even more hidden in the U.S. Black community than in the general society. Blacks are not alone in the anti-rape movement in their discomfort with the openly lesbian presence; dissension has also surfaced in the statewide Coalition, often between centers outside the major urban areas, which tend to be more conservative, and those from Los Angeles and the Bay Area. But locally, because a substantial number of the white women are lesbians and most of the Black women are heterosexual, the overlap of racial and sexuality differences exaggerates the schism. Both sides feel they have a moral cause for offense when someone from the other side is inadvertently racist or homophobic.

Despite the fact that all of the centers include these topics in their volunteer and staff training, these tensions affect both interpersonal interactions and organizational processes. Differences in life-style lead to divergent concerns. For example, several Black women mentioned that they wished there were support in the Alliance for dealing with husbands and families while working in rape crisis. This concern for intimate others was shared by heterosexual White women, but not by lesbians, because their partners were less likely to be threatened by their work with survivors of male violence. Lesbians, expecting Black women to be homophobic, sometimes have challenged and tested their sexuality. Even differences of style separated women—for example, the convention of dressing up in the Black community and of dressing down in White feminist circles.

Black women, like some Chicana women earlier, have also felt marginalized by being outside the shared reference system of White feminists. As Teresa Contreras of ELA put it:

> I'm fairly sure that some of us felt threatened by the jargon, the politics, the feminist politics, and the real assertiveness of the women involved in the rape crisis movement. And their confrontational style was totally contrary to the Chicano style. (Interview, April 26, 1988)

In interviews, some Black women noted that they did not really understand what "feminism" was and yet felt expected to know and support its precepts. Being thrown into the Alliance and the Coalition, where this was the political vocabulary, could be intimidating and alienating. Over time, however, some have come to put the name "feminist" to their own positions. Joan Crear, for example, after working in the anti-rape movement for over two years, was tentatively identifying herself as a feminist at the time I interviewed her. She said:

> It has become important for me to say, "I'm a feminist" to other women in my community, but I work on a definition where it doesn't sound like it's

such a big thing, because I believe that most women, or a lot of women are under . . . some of the things that feminism encompasses. . . . . [F]or me it means to want to be or to demand to share power in relationships, so I don't know if that's an appropriate term, because when I think about sharing power within relationships I have to look at that in terms of sharing power with my children, my boss, whether male or female, and so it means . . . I take responsibility for things that happen in my life. . . . I see myself as an adult woman, as an adult. (Interview, January 18, 1988)

Not all women of color live in South Central or East Los Angeles, so the existence of the ethnically based rape crisis centers is only one step toward serving all women and having a multiracial movement. The predominantly White hotlines in Los Angeles are still concerned about recruiting women of color, but face a dilemma when that goal conflicts with maintaining their integrity on feminism and homophobia. But according to Rochelle Coffey, director of the Pasadena hotline, the existence of the Black hotlines has helped give the predominantly White hotlines credibility with women of color in other parts of the county.

CONCLUSION

Whether states coopt or facilitate social movements is historically contingent on particular political forces (Tilly, 1978), and in the historical period described here, both processes occurred. Without state funding, the new Black anti-rape organizations might not exist. Their founding, however, also resulted in the further infusion of a bureaucratic orientation into the anti-rape movement, because the new organizations bear the stamp of their origins. But there is also a new source of resistance, in addition to the feminists, to the state's demands. The commitment of Rosa Parks and Compton to "serve their community" means that they make demands back to the state to shift its policies so that service is possible.

Despite conflicts, women in the Alliance, Black and White, lesbian and heterosexual, work together. The predictions from the early 1970s that women of color would need to establish their own organizations in order to become active in feminist causes seem to be borne out. Racially and ethnically homogeneous organizations have contributed more to diversifying the movement than integration within organizations. They successfully work together in mixed coalitions when they have powerful common interests, but independent bases.

REFERENCES

Bart, P., & O'Brien, P. H. (1985). *Stopping rape: Successful survival strategies.* New York: Pergamon.

Brownmiller, S. (1975). *Against our will: Men, women, and rape.* New York: Bantam.

Cleaver, E. (1968). *Soul on ice.* New York: Dell.

Davis, A. (1981). *Women, race, and class.* New York: Random House.

Dubrow, G., Flynn, C., Martinez, R., Peterson, J., Qayam, S., Segal, B., & Welch, M. B. (1986). Planning to end violence against women: Notes from a feminist conference at UCLA. *Women and Environments, 8,* 4-27.

Echols, A. (1989). *Daring to be bad: Radical feminism in America, 1967-1975.* Minneapolis: University of Minnesota.

Evans, S. (1979). *Personal politics.* New York: Vintage.

Ferree, M. M., & Hess, B. B. (1985). *Controversy and coalition: The new feminist movement.* Boston: Twayne.

Giddings, P. (1984). *When and where I enter: The impact of black women on race and sex in America.* New York: Bantam.

Hooks, B. (1981). *Ain't I a woman: Black women and feminism.* Boston: South End.

Kanuha, V. (1987). Sexual assault in Southeast Asian communities: Issues in intervention. *Response, 10,* 4-6.

Liebow, E. (1967). *Tally's corner.* Boston: Little, Brown.

Lum, J. (1988, March). Battered Asian women. *Rice,* pp. 50-52.

Mackle, N., Pernell, D., Shirchild, J., Baratta, C., & Groves, G. (1972). Dear *Aegis:* Letter from Santa Cruz Women Against Rape. *Aegis: Magazine on Ending Violence Against Women, 35,* 28-30.

New York Radical Feminists. (1974). *Rape: The first sourcebook for women* (N. Connell & C. Wilson, Eds.). New York: New American Library.

Office of Criminal Justice Planning. (1987). *California sexual assault victim services and prevention program guidelines.* Sacramento: State of California.

Rimonte, N. (1985). *Protocol for the treatment of rape and other sexual assault.* Los Angeles County Commission for Women.

Rodriguez, N. M. (1988). Transcending bureaucracy: Feminist politics at a shelter for battered women. *Gender & Society, 2,* 214-227.

Roth, S., & Baslow, R. (1984). Compromising positions at anti-rape conference. *Aegis: Magazine on Ending Violence Against Women, 38,* 38:56-58.

Schecter, S. (1982). *Women and male violence: The visions and struggles of the battered women's movement.* Boston: South End.

Southern California Rape Hotline Alliance. (1979-1988). [Minutes].

Southern California Rape Hotline Alliance. (1983). [Position paper]. Drafted by Emilia Bellone and Nilda Rimonte for the Committee to Develop OCJP Position Paper.

Stack, C. (1974). *All our kin: Strategies for survival in a black community.* New York: Harper & Row.

Tilly, C. (1978). *From mobilization to revolution.* Reading, MA: Addison-Wesley.

Zald, M. N., & Ash, R. (1966). Social movement organizations: Growth, decay and change. *Social Forces, 44,* 327-341.

14 July 18, 1988, at a Sexual Assault and Battered Women's Center

MARY SCOTT BORIA
CHRISTINA BEVILAQUA
HELEN GUALTIERI
YOLANDA HERNANDEZ
JAMIE A. JIMENEZ
ERIN SORENSON
DEBORAH WEBER
YWCA of Metropolitan Chicago
Women's Services

6:00 A.M.—WAKING UP

The 6-year-old "matriarch" of the family is awake. This is unusual for her, but because she went to bed at six the evening before, she was bright this morning, and as ever, talking a mile a minute. The nice thing about having her up so early was that we seldom get a chance, just the two of us, to talk. I'm usually fighting with her to get up and out, so her being up seems to lessen the anxiousness that I'm already feeling for today.

As I didn't get to bed until about 12:30 last night, the sight of 6:00 a.m. isn't so pleasant, and my eagerness to rise was tainted by the tiredness left in my system. No matter how anxious I feel to get "work" done, the basics are taking over my life. As I lie here on the floor, squeezed between a coffee table and a chair, I find myself stretching my body in ways I never imagined and thinking what could these pains be: age? multiple sclerosis? the heat? stress? poor body posture catching up with me? too small a bed? what? Nevertheless, my body is definitely telling me something. The thought occurs to me that my brain may work fine, but if my body is shot, how devastating that will be. So, reluctantly, at six in the morning, before the day has really begun, I'm forced to consider the balance in my life that absolutely has to include attention to my body's health.

7:00 A.M.—BATHING AND SAYING GOOD-BYES

My daughter looks so beautiful sitting at the table with her hair hanging in front of her half-open eyes as she looks down at the cats, who are begging for her attention. "Did you sleep well?" "Great," she says. I'm relieved because the night before she woke up crying hard from a dream she had where men were shooting me with arrows, and she couldn't stop them. I gulp some cold coffee and wonder if it's too early for a cigarette.

My husband screams good-bye and not to forget that he'll be late because it's his volleyball night. I start my bath and look over some notes I was typing for my qualifying exams. I think how much I hate studying all the time. In an act of defiance, I put my notes down and write my grocery list. "Mom, your bath is overflowing," my daughter calls. I bring my notes into the bathroom with me. They are still as boring as when I typed them up, and I give *Ms.* magazine a go. I see an article in the table of contents, "What's the Difference Between Men and Women?" "Well," I think to myself, "that might be interesting." What *are* some newsworthy differences between men and women? Hmmmm . . . women don't commit mass murders . . . women don't generally rape children . . . women aren't abandoning their children to poverty in mind-numbing numbers. I get to the article. I'm disappointed. It's about how long it takes women to go to the bathroom compared with men: 79 seconds, women; 43 seconds, men. There isn't even a policy recommendation. I wonder if I should call the editors and let them know that our child sexual assault program is averaging 10 referrals a week and we're only one agency of several that sees children specifically for this. I read somewhere that *Ms.* is trying to appeal to the "new feminists," whatever they are. I wonder if the "new feminists" care about these "old issues."

9:00 A.M.—STARTING WORK

I arrive at the office and turn on the answering machine. I receive a phone call from a colleague. She was with a friend at the hospital all night and probably will not be in today. Another colleague called in sick today. After wishing her good health, I receive two crises calls, both from survivors of domestic violence. The first caller is a battered woman who left her husband and needs legal assistance to pursue a divorce. The second caller asks for counseling for herself and wants to know what legal options she has available. Upon hanging up, I try to contact a rape survivor who wants to join our sexual assault survivor group. I call, and she says that she'd been waiting to join a support group for some time and that she is really looking forward to it and meeting other survivors. She asks my name and thanks me for calling. I tell her that I am looking forward to meeting her on group night.

I then look at the waiting list to see if there are any other individuals who have expressed an interest in our support group, and the list seems endless.

10 A.M.—THINKING ABOUT A CASE

I'm thinking of a case that I'm working on right now. The plaintiff is a waitress at a country club, and the assailant (or *ass* as I lovingly refer to these guys) is a member of the club, a retired small-time mobster whose life is his importance to his cronies in this club, and who saw fit to grab the plaintiff's hand and suck on her fingers as she was serving him lunch. He then followed her into an area off the kitchen and grabbed her from behind in a choke hold. She got away, told the powers that be, and they terminated his membership in the club. Of course, it was re-instated when he got an attorney to threaten them. Now he's calling the plaintiff and threatening her and her family. She called the police and got a court date next week. It's on a day when I can't go. I'll pick it up at the next court date, as it's bound to be continued.

They charged him with battery and not criminal sexual assault, and as I was thinking about the implications of this set of charges versus the other, I remembered another case and the fact that there's a specific court for sexual abuse cases. The abuse charges would be heard at one court and the battery charges at another. For the plaintiff, it means two separate cases, two separate courts to go to, one in downtown Chicago and one in the suburbs, and at the end of either case, what's the best she could hope for? He won't go to jail, he probably won't even get pro-bation. He'll end up with, if anything, supervision for 6 months to a year, and it'll come off his record when he's finished serving his supervision.

What frightens me in all this is my role as a legal advocate. As I become more and more familiar with the legal system's reality, when I think about a case, I jump immediately into the procedures, the court, the police, etc. I translate that reality for the survivors, who feel the reality from a very different perspective. Theirs is a perspective of specifics, of details, of what led to what, of their own very unique reactions, of their fear, their uncertainty, their anger, their shame. My job is to provide a bridge over the yawning chasm between the law, the SYSTEM—huge, unmovable, made of steel, totally unyielding—and the survivors' experience—ephemeral in many ways, indistinct, ubiquitous, their humiliation following them like a shadow. And how does the legal system translate their shadow? The pieces of the survivors' assault, to them the most dire, most imperative, most personal, are not recognized as anything by the SYSTEM's structure. So, in the end, their story, their reality is denied. But when I try to bridge that with them, try to make that steel structure yield as much as possible and simultaneously to prepare the survivor for its unyielding quality, the shakiness of the venture is always so apparent to me, and I'm never sure if I've explained the system to someone who needs to understand it and will use it. Am I really just making it easier for them to accept what should not be accepted?

I try to call the state's assistant attorney from last week's case: two Class X felony convictions. Two guys each were charged with aggravated criminal sexual assault. I want to congratulate the attorney for winning. It's political more than personal. She did a good job, lots of lawyerly brouhaha, but she's terrible with survivors. In the case last week, which was an acquaintance rape case, the defense produced an 11th-hour witness to testify for their side. The plaintiff knew who he was—she'd dated him when she was a teenager. "You dated that *scum?*" her attorney demanded, incredulous, as we were standing in the hallway waiting for the trial to resume. Her voice sounds amplified all the time, and she scowls, stamps her feet, shakes her finger at people, etc. She looks like Joan Crawford at her hardest and most abrasive, and sounds like her as well. But I've got another case with this attorney next week, so it won't hurt to congratulate her. Maybe it'll help when she's dealing with the survivor in the upcoming case.

Yesterday was sunny and lovely, so I went for a walk, not in my neighborhood, where catcalls are a way of life, but in a very yuppie, gentrified neighborhood. I was alone. I bought an ice cream cone and walked down the street with it. Men commented as I walked by, leered, leaned out of passing cars to suggest what they'd like to do to me, what they'd like me to do to them. I kept walking. It felt like a terrible day, the ice cream tasted terrible now. I thought, perhaps I'll go to law school, and then I'll devote my life to passing legislation enabling, even encouraging, women to carry loaded guns with which they would be permitted to shoot to *death* any man who makes any comment to them that is unsolicited. Maybe violence does beget violence; all this hostility and aggression toward us in our daily lives—on our jobs, in the courtroom, on a walk alone—makes me want murder to put a stop to it, to be able to be left alone, unbothered.

NOON—WAITING FOR A CLIENT

I've been in meetings all morning, and I'm starving because I skipped breakfast. I'm seeing a woman who's an incest survivor at noon, and I'm anticipating a difficult visit. I hope she's late. I need time to think. I've been working with sexual assault survivors of all ages for almost 8 years now and it never gets easier. Today I'll tell her that her carefully guarded and nurtured secret is out and her six children highly suspect that their grandfather is really their father. I anticipate this to be devastating news to her, as she is already confused and alone. Maybe it will just be one more devastation in a series of devastations. If I could spare her more pain I would. But her children are suffering under the burden of not knowing, so it seems that the truth is as painful as the lies. Usually, when a survivor speaks the truth, it's the beginning of a long healing—it's rewarding and precious to be a part of that process. In this family, as the truth is acknowledged, it is the opening of a wound that may never heal. I never wanted to cause pain. I hope she cancels . . . oh . . . I hear her children. They've arrived.

1:00 P.M.—LUNCH AND PHONE CALLS

I'm finishing my peanut butter sandwich at my desk, trying to save time and money. When will these salaries ever go up so I can take myself out to lunch?

I just filled out my time sheet and am thinking, "This is ridiculous. How can I break my work down into percentages? Let's see, is a client's rape and all the devastation it's done to her life a B17-Community Education or a D25-Individual Advocacy?"

A former colleague from the Department of Children and Family Services walks in. She says she is much happier now that she is not working for them. She's pregnant and plans on staying home. I would love to be able to stay home part-time with my kid.

I try to get back to my paperwork, and the phone rings. It's one of my battered women clients. We are working on "new relationships" that we hope will be different from the abusive one she was in. She calls, very upset because the guy she has been dating for the last month has all of a sudden become controlling, accusatory, and threatens to leave. Between her putting me on hold and answering calls (she's a switchboard operator at work), we are speaking about how she could handle and confront his new behavior. We are also talking about what it is that she may really want out of a relationship, but most of all we are talking about how scary it is to be alone.

As soon as I hang up, the phone rings again. It is a woman who is an incest survivor, who desperately wants to get into our group. I tell her, with sadness, that I think the group is already filled up. The number of calls is so overwhelming. I guess we do our best to help as many women as we can.

I spend the next half hour talking to another client about her excursion to a camp in Wisconsin where she believes she was ritualistically sexually abused as a child. She wants me to go back there with her to see if she can remember more. The friend she went with was too afraid to go in. She is fearing for her safety and wants me to know where her safe deposit box is, as it contains some tapes that she made, telling her story. She is afraid something might happen to her.

I hang up, finish my sandwich, and wonder what a real lunch hour would be like.

3:00 P.M.—JUST SITTING IN MY OFFICE

I just found out from a co-worker that the daughter of a colleague from a neighboring agency got assaulted last week. She's wondering if we have a kids' group going, and I told her about the group running right now, but I think it's filled. Working in the field does not make you immune.

A client at the center dropped in to say that she settled out of court with her husband. They were in court over visitation after a 2-year court involvement found him not guilty of sexually assaulting their then 3-year-old. She feels somewhat OK but said the financial burden for the legal stuff was too heavy. "At least," she says, "now that my daughter is 5, she can talk when he molests her again, and this time she can testify."

5:00 P.M.—CLOSING UP

As I take time to reflect on the events of today, I think about all the women who called in for assistance or just for someone to listen. I wonder how they are doing at this very moment. The last caller of the day was a battered woman who sounded confused about what to do with her abusive relationship. We spoke for 40 minutes. She asked my name and thanked me for listening to her and providing her with information. I wished her luck and told her to take care. Again she thanked me. Well, it's about time I turn on the answering machine again. I wonder how many women will be calling tonight.

9:00 P.M.—UNWINDING

It's been a hard day. A friend my age just lost the baby she's been trying forever to have. My own mother is turning 65 today, and we still don't have the relationship I'd like. I feel so old and tired. I pick up this month's *Ms.* and find an article called "AIDS—The New Burden for Rape Victims." How can it be that someone who has been assaulted and survived and perhaps is even firmly on the road to healing finds out she's dying from AIDS. What could this mean?

I need distracting, and my partner suggests a game of computer Monopoly. I like this version—it goes four times as fast as regular board Monopoly, and the computer handles all the money transactions! During the game, I get a call from Chicago NOW—it's their annual beg-a-thon. We talk a while, and the caller tells me she's having a successful evening. I wish our agency would have such good luck fund-raising. That reminds me that Wednesday we are supposed to "arrange shots" that best show what our center is about. These get presented in a show to various funders. I'm not ready for corporate America and the sanitized way we yank at their heartstrings. I'd like people to hear the crying and feel the pain and *really* understand what it is we do. Maybe the real answer is, I need to play the lottery.

11:00 P.M.—FALLING ASLEEP

My partner's been up late working, and I went to bed early. I'm usually not up this late, but tonight I can't sleep. He comes to bed and kisses my forehead. "Good night, I love you," he says. "I love you, too," I say. We lay silently next to each other, and I wonder if he's going to want to make love. We haven't made love in a couple of weeks, and I know he feels bad. But I keep having these visions when we start to make love—sometimes I become one of my child clients, and he becomes the abuser; sometimes I become one of the mothers of an assaulted child that I'm seeing, and he becomes the husband that they always thought was wonderful because he spent so much time with the kids; and sometimes he becomes the man who raped me when I was 15 years old, and I become a scared, lonely little girl. I fall asleep hoping he'll forgive me.

15 Feminism, Marxism, Method, and the State: Toward a Feminist Jurisprudence

CATHARINE A. MACKINNON
University of Michigan

Feminism has no theory of the state. It has a theory of power: Sexuality is gendered as gender is sexualized. Male and female are created through the erotization of dominance and submission. The man/woman difference and the dominance/submission dynamic define each other. This is the social meaning of sex and the distinctively feminist account of gender inequality.[1] Sexual objectification, the central process within this dynamic, is at once epistemological and political.[2] The feminist theory of knowledge is inextricable from the feminist critique of power because the male point of view forces itself upon the world as its way of apprehending it.

AUTHOR'S NOTE: For A. D. and D. K. H. In addition to all those whose help is acknowledged in the first part of this chapter, "Feminism, Marxism, Method, and the State: An Agenda for Theory," *Signs: Journal of Women in Culture and Society 7,* no. 3 (Spring 1982): 515-44 (hereafter cited as part 1), my students and colleagues at Yale, Harvard, and Stanford contributed profoundly to the larger project of which both articles are parts. Among them, Sonia E. Alvarez, Jeanne M. Barkey, Paul Brest, Ruth Colker, Karen E. Davis, Sharon Dyer, Tom Emerson, Daniel Gunther, Patricia Kliendienst Joplin, Mark Kelman, Duncan Kennedy, John Kaplan, Lyn Lemaire, Mira Marshall, Rebecca Mark, Martha Minow, Helen M. A. Neally, Lisa Rofel, Sharon Silverstein, Dean Spencer, Laurence Tribe, and Mary Whisner stand out vividly in retrospect. None of it would have happened without Lu Ann Carter and David Rayson. And thank you, Meg Baldwin, Annie McCombs, and Janet Spector.

Marxism appears in lower case, Black in upper case, for reasons explained in Part 1.

Reprinted with permission of the author and publisher from *Signs: Journal of Women in Culture and Society,* 8(4), 635-658, University of Chicago Press.

The perspective from the male standpoint[3] enforces women's definition, encircles her body, circumlocutes her speech, and describes her
life. The male perspective is systemic and hegemonic. The content of
the signification "woman" is the content of women's lives. Each sex has
its role, but their stakes and power are not equal. If the sexes are unequal, and perspective participates in situation, there is no ungendered
reality or ungendered perspective. And they are connected. In this context, objectivity—the nonsituated, universal standpoint, whether claimed
or aspired to—is a denial of the existence or potency of sex inequality
that tacitly participates in constructing reality from the dominant point
of view. Objectivity, as the epistemological stance of which objectification is the social process, creates the reality it apprehends by defining
as knowledge the reality it creates through its way of apprehending it.
Sexual metaphors for knowing are no coincidence.[4] The solipsism of
the approach does not undercut its sincerity, but it is interest that pre-
cedes method.

Feminism criticizes this male totality without an account of our capacity
to do so or to imagine or realize a more whole truth. Feminism affirms
women's point of view by revealing, criticizing, and explaining its impossibility. This is not a dialectical paradox. It is a methodological expression of women's situation, in which the struggle for consciousness
is a struggle for world: for a sexuality, a history, a culture, a community,
a form of power, an experience of the sacred. If women had consciousness or world, sex inequality would be harmless, or all women would
be feminist. Yet we have something of both, or there would be no such
thing as feminism. Why can women know that this—life as we have
known it—is not all, not enough, not ours, not just? Now, why don't all
women?[5]

The practice of a politics of all women in the face of its theoretical
impossibility is creating a new process of theorizing and a new form of
theory. Although feminism emerges from women's particular experience, it is not subjective or partial, for no interior ground and few if any
aspects of life are free of male power. Nor is feminism objective, abstract,
or universal.[6] It claims no external ground or unsexed sphere of generalization or abstraction beyond male power, no transcendence of the
specificity of each of its manifestations. How is it possible to have an
engaged truth that does not simply reiterate its determinations? *Dis*-
engaged truth only reiterates *its* determinations. Choice of method is choice
of determinants—a choice which, for women as such, has been unavailable because of the subordination of women. Feminism does not begin

with the premise that it is unpremised. It does not aspire to persuade an unpremised audience, because there is no such audience. Its project is to uncover and claim as valid the experience of women, the major content of which is the devalidation of women's experience. This defines our task not only because male dominance is perhaps the most pervasive and tenacious system of power in history, but because it is metaphysically nearly perfect.[7] Its point of view is the standard for point-of-viewlessness, its particularity the meaning of universality. Its force is exercised as consent, its authority as participation, its supremacy as the paradigm of order, its control as the definition of legitimacy. Feminism claims the voice of women's silence, the sexuality of our eroticized desexualization, the fullness of "lack," the centrality of our marginality and exclusion, the public nature of privacy, the presence of our absence. This approach is more complex than transgression, more transformative than transvaluation, deeper than mirror-imaged resistance, more affirmative than the negation of our negativity. It is neither materialist nor idealist; it is feminist. Neither the transcendence of liberalism nor the determination of materialism works for us. Idealism is too unreal; women's inequality is enforced, so it cannot simply be thought out of existence, certainly not by us. Materialism is too real; women's inequality has never not existed, so women's equality never has. That is, the equality of women to men will not be scientifically provable until it is no longer necessary to do so. Women's situation offers no outside to stand on or gaze at, no inside to escape to, too much urgency to wait, no place else to go, and nothing to use but the twisted tools that have been shoved down our throats. If feminism is revolutionary, this is why.

Feminism has been widely thought to contain tendencies of liberal feminism, radical feminism, and socialist feminism. But just as socialist feminism has often amounted to marxism applied to women, liberal feminism has often amounted to liberalism applied to women. Radical feminism is feminism. Radical feminism—after this, feminism unmodified —is methodologically post-marxist.[8] It moves to resolve the marxist-feminist problematic on the level of method. Because its method emerges from the concrete conditions of all women as a sex, it dissolves the individualist, naturalist, idealist, moralist structure of liberalism, the politics of which science is the epistemology. Where liberal feminism sees sexism primarily as an illusion or myth to be dispelled, an inaccuracy to be corrected, true feminism sees the male point of view as fundamental to the male power to create the world in its own image, the image of its desires, not just as its delusory end product. Feminism distinctively as such comprehends that what counts as truth is produced in the interest of those with power to shape reality, and that this process is as pervasive as it is necessary as it is changeable. Unlike the scientific strain in marxism or the Kantian imperative in liberalism, which in this context share most salient features, feminism neither claims universality nor, failing that, reduces to relativity. It does not seek a generality that subsumes its particulars or an abstract theory or a science of sexism. It rejects the approach of control over nature (including us) analogized to control over society (also including us) which has grounded the "science of society" project as the paradigm for political knowledge since (at least) Descartes. Both liberalism and marxism have been subversive on women's behalf. Neither is enough. To grasp the inadequacies for women of liberalism on one side and marxism on the other is to begin to comprehend the role of the liberal state and liberal legalism[9] within a post-marxist feminism of social transformation.

As feminism has a theory of power but lacks a theory of the state, so marxism has a theory of value which (through the organization of work in production) becomes class analysis, but a problematic theory of the state. Marx did not address the state much more explicitly than he did women. Women were substratum, the state epiphenomenon.[10] Engels, who frontally analyzed both, and together, presumed the subordination of women in every attempt to reveal its roots, just as he presupposed something like the state, or state-like social conditions, in every attempt to expose its origins.[11] Marx tended to use the term "political" narrowly to refer to the state or its laws, criticizing as exclusively political interpretations of the state's organization or behavior which took them as sui generis. Accordingly, until recently, most marxism has tended to consider political that which occurs between classes, that is, to interpret as "the political" instances of the marxist concept of inequality. In this broad sense, the marxist theory of social inequality has been its theory of politics. This has not so much collapsed the state into society (although it goes far in that direction) as conceived the state as determined by the totality of social relations of which the state is one determined and determining part—without specifying which, or how much, is which.

In this context, recent marxist work has tried to grasp the specificity of the institutional state: how it wields class power, or transforms class society, or responds to approach by a left aspiring to rulership or other changes. While liberal theory has seen the state as emanating power, and traditional marxism has seen the state as expressing power constituted elsewhere, recent marxism, much of it structuralist, has tried to analyze state power as specific to the state as a form, yet integral to a determinate social whole understood in class terms. This state is found "relatively autonomous." This means that the state, expressed through its functionaries, has a definite class character, is definitely capitalist or socialist, but also has its own interests, which are to some degree independent of those of the ruling class and even of the class structure.[12] The state as such, in this view, has a specific power and interest, termed "the political," such that class power, class interest expressed by and in the state, and state behavior, although inconceivable in isolation from one another, are nevertheless not linearly or causally linked or strictly coextensive. Such work locates "the specificity of the political" in a immediate "region"[13] between the state as its own ground of power (which alone, as in the liberal conception, would set the state above or apart from class) and the state as possessing no special supremacy or priority in terms of power, as in the more orthodox marxist view.

The idea that the state is relatively autonomous, a kind of first among equals of social institutions, has the genius of appearing to take a stand on the issue of reciprocal constitution of state and society while straddling it. Is the state essentially autonomous of class but partly determined by it, or is it essentially determined by class but not exclusively so? Is it relatively constrained within a context of freedom or relatively free within a context of constraint?[14] As to who or what fundamentally moves and shapes the realities and instrumentalities of domination, and where to go to do something about it, what qualifies what is as ambiguous as it is crucial. Whatever it has not accomplished, however, this literature has at least relieved the compulsion to find all law—directly or convolutedly, nakedly or clothed in unconscious or devious rationalia —to be simply bourgeois, without undercutting the notion that it is determinately driven by interest.

A methodologically post-marxist feminism must confront, on our own terms, the issue of the relation between the state and society within a theory of social determination adequate to the specificity of sex. Lacking even a tacit theory of the state of its own, feminist practice has instead oscillated between a liberal theory of the state on the one hand and a left theory of the state on the other. Both treat law as the mind of society: disembodied reason in liberal theory, reflection of material interest in left theory. In liberal moments the state is accepted on its own terms as a neutral arbiter among conflicting interests. The law is actually or potentially principled, meaning predisposed to no substantive outcome, thus available as a tool that is not fatally twisted. Women implicitly become an interest group within pluralism, with specific problems of mobilization and representation, exit and voice, sustaining incremental gains and losses. In left moments, the state becomes a tool of dominance and repression, the law legitimizing ideology, use of the legal system a form of utopian idealism or gradualist reform, each apparent gain deceptive or co-optive, and each loss inevitable.

Applied to women, liberalism has supported state intervention on behalf of women as abstract persons with abstract rights without scrutinizing the content of these notions in gendered terms. Marxism applied to women is always on the edge of counseling abdication of the state as an arena altogether—and with it those women whom the state does not ignore or who are, as yet, in no position to ignore it. Feminism has so far accepted these constraints upon its alternatives: either the state, as primary tool of women's betterment and status transformation, without analysis (hence strategy) for it as male; or civil society, which for women has more closely resembled a state of nature. The state, and with it the law, has been either omnipotent or impotent: everything or nothing.

The feminist posture toward the state has therefore been schizoid on issues central to women's survival: rape, battery, pornography, prostitution, sexual harassment, sex discrimination, abortion, and the Equal Rights Amendment, to name a few. Attempts to reform and enforce rape laws, for example, have tended to build on the model of the deviant perpetrator and the violent act, as if the fact that rape is a crime means that the society is against it, so law enforcement would reduce or delegitimize it. Initiatives are accordingly directed toward making the police more sensitive, prosecutors more responsive, judges more receptive, and the law, in words, less sexist. This may be progressive in the liberal or the left senses, but how is it empowering in the feminist sense? Even if it were effective in jailing men who do little different from what nondeviant men do regularly, how would such an approach alter women's rapability? Unconfronted are *why* women are raped and the role of the state in that. Similarly, applying laws against battery to husbands, although it can mean life itself, has largely failed to address, as part of the strategy for state intervention, the conditions that produce men who systematically express themselves violently toward women— women whose resistance is disabled—and the role of the state in this dynamic. Criminal enforcement in these areas, while suggesting that rape and battery are deviant, punishes men for expressing the images of masculinity that mean their identity, for which they are otherwise trained, elevated, venerated, and paid. These men must be stopped. But how does that change them or reduce the chances that there will be more like them? Liberal strategies entrust women to the state. Left theory abandons us to the rapists and batterers. The question for feminism is not only whether there is a meaningful difference between the two, but whether either is adequate to the feminist critique of rape and battery as systemic and to the role of the state and the law within that system. Feminism has descriptions of the state's treatment of the gender difference, but no analysis of the state as gender hierarchy. We need to know. What, in gender terms, are the state's norms of accountability, sources of power, real constituency? Is the state to some degree autonomous of the interests of men or an integral expression of them? Does the state embody and serve male interests in its form, dynamics, relation to society, and specific policies? Is the state constructed upon the subordination of women? If so, how does male power become state power? Can such a state be made to serve the interests of those upon whose powerlessness its power is erected? Would a different relation between state and society, such as may pertain under socialism, make a difference? If not, is masculinity inherent in the state form as such, or is some other form of state, or some other way of governing, distinguishable or imaginable? In the absence of answers to such questions, feminism has been caught between giving more power to the state in each attempt to claim it for women and leaving unchecked power in the society to men. Undisturbed, meanwhile, like the assumption that women generally consent to sex, is the assumption that we consent to this government. The question for feminism, for the first time on its own terms, is: What is this state, from women's point of view?

As a beginning, I propose that the state is male in the feminist sense.[15] The law sees and treats women the way men see and treat women. The liberal state coercively and authoritatively constitutes the social order in the interest of men as a gender, through its legitimizing norms, relation to society, and substantive policies. It achieves this through embodying and ensuring male control over women's sexuality at every level, occasionally cushioning, qualifying, or de jure prohibiting its excesses when necessary to its normalization. Substantively, the way the male point of view frames an experience is the way it is framed by state policy. To the extent possession is the point of sex, rape is sex with a woman who is not yours, unless the act is so as to make her yours. If part of the kick of pornography involves eroticizing the putatively prohibited, obscenity law will putatively prohibit pornography enough to maintain its desirability without ever making it unavailable or truly illegitimate. The same with prostitution. As male is the implicit reference for human, maleness will be the measure of equality in sex discrimination law. To the extent that the point of abortion is to control the reproductive sequelae of intercourse, so as to facilitate male sexual access to women, access to abortion will be controlled by "a man or The Man."[16] Gender, elaborated and sustained by behavioral patterns of application and administration, is maintained as a division of power.

Formally, the state is male in that objectivity is its norm. Objectivity is liberal legalism's conception of itself. It legitimizes itself by reflecting its view of existing society, a society it made and makes by so seeing it, and calling that view, and that relation, practical rationality. If rationality is measured by point-of-viewlessness, what counts as reason will be that which corresponds to the way things are, and practical will mean that which can be done without changing anything. In this framework, the task of legal interpretation becomes "to perfect the state as mirror of the society."[17] Objectivist epistemology is the law of law. It ensures that the law will most reinforce existing distributions of power when it most closely adheres to its own highest ideal of fairness. Like the science it emulates, this epistemological stance cannot see the social specificity of reflection as method or its choice to embrace that which it reflects. Such law not only reflects a society in which men rule women, it also rules in a male way: "The phallus means everything that sets itself up as a mirror."[18] The rule form, which unites scientific knowledge with state control in its conception of what law is, institutionalizes the objective stance as jurisprudence. A closer look at the substantive law of rape[19] in light of such an argument suggests that the relation between objectification (understood as the primary process of the subordination of women) and the power of the state is the relation between the personal and the political at the level of government. This is not because the state is presumptively the sphere of politics. It is because the state, in part through law, institutionalizes male power. If male power is systemic, it *is* the regime.

II

Feminists have reconceived rape as central to women's condition in two ways. Some see rape as an act of violence, not sexuality, the threat of which intimidates all women.[20] Others see rape, including its violence, as an expression of male sexuality, the social imperatives of which define all women.[21] The first, formally, in the liberal tradition, comprehends rape as a displacement of power based on physical force onto sexuality, a preexisting natural sphere to which domination is alien. Thus, Susan Brownmiller examines rape in riots, wars, pogroms, and revolutions; rape by police, parents, prison guards; and rape motivated by racism—seldom rape in normal circumstances, in everyday life, in ordinary relationships, by men as men.[22] Women are raped by guns, age, white supremacy, the state—only derivatively by the penis. The more feminist view to me, one which derives from victims' experiences, sees sexuality as a social sphere of male power of which forced sex is paradigmatic. Rape is not less sexual for being violent; to the extent that coercion has become integral to male sexuality, rape may be sexual to the degree that, and because, it is violent.

The point of defining rape as "violence not sex" or "violence against women" has been to separate sexuality from gender in order to affirm sex (heterosexuality) while rejecting violence (rape). The problem remains what it has always been: telling the difference. The convergence of sexuality with violence, long used at law to deny the reality of women's violation, is recognized by rape survivors, with a difference: Where the legal system has seen the intercourse in rape, victims see the rape in intercourse. The uncoerced context for sexual expression becomes as elusive as the physical acts come to feel indistinguishable.[23] Instead of asking, What is the violation of rape, what if we ask, What is the non-violation of intercourse? To tell what is wrong with rape, explain what is right about sex. If this, in turn, is difficult, the difficulty is as instructive as the difficulty men have in telling the difference when women see one. Perhaps the wrong of rape has proven so difficult to articulate[24] because the unquestionable starting point has been that rape is definable as distinct from intercourse, when for women it is difficult to distinguish them under conditions of male dominance.[25]

Like heterosexuality, the crime of rape centers on penetration.[26] The law to protect women's sexuality from forcible violation/expropriation defines the protected in male genital terms. Women do resent forced penetration. But penile invasion of the vagina may be less pivotal to women's sexuality, pleasure, or violation than it is to male sexuality. This definitive element of rape centers upon a male-defined loss, not coincidentally also upon the way men define loss of exclusive access. In this light, rape, as legally defined, appears more a crime against female monogamy than against female sexuality. Property concepts fail fully to comprehend this,[27] however, not because women's sexuality is not, finally, a thing, but because it is never ours. The moment we "have" it—"have sex" in the dual sexuality/gender sense—it is lost as ours. This may explain the male incomprehension that, once a woman has had sex, she loses anything when raped. To them we *have nothing* to lose. Dignitary harms, because nonmaterial, are remote to the legal mind. But women's loss through rape is not only less tangible, it is less existent. It is difficult to avoid the conclusion that penetration itself is known to be a violation and that women's sexuality, our gender definition, is itself stigmatic. If this is so, the pressing question for explanation is not why some of us accept rape but why any of us resent it.

The law of rape divides the world of women into spheres of consent according to how much say we are legally presumed to have over sexual access to us by various categories of men. Little girls may not consent; wives must. If rape laws existed to enforce women's control over our own sexuality, as the consent defense implies, marital rape would not be a widespread exception,[28] nor would statutory rape proscribe all sexual intercourse with underage girls regardless of their wishes. The rest of us fall into parallel provinces: Good girls, like children, are unconsenting, virginal, rapable; bad girls, like wives, are consenting, whores, unrapable. The age line under which girls are presumed disabled from withholding consent to sex rationalizes a condition of sexual coercion women never outgrow. As with protective labor laws for women only, dividing and protecting the most vulnerable becomes a device for not protecting everyone. Risking loss of even so little cannot be afforded. Yet the protection is denigrating and limiting (girls may not choose to be sexual) as well as perverse (girls are eroticized as untouchable; now reconsider the data on incest).

If the accused knows us, consent is inferred. The exemption for rape in marriage is consistent with the assumption underlying most adjudications of forcible rape: To the extent the parties relate, it was not really rape, it was personal.[29] As the marital exemptions erode, preclusions for cohabitants and voluntary social companions may expand. In this light, the partial erosion of the marital rape exemption looks less like a change in the equation between women's experience of sexual violation and men's experience of intimacy, and more like a legal adjustment to the social fact that acceptable heterosexual sex is increasingly not limited to the legal family. So although the rape law may not now always assume that the woman consented simply because the parties are legally one, indices of closeness, of relationship ranging from nodding acquaintance to living together, still contraindicate rape. Perhaps this reflects men's experience that women they know meaningfully consent to sex with them. That cannot be rape; rape must be by someone else, someone unknown. But *women* experience rape most often by men we know.[30] Men believe that it is less awful to be raped by someone one is close to: "The emotional trauma suffered by a person victimized by an individual with whom sexual intimacy is shared as a normal part of an ongoing marital relationship is not nearly as severe as that suffered by a person who is victimized by one with whom that intimacy is not shared."[31] But women feel as much, if not more, traumatized by being raped by someone we have known or trusted, someone we have shared at least an illusion of mutuality with, than by some stranger. In whose interest is it to believe that it is not so bad to be raped by someone who has fucked you before as by someone who has not? Disallowing charges of rape in marriage may also "remove a substantial obstacle to the resumption of normal marital relations."[32] That depends upon your view of normal. Note that the obstacle to normalcy here is not the rape but the law against it. Apparently someone besides feminists finds sexual victimization and sexual intimacy not all that contradictory. Sometimes I think women and men live in different cultures.

Having defined rape in male sexual terms, the law's problem, which becomes the victim's problem, is distinguishing rape from sex in specific cases. The law does this by adjudicating the level of acceptable force starting just above the level set by what is seen as normal male sexual behavior, rather than at the victim's, or women's, point of violation. Rape cases finding insufficient force reveal that acceptable sex, in the legal perspective, can entail a lot of force. This is not only because of the way specific facts are perceived and interpreted, but because of the way the injury itself is defined as illegal. Rape is a sex crime that is not a crime when it looks like sex. To seek to define rape as violent, not sexual, is understandable in this context, and often seems strategic. But assault that is consented to is still assault; rape consented to is intercourse. The substantive reference point implicit in existing legal standards is the sexually normative level of force. Until this norm is confronted as such, no distinction between violence and sexuality will prohibit more instances of women's experienced violation than does the existing definition. The question is what is *seen as* force, hence as violence, in the sexual arena. Most rapes, as women live them, will not be seen to violate women until sex and violence are confronted as mutually definitive. It is not only men convicted of rape who believe that the only thing they did different from what men do all the time is get caught.

The line between rape and intercourse commonly centers on some measure of the woman's "will." But from what should the law know woman's will? Like much existing law, Brownmiller tends to treat will as a question of consent and consent as a factual issue of the presence of force.[33] Proof problems aside, force and desire are not mutually exclusive. So long as dominance is eroticized, they never will be. Women are socialized to passive receptivity; may have or perceive no alternative to acquiescence; may prefer it to the escalated risk of injury and the humiliation of a lost fight; submit to survive. Some eroticize dominance and submission; it beats feeling forced. Sexual intercourse may be deeply unwanted—the woman would never have initiated it—yet no force may be present. Too, force may be used, yet the woman may want the sex—to avoid more force or because she, too, eroticizes dominance. Women and men know this. Calling rape violence, not sex, thus evades, at the moment it most seems to confront, the issue of who controls women's sexuality and the dominance/submission dynamic that has defined it. When sex is violent, women may have lost control over what is done to us, but absence of force does not ensure the presence of that control. Nor, under conditions of male dominance, does the presence of force make an interaction nonsexual. If sex is normally something men do to women, the issue is less whether there was force and more whether consent is a meaningful concept.[34]

To explain women's gender status as a function of rape, Brownmiller argues that the threat of rape benefits all men.[35] She does not specify in what way. Perhaps it benefits them sexually, hence as a gender: Male initiatives toward women carry the fear of rape as support for persuading compliance, the resulting appearance of which has been called consent. Here the victims' perspective grasps what liberalism applied to women denies: that forced sex as sexuality is not exceptional in relations between the sexes but constitutes the social meaning of gender: "Rape is a man's act, whether it is male or a female man and whether it is a man relatively permanently or relatively temporarily; and being raped is a woman's experience, whether it is a female or a male woman and whether it is a woman relatively permanently or relatively temporarily."[36] To be rap*able*, a position which is social, not biological, defines what a woman *is*.

Most women get the message that the law against rape is virtually unenforceable as applied to them. Our own experience is more often delegitimized by this than the law is. Women radically distinguish between rape and experiences of sexual violation, concluding that we have not "really" been raped if we have ever seen or dated or slept with or been married to the man, if we were fashionably dressed or are not provably virgin, if we are prostitutes, if we put up with it or tried to get it over with, if we were force-fucked over a period of years. If we probably couldn't prove it in court, it wasn't rape. The distance between most sexual violations of women and the legally perfect rape measures the imposition of someone else's definition upon women's experiences. Rape, from women's point of view, is not prohibited; it is regulated. Even women who know we have been raped do not believe that the legal system will see it the way we do. We are often not wrong. Rather than deterring or avenging rape, the state, in many victims' experiences, perpetuates it. Women who charge rape say they were raped twice, the second time in court. If the state is male, this is more than a figure of speech.

The law distinguishes rape from intercourse by the woman's lack of consent coupled with a man's (usually) knowing disregard of it. A feminist distinction between rape and intercourse, to hazard a beginning approach, lies instead in the *meaning* of the act from women's point of view. What is wrong with rape is that it is an act of the subordination of women to men. Seen this way, the issue is not so much what rape "is" as the way its social conception is shaped to interpret particular encounters. Under conditions of sex inequality, with perspective bound up with situation, whether a contested interaction is rape comes down to whose meaning wins. If sexuality is relational, specifically if it is a power relation of gender, consent is a communication under conditions of inequality. It transpires somewhere between what the woman actually wanted and what the man comprehended she wanted. Instead of capturing this dynamic, the law gives us linear statics face to face. Nonconsent in law becomes a question of the man's force or the woman's resistance or both.[37] Rape, like many crimes and torts, requires that the accused possess a criminal mind (mens rea) for his acts to be criminal. The man's mental state refers to what he actually understood at the time or to what a reasonable man should have understood under the circumstances. The problem is this: The injury of rape lies in the meaning of the act to its victims, but the standard for its criminality lies in the meaning of the same act to the assailants. Rape is an injury only from women's point of view. It is a crime only from the male point of view, explicitly including that of the accused.

Thus is the crime of rape defined and adjudicated from the male standpoint, that is, presuming that (what feminists see as) forced sex is sex. Under male supremacy, of course, it is. What this means doctrinally is that the man's perceptions of the woman's desires often determine whether she is deemed violated. This might be like other crimes of subjective intent if rape were like other crimes. But with rape, because sexuality defines gender, the only difference between assault and (what is socially considered) noninjury is the meaning of the encounter to the woman. Interpreted this way, the legal problem has been to determine whose view of that meaning constitutes what really happened, as if what happened objectively exists to be objectively determined, thus as if this task of determination is separable from the gender of the participants and the gendered nature of their exchange. Thus, even though the rape law oscillates between subjective tests and more objective standards invoking social reasonableness, it uniformly presumes a single underlying reality, not a reality split by divergent meanings, such as those inequality produces. Many women are raped by men who know the meaning of their acts to women and proceed anyway.[38] But women are also violated every day by men who have no idea of the meaning of their acts to women. To them, it is sex. Therefore, to the law, it is sex. That is the single reality of what happened. When a rape prosecution is lost on a consent defense, the woman has not only failed to prove lack of consent, she is not considered to have been injured at all. Hermeneutically unpacked, read: Because he did not perceive she did not want him, she was not violated. She had sex. Sex itself cannot be an injury. Women consent to sex every day. Sex makes a woman a woman. Sex is what women are *for.*

To a feminist analysis, men set sexual mores ideologically and behaviorally, define rape as they imagine the sexual violation of women through distinguishing it from their image of what they normally do, and sit in judgment in most accusations of sex crimes. So rape comes to mean a strange (read Black) man knowing a woman does not want sex and going ahead anyway. But men are systematically conditioned not even to notice what women want. They may have not a glimmer of women's indifference or revulsion. Rapists typically believe the woman loved it.[39] Women, as a survival strategy, must ignore or devalue or mute our desires (particularly lack of them) to convey the impression that the man will get what he wants regardless of what we want. In this context, consider measuring the genuineness of consent from the individual assailant's (or even the socially reasonable, i.e., objective, man's) point of view.

Men's pervasive belief that women fabricate rape charges after consenting to sex makes sense in this light. To them, the accusations *are* false because, to them, the facts describe sex. To interpret such events as rapes distorts their experience. Since they seldom consider that their experience of the real is anything other than reality, they can only explain the woman's version as maliciously invented. Similarly, the male anxiety that rape is easy to charge and difficult to disprove (also widely believed in the face of overwhelming evidence to the contrary) arises because rape accusations express one thing men cannot seem to control: the meaning to women of sexual encounters.

Thus do legal doctrines, incoherent or puzzling as syllogistic logic, become coherent as ideology. For example, when an accused wrongly but sincerely believes that a woman he sexually forced consented, he may have a defense of mistaken belief or fail to satisfy the mental requirement of knowingly proceeding against her will.[40] One commentator notes, discussing the conceptually similar issue of revocation of prior consent (i.e., on the issue of the conditions under which women are allowed to control access to the sexuality from one time to the next):

> Even where a woman revokes prior consent, such is the male ego that, seized of an exaggerated assessment of his sexual prowess, a man might genuinely believe her still to be consenting; resistance may be misinterpreted as enthusiastic cooperation; protestations of pain or disinclination, a spur to more sophisticated or more ardent love-making; a clear statement to stop, taken as referring to a particular intimacy rather than the entire performance.[41]

This equally vividly captures common male readings of women's indications of disinclination under all kinds of circumstances.[42] Now reconsider to what extent the man's perceptions should determine whether a rape occurred. From whose standpoint, and in whose interest, is a law that allows one person's conditioned unconsciousness to contraindicate another's experienced violation? This aspect of the rape law reflects the sex inequality of the society not only in conceiving a cognizable injury from the viewpoint of the reasonable rapist, but in affirmatively rewarding men with acquittals for not comprehending women's point of view on sexual encounters.

Whether the law calls this coerced consent or mistake of fact, the more the sexual violation of women is routine, the more beliefs equating sexuality with violation become reasonable, and the more honestly women can be defined in terms of our fuckability. It would be comparatively simple if the legal problem were limited to avoiding retroactive falsification of the accused's state of mind. Surely there are incentives to lie. But the deeper problem is the rape law's assumption that a single, objective state of affairs existed, one which merely needs to be determined by evidence, where many (maybe even most) rapes involve honest men and violated women. When the reality is split—a woman is raped but not by a rapist?—the law tends to conclude that a rape *did not happen*. To attempt to solve this by adopting the standard of reasonable belief without asking, on a substantive social basis, to whom the belief is reasonable and why—meaning, what conditions make it reasonable —is one-sided: male-sided. What is it reasonable for a man to believe concerning a woman's desire for sex when heterosexuality is compulsory? Whose subjectivity becomes the objectivity of "what happened" is a matter of social meaning; that is, it has been a matter of sexual politics. One-sidedly erasing women's violation or dissolving the presumptions into the subjectivity of either side are alternatives dictated by the terms of the object/subject split, respectively. These are alternatives that will only retrace that split until its terms are confronted as gendered to the ground.

Desirability to men is commonly supposed to be a woman's form of power. This echoes the view that consent is women's form of control over intercourse, different but equal to the custom of male initiative. Look at it: Man initiates, woman chooses. Even the ideal is not mutual. Apart from the disparate consequences of refusal, or openness of original options, this model does not envision a situation the woman controls being placed in, or choices she frames, yet the consequences are attributed to her as if the sexes began at arm's length, on equal terrain, as in the contract fiction. Ambiguous cases of consent are often archetypically referred to as "half won arguments in parked cars."[43] Why not half lost? Why isn't half enough? Why is it an argument? Why do men still want "it," feel entitled to "it," when women don't want them? That sexual expression is even framed as a matter of woman's consent, without exposing these presuppositions, is integral to gender inequality. Woman's so-called power presupposes her more fundamental powerlessness.[44]

III

The state's formal norms recapitulate the male point of view on the level of design. In Anglo-American jurisprudence, morals (value judgments) are deemed separable and separated from politics (power contests), and both from adjudication (interpretation). Neutrality, including judicial decision making that is dispassionate, impersonal, disinterested, and precedential, is considered desirable and descriptive. Courts, forums without predisposition among parties and with no interest of their own, reflect society back to itself resolved. Government of laws not men limits partiality with written constraints and tempers force with reasonable rule following. This law aspires to science: to the immanent generalization subsuming the emergent particularity, to prediction and control of social regularities and regulations, preferably codified. The formulaic "tests" of "doctrine" aspire to mechanism, classification to taxonomy. Courts intervene only in properly "factualized" disputes,[45] cognizing social conflicts as if collecting empirical data. But the demarcations between morals and politics, the personality of the judge and the judicial role, bare coercion and the rule of law,[46] tend to merge in women's experience. Relatively seamlessly they promote a dominance of men as a social group through privileging the form of power—the perspective on social life—feminist consciousness reveals as socially male. The separation of form from substance, process from policy, role from theory and practice, echoes and reechoes at each level of the regime its basic norm: objectivity.

Consider a central example. The separation of public from private is as crucial to the liberal state's claim to objectivity as its inseparability is to women's claim to subordination. Legally, it has both formal and substantive dimensions. The state considers formal, not substantive, the allocation of public matters to itself to be treated objectively, of private matters to civil society to be treated subjectively. Substantively, the private is defined as a right to "an inviolable personality,"[47] which is guaranteed by ensuring "autonomy or control over the intimacies of personal identity."[48] It is hermetic. It means that which is inaccessible to, unaccountable to, and unconstructed by anything beyond itself. Intimacy occurs in private; this is supposed to guarantee original symmetry of power. Injuries arise in violating the private sphere, not within and by and because of it. Private means consent can be presumed unless disproved. To contain a systematic inequality contradicts the notion itself. But feminist consciousness has exploded the private. For women, the measure of the intimacy has been the measure of the oppression. To see the personal as political means to see the private as public. On this level, women have no privacy to lose or to guarantee. We are not inviolable. Our sexuality, meaning gender identity, is not only violable, it *is* (hence we are) our violation. Privacy is everything women as women have never been allowed to be or to have; at the same time the private is everything women have been equated with and defined in terms of *men's* ability to have. To confront the fact that we have no privacy is to confront our private degradation as the public order. To fail to recognize this place of the private in women's subordination by seeking protection behind a right to that privacy is thus to be cut off from collective verification and state support in the same act.[49] The very place (home, body), relations (sexual), activities (intercourse and reproduction), and feelings (intimacy, selfhood) that feminism finds central to women's subjection form the core of privacy doctrine. But when women are segregated in private, one at a time, a law of privacy will tend to protect the right of men "to be let alone,"[50] to oppress us one at a time. A law of the private, in a state that mirrors such a society, will translate the traditional values of the private sphere into individual women's right to privacy, subordinating women's collective needs to the imperatives of male supremacy.[51] It will keep some men out of the bedrooms of other men.

Liberalism converges with the left at this edge of the feminist critique of male power. Herbert Marcuse speaks of "philosophies which are 'political' in the widest sense—affecting society as a whole, demonstrably transcending the sphere of privacy."[52] This does and does not describe the feminist political: "Women both have and have not had a common world."[53] Isolation in the home and intimate degradation, women share. The private sphere, which confines and separates us, is therefore a political sphere, a common ground of our inequality. In feminist translation, the private is a sphere of battery, marital rape, and women's exploited labor; of the central social institutions whereby women are deprived of (as men are granted) identity, autonomy, control, and self-determination; and of the primary activity through which male supremacy is expressed and enforced. Rather than transcending the private as a predicate to politics, feminism politicizes it. For women, the private necessarily transcends the private. If the most private also most "affects society as a whole," the separation between public and private collapses as anything other than potent ideology. The failure of marxism adequately to address intimacy on the one hand, government on the other, is the same failure as the indistinguishability between marxism and liberalism on questions of sexual politics.

Interpreting further areas of law, a feminist theory of the state will reveal that the idealism of liberalism and the materialism of the left have come to much the same for women. Liberal jurisprudence that the law should reflect society and left jurisprudence that all law does or can do is reflect existing social relations will emerge as two guises of objectivist epistemology. If objectivity is the epistemological stance of which women's sexual objectification is the social process, its imposition the paradigm of power in the male form, then the state will appear most relentless in imposing the male point of view when it comes closest to achieving its highest formal criterion of distanced perspectivity. When it is most ruthlessly neutral, it will be most male; when it is most sex blind, it will be most blind to the sex of the standard being applied. When it most closely conforms to precedent, to "facts," to legislative intent, it will most closely enforce socially male norms and most thoroughly preclude questioning their content as having a point of view at all. Abstract rights will authorize the male experience of the world. The liberal view that law is society's text, its rational mind, expresses this in a normative mode; the traditional left view that the state, and with it the law, is superstructural or epiphenomenal expresses it in an empirical mode. Both rationalize male power by presuming that it does not exist, that equality between the sexes (room for marginal corrections conceded) is society's basic norm and fundamental description. Only feminism grasps the extent to which the opposite is true: that antifeminism is as normative as it is empirical. Once masculinity appears as a specific position, not just as the way things are, its judgments will be revealed in process and procedure, as well as adjudication and legislation. Perhaps the objectivity of the liberal state has made it appear "autonomous of class." Including, but beyond, the bourgeois in liberal legalism, lies what is male about it. However autonomous of class the liberal state may appear, it is not autonomous of sex. Justice will require change, not reflection—a new jurisprudence, a new relation between life and law.

NOTES

1. Much has been made of the distinction between sex and gender. Sex is thought the more biological, gender the more social. The relation of each to sexuality varies. Since I believe sexuality is fundamental to gender and fundamentally social, and that biology is its social meaning in the system of sex inequality, which is a social and political system that does not rest independently on biological differences in any respect, the sex/gender distinction looks like a nature/culture distinction. I use sex and gender relatively interchangeably. *Sexual Harassment of Working Women: A Case of Sex Discrimination* (New Haven: Yale University Press, 1979).

2. This analysis is developed in Part 1. I assume here your acquaintance with the arguments there.

3. Male is a social and political concept, not a biological attribute. As I use it, it has *nothing whatever* to do with inherency, preexistence, nature, inevitability, or body as such. It is more epistemological than ontological, undercutting the distinction itself, given male power to conform being with perspective. The perspective from the male standpoint is not always each man's opinion, although most men adhere to it, unconsciously and without considering it a point of view, as much because it makes sense of their experience (the male experience) as because it is in their interest. It is rational for them. A few men reject it; they pay. Because it is the dominant point of view and defines rationality, women are pushed to see reality in its terms, although this denies their vantage point as women in that it contradicts (at least some of) their lived experience. Women who adopt the male standpoint are passing, epistemologically speaking. This is not uncommon and is rewarded. The intractability of maleness as a form of dominance suggests that social constructs, although they flow from human agency, can be less plastic than nature has proven to be. If experience trying to do so is any guide, it may be easier to change biology than society.

4. In the Bible, to know a woman is to have sex with her. You acquire carnal knowledge. Many scholarly metaphors elaborate the theme of violating boundaries to appropriate from inside to carry off in usable form: "a penetrating observation," "an incisive analysis," "piercing the veil." Mary Ellman writes, "The male mind . . . is assumed to function primarily like a penis. Its fundamental character is seen to be aggression,and this quality is held essential to the highest or best working of the intellect" *(Thinking about women* [New York: Harcourt Brace Jovanovich, 1968], p. 23). Feminists are beginning to understand that to know has meant to fuck. See Evelyn Fox Keller, "Gender and Science," *Psychoanalysis and Contemporary Thought* 1, no. 3 (1978): 409-33, esp. 413; and Helen Roberts, ed. *Doing Feminist Research* (London: Routledge & Kegan Paul, 1981). The term "to fuck" uniquely captures my meaning because it refers to sexual activity without distinguishing rape from intercourse. At least since Plato's cave, visual metaphors for knowing have been central to Western theories of knowledge, the visual sense prioritized as a mode of verification. The relationship between visual appropriation and objectification is now only beginning to be explored. "The knowledge gained through still photographs will always be . . . a semblance of knowledge, a semblance of wisdom, as the act of taking pictures is a semblance of wisdom, a semblance of rape. The very muteness of what is, hypothetically, comprehensible in photographs is what constitutes their attraction and provocativeness" (Susan Sontag, *On Photography* [New York: Farrar, Straus & Giroux, 1980], p. 24).

5. Feminism aspires to represent the experience of all women as women see it, yet criticizes antifeminism and misogyny, including when it appears in female form. This tension is compressed in the epistemic term of art "the standpoint of all women." We are barely beginning to unpack it. Not all women agree with the feminist account of women's situation, nor do all feminists agree with any single rendition of feminism. Authority of interpretation—the claim to speak as a woman—thus becomes methodologically complex and politically crucial for the same reasons. Consider the accounts of their own experience given by right-wing women and lesbian sadomasochists. How can patriarchy be diminishing to women when women embrace and defend their place in it? How can dominance and submission be violating to women when women eroticize it? Now what is the point of view of the experience of all women? Most responses in the name of feminism,

stated in terms of method, either (1) simply regard some women's views as "false consciousness," or (2) embrace any version of women's experience that a biological female claims as her own. The first approach treats some women's views as unconscious conditioned reflections of their oppression, complicitous in it. Just as science devalues experience in the process of uncovering its roots, this approach criticizes the substance of a view because it can be accounted for by its determinants. But if both feminism and antifeminism are responses to the condition of women, how is feminism exempt from devalidation by the same account? That feminism is critical, and antifeminism is not, is not enough, because the question is the basis on which we know something is one or the other when women, all of whom share the condition of women, disagree. The false consciousness approach begs this question by taking women's self-reflections as evidence of their stake in their own oppression, when the women whose self-reflections are at issue question whether their condition is oppressed at all. The second response proceeds as if women are free. Or, at least, as if we have considerable latitude to make, or to choose, the meanings if not the determinations of our situation. Or, that the least feminism can do, since it claims to see the world through women's eyes, is to validate the interpretations women choose. Both responses arise because of the unwillingness, central to feminism, to dismiss some women as simply deluded while granting other women the ability to see the truth. These two resolutions echo the object/subject split: objectivity (my consciousness is true, yours false, never mind why) or subjectivity (I know I am right because it feels right to me, never mind why). Thus is determinism answered with transcendence, traditional marxism with traditional liberalism, dogmatism with tolerance. The first approach claims authority on the basis of its lack of involvement, asserting its view independent of whether the described concurs—sometimes because its does not. It also has no account, other than its alleged lack of involvement, of its own ability to provide such an account. How can some women see the truth and other women not? The second approach claims authority on the basis of its involvement. It has no account for different interpretations of the same experience or any way of choosing among conflicting ones, including those between women and men. It tends to assume that women, as we are, have power and are free in exactly the ways feminism, substantively, has found we are not. Thus, the first approach is one-sidedly outside when there is no outside, the second one-sidedly inside when someone (probably a woman) is inside everything, including every facet of sexism, racism, and so on. So our problem is this: The false consciousness approach cannot explain experience as it is experienced by those who experience it. The alternative can only reiterate the terms of that experience. This is only one way in which the object/subject split is fatal to the feminist enterprise.

6. To stress: The feminist criticism is not that the objective stance fails to be truly objective because it has social content, all the better to exorcise that content in the pursuit of the more truly point-of-viewless viewpoint. The criticism is that objectivity is largely accurate to its/the/a world, which world is criticized, and that it becomes more accurate as the power it represents and extends becomes more total. Analogous criticisms have arisen in the natural sciences, without being seen as threatening to the "science of society" project, or calling into question that project's tacit equation between natural and social objects of knowledge. What if we extend Heisenberg's uncertainty principle to social theory? (Werner Heisenberg, *The Physical Principles of the Quantum Theory* [Chicago: University of Chicago Press, 1930], pp. 4, 20, 62-65). What of the axiomatic method after Gödel's proof? (See Ernest Nagel and James R. Newman, *Gödel's Proof* [New York: New York University Press, 1958]).

7. Andrea Dworkin helped me express this.

8. I mean to imply that contemporary feminism that is not methodologically post-marxist is not radical, hence not feminist on this level. For example, to the extent Mary Daly's *Gyn/Ecology: The Meta ethics of Radical Feminism* (Boston: Beacon Press, 1978) is idealist in method—meaning that the subordination of women is an idea such that to think it differently is to change it—it is formally liberal no matter how extreme or insightful. To the extent Shulamith Firestone's analysis (*The Dialectic of Sex: The Case for Feminist Revolution* [New York: William Morrow, 1972]) rests on a naturalist definition of gender, holding that women are oppressed by our bodies rather than their social meaning, her radicalism, hence her feminism, is qualified. Susan Griffin's *Pornography and Silence: Culture's Revolt against Nature* (San Francisco: Harper & Row, 1982) is classically liberal in all formal respects including, for instance, the treatment of pornography and eros as a distinction that is fundamentally psychological rather than interested, more deeply a matter of good and bad (morality) than of power and powerlessness (politics). Andrea Dworkin's work, esp. *Pornography: Men Possessing Women* (New York: Perigee Books, 1981), and Adrienne Rich's poetry and essays, exemplify feminism as a methodological departure. This feminism seeks to define and pursue women's interest as the fate of all women bound together. It seeks to extract the truth of women's commonalities out of the lie that all women are the same. If whatever a given society defines as sexual defines gender, and if gender means the subordination of women to men, woman means—is not qualified or undercut by—the uniqueness of each woman and the specificity of race, class, time, and place. In this sense, lesbian feminism, the feminism of women of color, and socialist feminism are converging in a feminist politics of sexuality, race, and class, with a left to right spectrum of its own. This politics is struggling for a practice of unity that does not depend upon sameness without dissolving into empty tolerance, including tolerance of all it exists to change whenever that appears embodied in one of us. A new community begins here. As critique, women's communality describes a fact of male supremacy, of sex "in itself" no woman escapes the meaning of being a woman within a gendered social system, and sex inequality is not only pervasive but may be universal (in the sense of never having not been in some form) although "intelligible only in . . . locally specific forms" (M. A. Rosaldo, "The Use and Abuse of Anthropology: Reflections on Feminism and Cross-cultural Understanding," *Signs: Journal of Women in Culture and Society* 5, no. 3 [Spring 1980]: 389-417, 417). For women to become a sex "for ourselves" moves community to the level of vision.

9. See Karl Klare, "Law-Making as Praxis," *Telos* 12, no. 2 (Summer 1979): 123-35; Judith Shklar, *Legalism* (Cambridge, Mass.: Harvard University Press, 1964). To examine law as state is not to decide that all relevant state behavior occurs in legal texts. I do think that legal decisions expose power on the level of legitimizing rationale, and that law, as words in power, is central in the social erection of the liberal state.

10. Karl Marx, *Capital, Selected Works* 3 vols. (Moscow: Progress Publishers, 1969), 2:120, 130-40; *The German Ideology* (New York: International Publishers, 1972), pp. 48-52; *Introduction to Critique of Hegel's Philosophy of Right,* ed. Joseph O'Malley, trans. Annette Jolin (Cambridge: Cambridge University Press, 1970), p. 139; Marx to P. V. Annenkov, 1846, in *The Poverty of Philosophy* (New York: International Publishers, 1963), pp. 179-93, 191.

11. I am criticizing Engels's assumptions abut sexuality and women's place, and his empiricist method, and suggesting that the two are linked. Friedrich Engels, *Origin of the Family, Private Property and the State* (New York: International Publishers, 1942).

12. Representative works include Fred Block, "The Ruling Class Does Not Rule: Notes on the Marxist Theory of the State," *Socialist Revolution* 33 (May-June 1977): 6-28; Ralph Miliband, *The State in Capitalist Society* (New York: Basic Books, 1969); Nicos Poulantzas, *Classes in Contemporary Capitalism* (London: New Left Books, 1975), and *Political Power and Social Classes* (London: New Left Books, 1975); Goran Therborn, *What Does the Ruling Class Do When It Rules?* (London: New Left Books, 1975); Norberto Bobbio, "Is There a Marxist Theory of the State?" *Telos 35 (Spring 1978): 5-16.* Theda Skocpol, *States and Social Revolution: A Comparative Analysis of France, Russia and China* (Cambridge: Cambridge University Press, 1979), pp. 24-33, ably reviews much of this literature. Applications to law include Isaac Balbus, "Commodity Form and Legal Form: An Essay on the 'Relative Autonomy' of the Law," *Law and Society Review* 11, no. 3 (Winter 1977): 571-88; Mark Tushnet, "A Marxist Analysis of American Law," *Marxist Perspectives* 1, no. 1 (Spring 1978): 96-116; and Klare (n. 9 above).

13. Poulantzas's formulation follows Althusser. (Louis Althusser and Etienne Balibar, *Reading Capital,* trans. Ben Brewster [London: New Left Books, 1968]). For Poulantzas, the "specific autonomy which is characteristic of the function of the state . . . is the basis of the specificity of the political" (*Political Power and Social Classes* [n. 12 above], pp. 14, 46)—whatever that means. On structural causality between class and state, see p. 14.

14. See Ernesto Laclau's similar criticism of Miliband in *Politics and Ideology in Marxist Theory* (London: New Left Books, 1977), p. 65.

15. See Susan Rae Peterson, "Coercion and Rape: The State as a Male Protection Racket," in *Feminism and Philosophy,* ed. Mary Vetterling-Braggin, Frederick A. Elliston, and Jane English (Totowa, NJ: Littlefield, Adams & Co., 1977), pp. 360-71; Janet Rifkin, "Toward a Theory of Law Patriarchy," *Harvard Women's Law Journal* 3 (Spring 1980): 83-92.

16. Johnnie Tillmon, "Welfare Is a Women's Issue," *Liberation News Service* (February 26, 1972), in *America's Working Women: A Documentary History, 1600 to the Present,* ed. Rosalyn Baxandall, Linda Gordon, and Susan Reverby (New York: Vintage Books, 1976), pp. 357-358.

17. Laurence Tribe, "Constitution as Point of View" (Harvard Law School, Cambridge, Mass., 1982, mimeographed), p. 13.

18. Madeleine Gagnon, "Body I," in *New French Feminisms,* ed. Elaine Marks and Isabelle de Courtivron (Amherst: University of Massachusetts Press, 1980), p. 180. Turns on the mirroring trope, which I see as metaphoric analyses of the epistemological/political dimension of objectification, are ubiquitous in feminist writing: "Into the room of the dressing where the walls are covered with mirrors. Where mirrors are like eyes of men, and the women reflect the judgments of mirrors" (Susan Griffin, *Woman and Nature: The Roaring Inside Her* [New York: Harper & Row, 1979] p. 155). See also Mary Daly, *Beyond God the Father: Toward a Philosophy of Women's Liberation* (Boston: Beacon Press, 1975), pp. 195, 197; Sheila Rowbotham, *Women's Consciousness, Man's World* (Harmondsworth: Pelican Books, 1973), pp. 26-29. "She did suffer, the witch/trying to peer round the looking/glass, she forgot/someone was in the way" (Michelene, "Reflexion," quoted in Rowbotham, p. 2). Virginia Woolf wrote the figure around ("So I reflected . . ."), noticing "the necessity that women so often are to men" of serving as a looking glass in which a man can "see himself at breakfast and at dinner at least twice the size he really is." Notice the doubled sexual/gender meaning: "Whatever may be their use in civilized societies, mirrors are essential to all violent and heroic action. That is why Napoleon and Mussolini both insist so emphatically upon the inferiority of women,

for if they were not inferior, they would cease to enlarge" (*A Room of One's Own* [New York: Harcourt, Brace & World, 1969], p. 36).

19. Space limitations made it necessary to eliminate sections on pornography, sex discrimination, and abortion. For the same reason, most supporting references, including those to case law, have been cut. The final section of this paper accordingly states the systemic implications of the analysis more tentatively than I think them, but as strongly as I felt I could, on the basis of the single substantive examination that appears here.

20. Susan Brownmiller, *Against Our Will: Men, Women and Rape* (New York: Simon & Schuster, 1976), p. 15.

21. Diana E. H. Russell, *The Politics of Rape: The Victim's Perspective* (New York: Stein & Day, 1977); Andrea Medea and Kathleen Thompson, *Against Rape* (New York: Farrar, Straus & Giroux, 1974); Lorenne M. G. Clark and Debra Lewis, *Rape: The Price of Coercive Sexuality* (Toronto: The Women's Press, 1977); Susan Griffin, "Rape: The All-American Crime," *Ramparts* (September 1971), pp. 26-35; Ti-Grace Atkinson connects rape with "the institutions of sexual intercourse" (*Amazon Odyssey: The First Collection of Writings by the Political Pioneer of the Women's Movement* [New York: Links Books, 1974], pp. 13-23); Kalamu ya Salaam, "Rape: A Radical Analysis From the African-American Perspective," in *Our Women Keep Our Skies From Falling* (New Orleans: Nkombo, 1980), pp. 25-40.

22. Racism, clearly, is everyday life. Racism in the United States, by singling out Black men for allegations of rape of white women, has helped obscure the fact that it is men who rape women, disproportionately women of color.

23. "Like other victims, I had problems with sex, after the rape. There was no way that Arthur could touch me that it didn't remind me of having been raped by this guy I never saw" (Carolyn Craven, "No More Victims: Carolyn Craven Talks About Rape, and About What Women and Men Can Do to Stop It," ed. Alison Wells [Berkeley, Calif., 1978, mimeographed]), p. 2.

24. Pamela Foa, "What's Wrong with Rape?" in Vetterling-Braggin, Elliston, and English (n. 15 above), pp. 347-59; Michael Davis, "What's So Bad about Rape?" (paper presented at the annual meeting of the Academy of Criminal Justice Sciences, Louisville, KY, March 1982).

25. "Since we would not want to say that there is anything morally wrong with sexual intercourse per se, we conclude that the wrongness of rape rests with the matter of the woman's consent" (Carolyn M. Shafer and Marilyn Frye, "Rape and Respect," in Vetterling-Braggin, Elliston, and English [n. 15 above], p. 334). "Sexual contact is not inherently harmful, insulting or provoking. Indeed, ordinarily it is something of which we are quite fond. The difference between ordinary sexual intercourse and rape is that ordinary sexual intercourse is more or less consented to while rape is not" (Davis [n. 24 above], p. 12).

26. Sec. 213.0 of the *Model Penal Code* (Official Draft and Revised Comments 1980), like most states, defines rape as sexual intercourse with a female who is not the wife of the perpetrator "with some penetration however slight." Impotency is sometimes a defense. Michigan's gender-neutral sexual assault statute includes penetration by objects (sec. 520a[h]; 520[b]). See *Model Penal Code,* annotation to sec. 213.1(d) (Official Draft and Revised Comments 1980).

27. Although it is true that men possess women and that bodies are, socially, men's things, I have not analyzed rape as men treating women like property. In the manner of many socialist-feminist adaptations of marxian categories to women's situation, that analysis short-circuits analysis of rape as male sexuality and presumes rather than develops

links between sex and class. We need to rethink sexual dimensions of property as well as property dimensions of sexuality.

28. For an excellent summary of the current state of the marital exemption, see Joanne Schulman, "State-by-State Information on Marital Rape Exemption Laws," in *Rape in Marriage,* Diana E. H. Russell (New York: Macmillan, 1982), pp. 375-81.

29. On "social interaction as an element of consent," in a voluntary social companion context, see *Model Penal Code,* sec. 213.1. "The prior *social* interaction is an indicator of consent in addition to actor's and victim's *behavioral* interaction during the commission of the offense" (Wallace Loh, "Q: What Has Reform of Rape Legislation Wrought? A: Truth in Criminal Labeling," *Journal of Social Issues 37,* no. 4 [1981]: 28-52, 47). Perhaps consent should be an affirmative defense, pleaded and proven by the defendant.

30. Pauline Bart found that women were more likely to be raped—that is, less able to stop a rape in progress—when they knew their assailant, particularly when they had a prior or current sexual relationship ("A Study of Women Who Both Were Raped and Avoided Rape," *Journal of Social Issues* 37, no. 4 [1981]:123-37, 132). See also Linda Belden, "Why Women Do Not Report Sexual Assault" (City of Portland Public Service Employment Program, Portland Women's Crisis Line, Portland, Ore., March 1979, mimeographed); Diana E. H. Russell and Nancy Howell, "The Prevalence of Rape in the United States Revisited," *Signs: Journal of Women in Culture and Society* 8, no. 4 (1983); and Menachem Amir, *Patterns in Forcible Rape* (Chicago: University of Chicago Press, 1971), pp. 229-52.

31. Answer Brief for Plaintiff-Appellee at 10, People v. Brown, 632 P.2d 1025 (Colo. 1981).

32. Brown, 632 P.2d at 1027 (citing Comment, "Rape and Battery between Husband and Wife," *Stanford Law Review* 6 [1954]: 719-28, 719, 725).

33. Brownmiller (n. 20 above), pp. 8, 196, 400-407, 427-36.

34. See Carol Pateman, "Women and Consent," *Political Theory* 8, no. 2 (May 1980): 149-68.

35. Brownmiller (n. 20 above), p. 5.

36. Shafer and Frye (n. 25 above), p. 334. Battery of wives has been legally separated from marital rape not because assault by a man's fist is so different from assault by a penis. Both seem clearly violent. I am suggesting that both are also sexual. Assaults are often precipitated by women's noncompliance with gender requirements. See R. Emerson Dobash and Russell Dobash, *Violence against Wives: A Case against the Patriarchy* (New York: Free Press, 1979), pp. 14-20. Nearly all incidents occur in the home, most in the kitchen or bedroom. Most murdered women are killed by their husbands, most in the bedroom. The battery cycle accords with the rhythm of heterosexual sex (see Leonore Walker, *The Battered Woman* [New York: Harper & Row Publishers, 1979], pp. 19-20). The rhythm of lesbian S/M appears similar (Samois, ed. *Coming to Power* [Palo Alto, Calif.: Up Press, 1981]). Perhaps most interchanges between genders, but especially violent ones, make sense in sexual terms. However, the larger issue for the relation between sexuality and gender, hence sexuality and violence generally, including both war and violence against women, is: What *is* heterosexuality? If it is the erotization of dominance and submission, altering the participants' gender is comparatively incidental. If it is males over females, gender matters independently. Since I see heterosexuality as the fusion of the two, but with gender a social outcome (such that the acted upon is feminized, is the "girl" regardless of sex, the actor correspondingly masculinized), battery appears sexual on a deeper level. In baldest terms, sexuality is violent, so violence is sexual,

violence against women doubly so. If this is so, wives are beaten as well as raped, *as women*—as the acted upon, as gender, meaning sexual, objects. It further follows that all acts *by anyone* which treat a woman according to her object label "woman" are *sexual* acts. The extent to which sexual acts are acts of objectification remains a question of our account of our freedom to make our own meanings. It is clear, at least, that it is centering sexuality upon genitality that distinguishes battery from rape at exactly the juncture that both the law, and seeing rape as violence, not sex, does.

37. Even when nonconsent is not a legal element of the offense (as in Michigan), juries tend to infer rape from evidence of force or resistance.

38. This is apparently true of undetected as well as convicted rapists. Samuel David Smithyman's sample, composed largely of the former, contained self-selected respondents to his ad, which read: "Are you a rapist? Researchers Interviewing Anonymously by Phone to Protect Your Identity. Call . . ." Presumably those who chose to call defined their acts as rapes, at least at the time of responding ("The Undetected Rapist" [Ph.D. diss., Claremont Graduate School, 1978], pp. 54-60, 63-76, 80-90, 97-107).

39. "Probably the single most used cry of rapist to victim is 'You bitch . . . slut . . . you know you want it. You *all* want it' and afterward, 'There now, you really enjoyed it, didn't you?'" (Nancy Gager and Cathleen Schurr, *Sexual Assault: Confronting Rape in America* [New York: Grosset & Dunlap, 1976], p. 244).

40. See Director of Public Prosecutions v. Morgan, 2411 E.R.H.L. 347 (1975); Pappajohn v. The Queen, 11 D.L.R. 3d 1 (1980); People v. Mayberry, 15 Cal. 3d 143, 542 P.2d 1337 (1975).

41. Richard H. S. Tur, "Rape: Reasonableness and Time," *Oxford Journal of Legal Studies* 3 (Winter 1981): 432-41, 441. Tur, in the context of the Morgan and Pappajohn cases, says the "law ought not to be astute to equate wickedness and wishful, albeit mistaken, thinking" (p. 437). In feminist analysis, a rape is not an isolated or individual or moral transgression but a terrorist act within a systematic context of group subjection, like lynching.

42. See Silke Volgelmann-Sine et al., "Sex Differences in Feelings Attributed to a Woman in Situations Involving Coercion and Sexual Advances," *Journal of Personality* 47, no. 3 (September 1979): 420-31, esp. 429-30.

43. Note, "Forcible and Statutory Rape: An Exploration of the Operation and Objectives of the Consent Standard," *Yale Law Journal* 62 (1952): 55-56.

44. A similar analysis of sexual harassment suggests that women have such "power" only so long as we behave according to male definitions of female desirability, that is, only so long as we accede the definition of our sexuality (hence, ourselves, as gender female) to male terms. We have this power only so long as we remain powerless.

45. Peter Gabel, "Reification in Legal Reasoning" (New College Law School, San Francisco, 1980, mimeographed), p. 3.

46. Rawls's "original position," for instance, is a version of my objective standpoint (John Rawls, *A Theory of Justice* [Cambridge, Mass.: Harvard University Press, 1971]). Not only apologists for the liberal state, but also some of its most trenchant critics, see a real distinction between the rule of law and absolute arbitrary force. See E. P. Thompson, *Whigs and Hunters: The Origin of the Black Act* (New York: Pantheon Books, 1975), pp. 258-269. Douglas Hay argues that making and enforcing certain acts as illegal reinforces a structure of subordination ("Property, Authority, and the Criminal Law," in *Albion's Fatal Tree: Crime and Society in Eighteenth Century England,* ed. D. Hay et al. [New York: Pantheon Books, 1975], pp. 17-31). Michael D. A. Freeman ("Violence

against Women: Does the Legal System Provide Solutions or Itself Constitute the Problem?" [Madison, Wis., 1980, mimeographed], p. 12, n. 161) applies this argument to domestic battery of women. Here I extend it to women's situation as a whole, without suggesting that the analysis can *end* there.

47. S. D. Warren and L. D. Brandeis, "The Right to Privacy," *Harvard Law Review* 12, no. 2 (Spring 1977): 236.

48. Tom Gerety, "Redefining Privacy." *Harvard Civil Rights—Civil Liberties Law Review* 12, no. 2 (Spring 1977), 236.

49. Harris v. McRae, 448 U. S. 287 (190), which holds that withholding public funds for abortions does not violate the federal constitutional right to privacy, illustrates. See Zillah Eisentein, *The Radical Future of Liberal Feminism* (New York: Longman, 1971), p. 240.

50. Robeson v. Rochester Folding Box Co. 171 NY 538 (1902). Cooley, *Torts,* sec. 135, 4th ed. (Chicago: Callaghan, 1932).

51. This argument learned a lot from Tom Grey's article, "Eros, Civilization and the Burger Court," *Law and Contemporary Problems* 43, no. 3 (Summer 1980): 83-99.

52. Herbert Marcuse, "Repressive Tolerance," in *A Critique of Pure Tolerance,* ed. Robert Paul Wolff, Barrington Moore, Jr., and Herbert Marcuse (Boston: Beacon Press, 1965), pp. 81-117, esp. p. 91.

53. Adrienne Rich, "Conditions for Work: The Common World of Women," in *Working It Out: Twenty-three Women Writers, Artists, Scientists, and Scholars Talk about Their Lives and Work,* ed. Sara Ruddick and Pamela Daniels (New York: Pantheon Books, 1977), esp. pp. xiv-xxiv, p. xiv.

Part IV

Research Implications of Experiencing and Studying Violence Against Women

Introduction

CONTRIBUTIONS OF FEMINIST THEORY AND METHODOLOGY

Feminist analyses succeeded in politicizing the abuse of women and undermining the conventional wisdom that defined the abuse of women as a private matter, interpersonal relationships gone awry. Challenging this bias toward interpersonal definitions of such abuse, feminists depicted such behavior as criminal. Advocates succeeded in making sexual harassment, rape, incest, battery, and pornography public issues, and undercut the social supports that generally blamed women and children for being victimized. The heart of these feminist analyses was that normal men, not psychopaths, received social support for applying sanctions, including threats and abuse, to keep women in their place, subordinated at home and on the job. This powerful male bias, always asking what the victim did, has not yet been extinguished: It comes across in every debate about the innocence of the victim after an incident of sexual assault or battery.

Feminism, in academia, as in activism, had a major impact. This was strongest in social science where it fostered an enormous body of research on women. The data dramatically undermined our perspectives as social scientists, particularly our optimism about the capacity of the society to provide opportunities and progressively eliminate racial and gender discrimination. For example, the "hard data" that documented how much education was worth in future earnings was based on the experiences of White men, with most social scientists deploring the racial patterns uncovered but optimistic that educational access would resolve it. When people of color and all women are added to the tables, the system's discrimination was exposed, eroding the liberal optimism about its ability to change. Reform feminists applied a civil rights model to gender inequality, expecting that exposing gender stereotypes and discrimination would itself seriously undermine these inequities. The persistence of race and gender inequality undermines the conception of the United States as a society where rewards are based on achievement rather than on ascriptive criteria.

The most significant contributions in social science come from those who suggest viewing our social world from a different angle. Feminist theory and research offered a new paradigm for examining the experiences of women and men, and connected the private and public spheres of our social world. The insight of the secretary as "office wife" and the wife as "employee" linked the sexual division of labor at home and at work. In both settings women were cast as the helpmates, the assistants of men, and men expected and received deference in both arenas.

The research on violence against women, and particularly the understanding of violence as an issue of social control, of men's controlling women, connects women's experiences of abuse. These studies show that abusing and assaulting women is prevalent and rooted in misogyny, signifying that this violence reinforces men as a class controlling women as a class. One can conceptualize it as the linchpin of our subordination.

Despite the contributions of the work in this volume, these analyses probably will not make a strong contribution to policy at the highest levels. The principal questions that organize policy efforts are ultimately quantitative—How many? Who? Where? How bad are the consequences? How much will it cost? We know that the answers to such questions can be staggering, but we are unable to marshal reliable national estimates with which to answer them in the detail required.

Studies of violence against women fashioned in accordance with highly fundable mainstream research canons typically produce the lowest and least reliable estimates (Brush, Chapter 17). Social science in general has erased or gender-neutralized the violence women experience with such concepts as "family violence" (Kurz, Chapter 18). A major theme uniting the work presented here is that much of the research was conducted on a shoestring, and as is often the case, is rather more creative on this account. The strength of such methods lies in their efficacy for capturing subtleties of culture, context, and process that typically elude large-scale data collection efforts.

In this section, Lisa Brush and Demie Kurz criticize the conclusions and the public policy implications of such studies for failing to take feminist critics into account, that is, to recognize men's dominance of women, and the institutional supports for that dominance, as central to understanding the high incidence of battery. Brush's analysis of the data from the National Survey of Families and Households (NSFH) differentiates violent acts from injuries. It shows that although both partners commit violent acts as married couples, wives were significantly more likely to sustain injuries. This survey "reproduced the most serious failing of quantitative research on intimate violence because it did not enable researchers to investigate the context (other than disagreements) or meanings of violent acts and their outcomes for perpetrators or survivors of violence" (Brush, Chapter 17). What does it mean that men report fewer injuries to their wives than the wives apparently sustain? If denial is expected in addressing this behavior, under what circumstances would interview data be more reliable? Kurz challenges the analysis of the "family violence or spouse abuse" perspective for failing to check the findings against the data of police and hospital emergency rooms. The insights, as well as the questions raised, by the qualitative data available, should be taken into account in designing future qualitative or quantitative research.

Of course, the methods used in such large quantitative studies could be supplemented to produce richer data with greater validity, but such a strategy is labor intensive and therefore extremely expensive. It also raises hard questions about the rights of human subjects. Any proposed project that surmounts these obstacles is bound to produce bad and potentially expensive news of the sort that is increasingly unpopular in the prevailing economic and political climate.

CONSEQUENCES FOR RESEARCHERS AND ADVOCATES

Feminist methodology demands that we believe women's accounts of our lives, our lived experiences (Smith, 1987). Once women knew they would be believed, they started disclosing rape, battery, and incest. Andrea

Dworkin, herself a battered wife, wrote that she welcomed death and
yearned for prison after being severely beaten, rendered invisible by the
lack of recognition of her situation, her sense of self destroyed. Only the
perpetrator is presumed to have no free will. He can't help himself, but
why, we ask, didn't she help herself? Janet Lee found that as survivors
disclosed their experiences, "We were overwhelmed by the pervasiveness of violence, although reassured that it was not our private problem
but a public issue" (Chapter 19).

The reports of service providers in Chapters 14 (Boria et al.) and 20
(Fine) highlight the gap between feminist analyses of violence against
women and the practical, political, and ethical issues that counselors,
advocates, and teachers address. The prevalence of male violence in
women's lives and its effects are confirmed by researchers and by advocates, but Lee's experience in the classroom dramatizes the ways in which
violence permeates women's lives. Yet, most of us function by routinely
denying or discounting the dangers present in our daily lives. Thus, it
is not only structural factors that silence our widespread experience of
violation. Most of us find that working on violence unavoidably brings
fear and caution to the surface of our consciousness. This awareness
distances us from even our feminist colleagues who are struggling to
deny these social facts. This is very disturbing knowledge to walk around
with! Textbooks on gender and feminist conferences omit or minimize
the impact of violence in women's lives.

Those working with survivors (Boria et al., Chapter 14) mirror our
own experience in disclosing the toll exacted by studying and working
with violence against women and children. We are not as much fun at
parties, and some social interaction becomes strained because we cannot engage in the bantering that is normative in discussing work. And
we do not laugh at rape jokes (yes, they still make them). We are told
to lighten up. We do not. So it is understandable, albeit regrettable, that
people are not eager to become involved in systemic (rather than intra-
psychic) analyses of our vulnerability. Furthermore, because we report
primarily the harm normal men do to women, and the university, like
other institutions, has men at the top, it does not do much for our careers.
Male colleagues and students are particularly threatened by the systemic analyses, taking very personally the critical accounts of the structural supports for abuse. It's easier to isolate the messengers who bring
such bad news, just as there are attempts on campuses to isolate feminist
students as eccentric fringe groups.

THE NEED FOR A RESEARCH AGENDA

Feminist scholars who examine violence against women and children must critically view not only the mainstream research being produced but also the claims of feminist activists and leaders within the movements to stop battery and sexual assault. In doing the qualitative work that provides direct access to both abused women and advocates, Fine encourages researchers to accurately report the differences between the way abused women describe themselves, their relationships, and their experiences, and their description by advocates. Accurate research will report the contradictions found and better inform public policy than the uncritical echoing of the claims of service providers. Although Fine ably identifies the reforms feminists have accomplished on behalf of survivors of male violence, she urges feminist researchers to address the questions advocates need answered. She wants feminist analyses to be a catalyst that accelerates the social changes that would give women greater protection.

The failure of the criminal justice system to protect women led victims' advocates to press for reforms to remedy the situation. There was an assumption that other criminal assaults were taken seriously. Ferraro's analysis indicates that neither the court nor the police can get beyond the patriarchal biases of their institutions. Nor can victims escape the class, race, and ethnic barriers to equal protection under the law. Her work indicates that not only must researchers address advocates' questions, but they also must ask some of their own. As victims' services are increasingly institutionalized, they too develop vested interests, or perhaps a limited view of how women can best be assisted. For example, only a tiny proportion of battered women ever enter shelters to escape their partners' violence, so shelter advocates do not speak for all battered women. The first shelters were thought of as short-term interventions and were a means to keep families away from the batterer. But the absence of affordable housing means that many battered women and their children stay longer than 3 months in shelters. With scarce resources, do we need more housing or more shelters, or some mixture? Ferraro ably argues that women would be helped more if funds went to provide low-cost housing instead of studies of criminal justice procedures. Again, the system responds quickly to threats to its legitimacy, and to its liability, without altering the situations that increase the vulnerability of women and children (MacKinnon, Chapter 15). Some claim that battered women's shelters are barraged with requests for shelter from women who are "primarily homeless." Yet in New York State, social service workers find that one in three homeless families has a history of battery. Consequently, how important is it to screen out "primarily homeless" families? Some secondary analysis of existing records, collected by hospitals, clinics, courts, police, schools, and counseling services, might lead to shifts in public policy that could increase our understanding of the institutional impact of violence on families and other institutions.

What kinds of research would demonstrate the institutional supports for male violence? How can research expose the media's predisposition to view violent attacks on women as aberrations? Television includes rape, battery, and murder in its news coverage as well as its fictional dramas. Do these stories shock, titillate, scare, misinform, or inform viewers about violence? Who benefits from this culture's preference for psychological, rather than structural, explanations of events? Are the media images of victims and assailants stereotyped? Does the violence of pornography affect behavior? How? What images are the media defining as romantic? What are the messages in song lyrics? How have they changed in the past 50 years?

Feminist analyses identify the cultural supports for men's control of women. This is an argument distinct from concerns of personal accountability and responsibility. Shifting the focus from the victims to the perpetrators clarifies the patterns that reinforce victims being blamed for the assaults while removing culpability from violent men. Kurz reminds us of the research that focuses on the institutions outside the family where men learn to be violent, such as the military (Russell, 1989), sports (Messner, 1990), and fraternities (Martin & Hummer, Chapter 8). She also identifies the failure of legal and medical professionals to recognize their systemic support for violence against women (see also Warshaw, Chapter 10). Religious and educational institutions also contribute to the cultural climate that affirms men's and boys' rights and privileges relative to women and girls. What roles do schools continue to play in reproducing gender inequality and in the socialization that associates masculinity and femininity with aggressiveness and passiveness respectively? Our language ("Did you score?") reflects the persistence of images of conquest and antagonism between women and men. The eroticization of violence is also embedded in our language. What does it mean that a man successful with women is called a "ladykiller," that showing sexual interest in a woman is called "hitting on her," and that in many groups the most common hostile epithet is "fuck you"? Indeed one is insulted by being called a slang term for one's genitals.

For women to be safe, not only must researchers and advocates collaborate to change public policy, they must shift the focus from the perception of male violence as a psychological problem to the structural and institutional supports for violence against women. Patriarchy encourages male violence against women and children by legitimizing men's rights to control women and adults' rights to control children. Physical force and the threat of violence are routinely employed if other means of control fail. Feminist research must take into account the continuum of controls men utilize to maintain dominance. In all settings, on campuses and in communities, in government agencies and legislatures, our message is that male violence is systemic and institutionally shaped.

REFERENCES

MacKinnon, C. (1983, Summer). Feminism, marxism, method, and the state: Toward a feminist jurisprudence. *Signs, 8*(4), 635-658.
Messner, M. (1990). When bodies are weapons: Masculinity and violence in sport. *International Review of the Sociology of Sport.*
Russell, D.E.H. (1989). Sexism, violence, and the nuclear mentality. In *Exposing nuclear phallocies* (pp. 63-74). New York: Pergamon.
Smith, D. (1987). *The everyday world as problematic.* Boston: Northeastern University Press.

Feiffer

© Copyright 1989 Jules Feiffer

16 Living in Terror, Pain: Being a Battered Wife

ANDREA DWORKIN

On November 1, 1987, Joel Steinberg, a criminal defense lawyer, beat his illegally adopted daughter, Lisa, into a coma. She died November 5. Hedda Nussbaum, who had lived with Steinberg since 1976, was also in the apartment. Her face and body were deformed from his assaults, she had a gangrenous leg from his beatings. With 6-year-old Lisa lying on the bathroom floor, Steinberg went out for dinner and drinks. Nussbaum stayed behind. When Steinberg came home, he and Nussbaum freebased cocaine. Early the next day, Lisa stopped breathing and Nussbaum called 911. She was arrested with Steinberg, then given immunity for testifying against him.

Steinberg had started beating Nussbaum in 1978. In that year alone, she reportedly suffered at least 10 black eyes. In 1981, he ruptured her spleen. During this time, she worked as a children's book editor at Random House. She was fired in 1982 for missing too much work. Socially speaking, she was "disappeared."

Many say Lisa's death is Nussbaum's fault. They mourn Lisa, they blame Nussbaum. A perception is growing that Nussbaum is responsible legally and morally for the death of Lisa Steinberg.

I don't think Nussbaum is "innocent." I don't know any innocent adult women; life is harder than that for everyone. But adult women who have been battered are especially not innocent. Battery is a forced descent into hell and you don't get by in hell by moral goodness. You disintegrate. You don't survive as a discrete personality with a sense of right and wrong. You live in a world of pain, in isolation, on the verge of death, in terror; and when you get numb enough not to care whether

---

© Copyright 1989 by Andrea Dworkin. Originally published in the *Los Angles Times*.

you live or die you are experiencing the only grace God is going to send your way. Drugs help.

I was battered when I was married and there are some things I wish people would understand. I thought things had changed but it is clear from the story of Hedda Nussbaum that nothing has.

Your neighbors hear you screaming. They do nothing. The next day they look through you. If you scream for years they will look through you for years. Your neighbors, friends, and family see the bruises and injuries—and do nothing. They will not intercede. They send you back. They say it's your fault or you like it or they deny it is happening. Your family believes you belong with your husband.

If you scream and no one helps and no one acknowledges it and people look right through you, you begin to feel you don't exist. If you existed and you screamed, someone would help you. If you existed and were visibly injured, someone would help you. If you existed and asked for help in escaping, someone would help you.

When you go to the doctor or to the hospital because you are injured and they don't listen or help you or they give you tranquilizers or threaten to commit you because they say you are disoriented, paranoid, you begin to believe that he can hurt you as much as he wants and no one will help you. When the police refuse to help you, you begin to believe that he can hurt you or kill you and it will not matter because you do not exist.

You become unable to use language because it stops meaning anything. If you try to say you have been hurt and by whom and you point to visible injuries and are treated as if you made it up or as if it doesn't matter or as if it is your fault or as if you are worthless, you become afraid to say anything. You cannot talk to anyone because they will not help you and if you do talk, the man who is battering you will hurt you more. Once you lose language, your isolation is absolute.

Eventually I waited to die. I wanted to die. I hoped the next beating would kill me. When I would come to after being beaten unconscious, the first feeling I had was a sorrow that I was alive.

I would ask God to let me die now. My breasts were burned with lit cigarettes. My husband beat my legs with a wood beam so that I couldn't walk. I was present when he did immoral things to other people. When he hurt other people, I didn't help them. Nussbaum's guilt is not foreign to me.

A junkie said he would give me a ticket to far away and $1,000 if I would carry a briefcase through customs. I said I would. I knew it had heroin in it. I kept hoping I would be caught and sent to jail because in jail he couldn't beat me.

I had been sexually abused in the Women's House of Detention in New York City (arrested for an anti-Vietnam War demonstration) so I didn't have the idea that jail was a friendly place. I just hoped I would get 5 years and for 5 years I could sit in a jail cell and not be hit by him. In the end the junkie didn't give me the briefcase to carry, so I didn't get the $1,000. He did kindly give me the ticket. I stole the money I needed. Escape is heroic, isn't it?

I've been living with a kind and gentle man I love for the last 15 years. For 8 of those years, I would wake up screaming in blind terror, not knowing who I was, where I was, who he was, cowering and shaking. I'm more at peace now, but I've refused until recently to have my books published in the country where my former husband lives, and I've refused important professional invitations to go there. Once I went there in secret for 4 days to try to face it down. I couldn't stop trembling and sweating. I could barely breathe. There still isn't a day when I don't feel fear that I will see him and he will hurt me.

Death looks different to a woman who has been battered. It seems not nearly so cruel as life. I'm upset by the phony mourning for Lisa Steinberg—the hypocritical sentimentality of a society that would not really mind her being beaten to death once she was an adult.

If Lisa hadn't died, she would be on West 10th Street being tortured—now. Why was it that we wanted her to live? So that when the child became a woman and then was raped or beaten or prostituted we could look right through her? It's bad to hit a girl before she's of age. It's bad to torture a girl before she's of age. Then she's of age and, well, it isn't so bad, because she wants it, she likes it, she chose it.

Why is it all right to hurt adult women? Those who love children but don't think adult women deserve much precisely because we are not innocent—we are used and compromised and culpable—should try to remember this: The only way to have helped Lisa Steinberg was to have helped Nussbaum. But to do it, you would have had to care that an adult woman was being hurt—care enough to rescue her.

There was a little boy there too, Mitchell, 17 months old, tied up and covered in feces. And the only way to have spared him was to rescue Hedda. Now he has been tortured and he did not die. What kind of man will he grow up to be? I wish there was a way to take the hurt from him. There isn't. Is there a way to stop him from becoming a batterer? Is there?

17 Violent Acts and Injurious Outcomes in Married Couples: Methodological Issues in the National Survey of Families and Households

LISA D. BRUSH
University of Wisconsin—Madison

In this chapter, I present the results of a study of violence and injury in married couples. The first section covers feminist and nonfeminist approaches to violence in married couples. The second section presents an empirical dispute between the two approaches. The third section introduces the data set (the National Survey of Families and Households [NSFH]) and delineates the research design used to rebut the "battered husband syndrome" reported by previous researchers. The fourth section presents the findings of a multivariate log-linear analysis of the data on violent acts and injuries in the 5,474 married couples in the

AUTHOR'S NOTE: The National Survey of Families and Households was funded by a grant (HD21009) from the Center for Population Research at the National Institute of Child Health and Human Development. The survey was designed and carried out at the Center for Demography and Ecology at the University of Wisconsin—Madison under the direction of Larry Bumpass and James Sweet. The field work was done by the Institute for Survey Research at Temple University. The author acknowledges the support of Julia Adams, Hank Bromley, Larry Bumpass, Myra Marx Ferree, Elaine Fielding, Aldi Hagenaars, Nathan Janusz, Mary Klobucar, Judith Lorber, Lynn Magdol, Wendy Manning, Sara McLanahan, Patricia Miller, Beth Reninger, Laura Sanchez, Daniel Saunders, Judith Seltzer, James Sweet, and Elizabeth Thomson. Although this chapter would have been impossible without them, none of the people acknowledged above is responsible for errors of commission or omission remaining in the analysis or discussion.

NSFH. The chapter concludes with a discussion of the problems of using NSFH-type survey data to study intimate violence.

PARADIGMS

Researchers interested in intimate violence deploy two main frameworks in their investigations. One group of researchers conduct their inquiries and present their results in the context of "family systems." Researchers like Straus and his collaborators view violent acts in married couples as a specific instance of the violence endemic to society, which they deplore. Their research has contributed to our understanding of the household as a dangerously violent place for many people and has pioneered the use of surveys to gather data on domestic violence. Methodologically, these researchers are primarily concerned with generating reliable measures of the incidence of violent acts. Researchers use variants of Straus's Conflict Tactics Scale (CTS) to measure the frequency with which respondents report a continuum of confrontational tactics, such as using reason, bringing in someone else to support a position, shouting, hitting, and threatening with a weapon (e.g., Gelles & Straus, 1988; Straus, 1987; Straus & Gelles, 1986; Straus, Gelles, & Steinmetz, 1980).

According to feminist critics of this approach, the measures of violence in Straus's CTS are inadequate to the task of describing or analyzing intimate violence because they confound acts with outcomes and lump together settings and persons. A family systems approach, critics claim, overlooks important gendered variations in norms, legitimation, and above all, power. A man's striking a woman has different effects, consequences, and meanings than a woman's striking a man, these feminists hold, which the universalizing effect of the family systems approach obscures. In the family systems paradigm, the vital question of self-defense and the context of violent acts goes unexplored, women's actions are misinterpreted and misrepresented, and the dynamics of domestic violence are misunderstood (Breines & Gordon, 1983; Dobash & Dobash, 1979; Kurz, 1989; Saunders, 1988a, 1988b).

Some researchers and activists combine the concern with power dynamics and woman abuse from the feminist approach and the concern with domestic violence in general from the more universalistic family systems perspective. These investigators analyze abuse of an intimate partner ("battering") as a social relation. They focus on relationships of domination rather than individual acts of violence. According to this approach, although acts of violence may be mutual, power relations are not; it is impossible to be dominant and subordinate in the same relationship simultaneously (Card, 1988). This analysis recognizes the prevalence of violence in society and women's own violence. At the same time, it emphasizes women's definition and analysis of their experiences and promotes a feminist critique of intimacy, power, and safety. In particular, Hart's work (1986) on battered lesbians indicates that there is more to woman abuse than gender issues and suggests that researchers must be clearer about what questions, data, and analysis advance understanding of the complex and painful issue of violence between intimate partners.

AN EMPIRICAL DISPUTE

A long-standing empirical dispute in violence research involves quantitative comparisons of reports of violent acts by husbands and wives. Straus et al. (1980) reported that 12.1 percent of male and 11.6 percent of female respondents reported violent acts toward their partners during the course of a conflict in the year covered by their survey of 2,143 opposite-gender couples. An update of these results by Straus and Gelles (1986) showed that the overall rate of husband-to-wife violence was 11.3 percent and the overall rate of wife-to-husband violence was 12.1 percent in 1985. The differences between the two periods were not statistically significant, nor were the differences between the reported rates of husbands' violence toward wives and wives' violence toward husbands in either period. Steinmetz (1978; see also Steinmetz & Lucca, 1988) cited evidence from the original survey and other sources to support her claim that women's violence toward their partners constituted a "battered husband syndrome." Her results continue to be cited by men's rights groups lobbying for custody, child support, and shelter reforms (Ansberry, 1988; Fathers for Equal Rights Organization, 1988; McNeely & Robinson-Simpson, 1987). In part because they were appropriated by antifeminist groups, the findings stirred controversy, despite disclaimers attached to the report and subsequent reappraisals by at least one of the principal investigators (Straus, 1987).

Many researchers questioned the methods and assumptions behind Steinmetz's initial report of a "battered husband syndrome." Their comments fell into three categories. The earliest critics claimed that Steinmetz distorted her research findings and fabricated her claim from improperly reported data (Pleck, Pleck, Grossman, & Bart, 1978). A second group concentrated on extending the analysis of data similar to that used by Steinmetz in ways that temper the potentially antifeminist implications of Steinmetz's results (e.g., Wendt, 1986). A third group, made up primarily of feminist critics, specifically questioned the focus on violent acts instead of on the outcomes of those acts (Breines & Gordon, 1983; Dobash & Dobash, 1979).

In an effort to resolve the debate over the "battered husband syndrome," this study used quantitative data from a random national survey to look not only at the incidence of acts of violence but also at the incidence of injurious outcomes of those violent acts. In this chapter, I report the analysis of data collected in the NSFH. The analysis replicated the finding of no significant difference between men and women in committing violent acts but refuted the "battered husband syndrome" by showing that women were more likely to be hurt than men were, even in situations in which both partners were reported as being violent.

RESEARCH DESIGN

Data

The NSFH was a national, multistage, area probability sample survey of the U.S. population of persons aged 19 and older, living in households. Respondents were interviewed in either English or Spanish. Data were collected in face-to-face interviews over a 14-month period ending in May 1988. The survey included a cross-section sample of 9,643 households plus a double sampling of blacks, Puerto Ricans, Mexican Americans, single-parent families, families with stepchildren, cohabiting couples, and recently married couples. The total sample (main plus oversample) consisted of 13,017 primary respondents (for details on sampling method, oversample, interviewer training, and survey content and development, see Sweet, Bumpass, & Call, 1988). A self-enumerated section of the questionnaire posed questions about couple relationships, including violence. In an effort to produce figures at least roughly comparable to previous surveys, the analysis was limited to married primary respondents living with a spouse (unweighted total $N=5,474$) in the main and oversamples.

The self-enumerated portion of the questionnaire included a section on how couples handle disagreements, with questions about the frequency with which disagreements "become physical" and result in the respondent or partner (or both) acting violently and being hurt. The questionnaire asked specifically if the respondent or partner (or both) was hurt, not if one or the other of them had to seek medical attention or call the police. Thus help-seeking behavior was not confounded with injuries (this has been a consistent problem in violence research; see, e.g., Gelles & Straus, 1985, p. 14). For the questions about violent acts, the time frame was "during the past year." For the questions about injury, the time frame was "ever [in the current relationship]." The response rate on the questions of interest was about 90 percent for both male and female respondents.

Variables

Four questions from the self-enumerated questionnaire of the NSFH explicitly measured couple violence and injury. Two questions asked about violent acts: *During the past year, how many fights with your partner resulted in YOU hitting, shoving, or throwing things at him/her?* and *During the past year, how many fights with your partner resulted in HIM/ HER hitting, shoving, or throwing things at you?* These two questions were coded on a frequency scale (none, once, twice, three or more times), but because of the rareness of the event, they were recorded as dichotomous variables. Two additional questions asked about injurious outcomes: *Have YOU ever been cut, bruised, or seriously injured in a fight with your partner?* and *Has your PARTNER ever been cut, bruised, or seriously injured in a fight with you?* These two questions were coded as dichotomous variables. Both pairs of questions followed what was intended to act as a sort question about how often disagreements became "physical" and thus were supposed to be answered only if fights actually "became physical."

These questions yielded two sets of dependent variables. First, a set of dichotomous variables indicated whether or not a given respondent reported being violent toward his or her partner (*rhit*), the partner's being violent toward the respondent (*phit*), the respondent's being injured by the partner (*rhurt*), or the partner's being injured by the respondent (*phurt*). Second, reports were categorized according to whether neither partner, both partners, the man only, or the woman only was reported as hitting (*hit*) or being hurt (*hurt*).

The primary independent variable was gender of respondent (man was the excluded category). Control variables, all constructed as dummy variables, included age (under 30 was the excluded category), race (white was the excluded category), marriage (first marriage was the excluded category), education (no high school degree was the excluded category), and presence of children under 18 in the household (no children was the excluded category). These variables were chosen to control for the effects of using the entire sample (which overrepresented some age, race, marriage, and parenting groups) and to control for effects previous researchers have hypothesized as important in explaining the variance in violence across different groups (see, e.g., Straus et al., 1980).

FINDINGS

The NSFH data confirmed earlier evidence of women's acting violently in couples. There was no significant difference between wives and husbands in these respondents' reports of hitting, shoving, or throwing things in the current relationship. As one would expect from previously reported studies, among couples in which any violence occurred, the most common response (women, 3.4 percent; men 2.9 percent) was that both partners acted violently.

Critics of results based on the CTS have concentrated on the different outcomes of violence for men and women. A woman is more likely to sustain injury from violent acts by a man than vice versa, the argument goes. The NSFH data indicated that women were more likely than men (1.1 to 0.2 percent) to report that the woman was injured and also that only the man was injured (0.4 to 0.2 percent). Women's reports of their own injuries were 2.5 times men's reports of women's injuries in all cases in which women were hurt. Moreover, in cases in which women alone were reported injured, women reported a rate 5.5 times that which men reported about them. Thus, although men reported that men and women were hurt with equal frequency, women reported that women were hurt 2.75 times more than men.

Further analysis of the injury variable required testing the significance of the gender difference, controlling for other variables. It was female respondents' reports of their own injuries that accounted for differences between the levels of injury male and female respondents reported; therefore, only the *rhurt* variable was used in the remaining analyses. Because the dependent variable, *rhurt,* was dichotomous, and injury was a rare event, a log-linear model was used. Logit analyses using the control variables specified above did not eliminate the gender difference in reporting respondent's injury. Although there was a significant improvement in the fit of the models when the control variables were added, the difference in the probabilities of male and female

TABLE 17.1 Maximum Likelihood Estimates of Log-Odds of
Respondent's Being Cut, Bruised, or Seriously Injured

	Base Model		Full Model	
	Coefficient	Standard Error	Coefficient	Standard Error
Intercept	−5.063	0.259	−4.543	0.485
Gender				
Women	0.873*	0.307	0.796*	0.310
Race				
Black			0.466	0.422
Other			0.754	0.413
Marital Status				
Second or more marriage			0.260	0.343
Age				
Over 30			−0.832*	0.300
Education				
High school, GED			0.041	0.374
Postsecondary			−0.292	0.454
College degree			−1.074	0.595
Children under 18				
One			0.012	0.393
Two			0.473	0.344
Three or more			−0.422	0.512
Log-likelihood	−283.30		−271.79**	
df	1		11	
N=5474				

SOURCE: National Survey of Families and Households data file, version 1212. The data here include
all married couples with spouse present in the household, in the main and oversamples, unweighted.
*Coefficient significant at .05 level.
**chi-square test of improvement of fit between models is significant at .025 level.

respondents' being hurt remained significant. Age was the only other
significant variable, with the probability of injury decreasing for respondents over 30 years of age (see Table 17.1).

The final step in the analysis of the NSFH data was to look specifically at respondents' reports of injuries when both partners were reported
as acting violently. From the entire sample, the 154 cases in which both
partners were violent were selected and then tested for gender differences in responses in the *rhurt* variable. Although adding the control
variables to the model did not significantly improve the fit of the model,
in the full model, the probability of female respondents being hurt was
significantly higher than for male respondents. Having three or more chil-

TABLE 17.2   Maximum Likelihood Estimates of Log-Odds of
Respondent's Being Cut, Bruised, or Seriously Injured,
Given Both Partners Are Reported as Acting Violently

| | Base Model | | Full Model | |
	Coefficient	Standard Error	Coefficient	Standard Error
Intercept	−1.680	0.328	−1.682	0.639
Gender				
Women	0.704	0.410	0.937*	0.451
Race				
Black			−0.093	0.608
Other			1.142	0.710
Marital status				
Second or more marriage			−0.064	0.530
Age				
Over 30			0.926	0.473
Education				
High school, GED			0.537	0.579
Postsecondary			−0.777	0.694
College degree			−0.767	0.795
Children under 18				
One			−1.058	0.575
Two			−0.555	0.555
Three or more			−1.759*	0.816
Log-likelihood	−79.75		−71.07	
df	1		11	
N=154				

SOURCE: National Survey of Families and Households data file, version 1212. The data here include all married couples with spouse present in the household, in the main and oversamples, unweighted, in which both partners are reported as acting violently.
*Coefficient significant at .05 level.

dren under 18 in the household was the only other significant variable (see Table 17.2).

DISCUSSION

The data analysis presented in this chapter showed that although NSFH respondents confirmed that women were not any more pacific than men in the course of disagreements, women were more likely than men to report that they were injured in the course of disagreements with their partners. This result held even for those cases in which both men and women were violent. These findings empirically refute the "battered husband syndrome." At the same time, they demonstrate the importance of developing innovative methods of eliciting information about intimate violence from survey respondents.

The overall levels of reported violent acts were considerably lower in the NSFH than in previous surveys. There are several plausible explanations. First, no questions directly comparable to those asked in previous studies appeared in the NSFH. Second, the short series of questions in the NSFH did not have the same desensitizing effect as the longer series in surveys based more closely on the CTS, which may have made respondents less willing to respond honestly to the NSFH. Third, the NSFH questions appeared in the middle of a lengthy interview, so respondents were more likely to be tired or inattentive than in surveys aimed exclusively at determining the incidence of domestic violence. Fourth, the NSFH asked only general questions about acts and outcomes, compared to the detail of studies based more closely on Straus's CTS. Although the NSFH questions did not mix acts of physical and verbal aggression in the same question, the questions did include a range of acts or outcomes in a single measure, which may have produced underestimates of the incidence of violence and injury. Fifth, the time spans covered by the NSFH questions about violent acts and injurious outcomes do not replicate exactly previous research, rendering comparisons of incidence problematic. Finally, the salience of the issue may also be lower in the minds of respondents to NSFH than in the minds of respondents to surveys specifically aimed at the violence issue, again leading to underestimates of violence and injury.

The NSFH overcame a serious flaw in earlier research on intimate violence by asking questions that differentiated between violent acts and injurious outcomes. But because it was designed in part to facilitate replication of earlier results, the violence section of the NSFH reproduced some of the problems of earlier studies, including underestimation of violence rates. Like the CTS, the NSFH interview schedule referred to violence only in the context of disagreements, although violent and nonviolent abuse may occur without a precipitating disagreement. Similarly, the NSFH included no measure of sexual violence. The NSFH failed to consider the extent to which nonviolent argumentative techniques are used as tools of intimidation and domination in abusive relationships. The questionnaire did not ask about the use of suicide threats or the use of violence or threats of violence to property, pets, children, or other relatives as forms of domination and control. It did not ask who initiated the violence or consider self-defense. Furthermore, the NSFH survey reproduced the most serious failing of quantitative research on intimate violence because it did not enable researchers to investigate the context (other than disagreements) or meanings of violent acts and their outcomes for the perpetrators or survivors of violence. Thus the NSFH not only precluded any graduated analysis of the severity of violent acts and injuries but also failed to measure any gender differences in the consequences (other than injury) and meanings of intimate violence.

Survey instruments characteristically used to conduct quantitative research on intimate violence have reproduced a bias toward nonfeminist interpretations of power and violence in relationships. The flaws in survey instruments that generate this bias are not limited to the content of interview questions. The most important barrier to adequate assessments of the extent and dimensions of intimate violence through surveys is the context of the interaction between interviewer and interviewee. To elicit adequate information about the highly stigmatized, traumatic phenomenon of battering requires an infusion of trust, safety, and intimacy into the interviewing relationship. Methods of empirical inquiry used in battered women's shelters, rape crisis centers, consciousness-raising groups, and explicitly feminist research provide models for the transformation in survey methods that would establish new research practices and relationships appropriate to studying violence (see Heldke, 1988; Knorr-Cetina, 1981, 1982; Smith, 1979, 1987).

Despite being the only likely remedy to the problems of standard survey research, experimental survey methods like those advocated and practiced by some feminists are unlikely to receive financial support in the current research climate. Nationwide, face-to-face surveys are expensive to mount, and funding is scarce and dependent largely on male-dominated state and scientific bureaucracies. The principal investigators on such projects are generally researchers with little or no commitment to feminist scholarship. Moreover, feminist analysts of violence exhibit a pervasive and profound skepticism of quantitative survey methods. Thus the researchers most likely to be able and motivated to make the necessary improvements in the content and context of surveys on violence are least likely to have access to the resources such changes require. Nevertheless, this is the direction in which the feminist critique of recent quantitative violence research calls investigators to move.

REFERENCES

Ansberry, C. (1988, May 5). Calling sexes equal in domestic violence article stirs clash among rights groups. *Wall Street Journal*, p. 1.

Breines, W., & Gordon, L. (1983). The new scholarship on family violence. *Signs, 8,* 490-531.

Card, C. (1988, November). Lesbian battering. *Newsletter on Feminism and Philosophy* (American Philosophical Association), *1,* 3-7.

Dobash, R. E., & Dobash, R. (1979). *Violence against wives: A case against the patriarchy.* New York: Free Press.

Fathers for Equal Rights Organization. (1988, February). *Father's Review,* p. 1.

Gelles, R. J., & Straus, M. A. (1985). *Physical violence in American families—A resurvey* (Typescript of questionnaire). New York: Louis Harris and Associates.

Gelles, R. J., & Straus, M. A. (1988). *Intimate violence.* New York: Simon & Schuster.

Hart, B. (1986). Lesbian battering: An examination. In K. Lorbel (Ed.), *Naming the violence: Speaking out about lesbian battering* (pp.173-189). Seattle: Seal.

Heldke, L. (1988). Recipes for theory making. *Hypatia, 3,* 15-29.

Knorr-Cetina, K. D. (1981). *The manufacture of knowledge.* New York: Pergamon.

Knorr-Cetina, K. D. (1982). The constructivist programme in the sociology of science: Retreats or advances? *Social Studies of Science, 12,* 320-324.

Kurz, D. (1989). Social science perspectives on wife abuse: Current debates and future directions. *Gender & Society, 3,* 489-505.

McNeely, R. L., & Robinson-Simpson, G. (1987). The truth about domestic violence: A falsely framed issue. *Social Work, 32,* 485-490.

Pleck, E., Pleck, J. H., Grossman, M., & Bart, P. (1978). The battered data syndrome: A comment on Steinmetz's article. *Victimology, 2,* 680-684.

Saunders, D. G. (1988a). Wife abuse, husband abuse, or mutual combat? A feminist perspective on the empirical findings. In K. Ylló & M. Bograd (Eds.), *Feminist perspectives on wife abuse* (pp. 90-113). Newbury Park, CA: Sage.

Saunders, D. G. (1988b). Other "truths" about domestic violence: A reply to McNeely and Robinson-Simpson. *Social Work, 33,* 179-183.

Smith, D. (1979). A sociology for women. In J. Sherman & E. T. Beck (Eds.), *The prism of sex: Essays in the sociology of knowledge* (pp. 135-187). Madison: University of Wisconsin Press.

Smith, D. (1987). *The everyday world as problematic: A feminist sociology.* Boston: Northeastern University Press.

Steinmetz, S. K. (1978). The battered husband syndrome. *Victimology, 2,* 499-509.

Steinmetz, S. K., & Lucca, J. S. (1988). Husband battering. In V. B. Van Hasselt, R. L. Morrison, A. S. Bellack, & M. Hersen (Eds.), *Handbook of family violence* (pp. 223-246). New York: Plenum.

Straus, M. A. (1987). *The Conflict Tactics Scales: An evaluation and new data on validity, reliability, norms, and scoring methods.* Paper presented at the annual meeting of the National Council on Family Relations.

Straus, M. A., & Gelles, R. J. (1986). Societal change and change in family violence from 1975 to 1985 as revealed by two national surveys. *Journal of Marriage and the Family, 48,* 465-479.

Straus, M. A., Gelles, R. J., & Steinmetz, S. K. (1980). *Behind closed doors: Violence in the American family.* Garden City, NY: Anchor.

Sweet, J., Bumpass, L, & Call, V. (1988). The design and contents of the National Survey of Families and Households (working paper). Madison: University of Wisconsin, Center for Demography and Ecology.

Wendt, M. J. (1986). *Violent interaction between American couples.* Unpublished master's thesis, University of Wisconsin—Madison.

18 Social Science Perspectives on Wife Abuse: Current Debates and Future Directions

DEMIE KURZ
University of Pennsylvania

In the last decade, there has been much scholarly, public, and policy attention to the problem of the physical abuse of wives by husbands (*Attorney General's Task Force on Family Violence,* 1984; Pagelow, 1987; Straus, Gelles, & Steinmetz, 1980). The battered women's movement was the first to identify this issue and, aided by other reformers, to bring it to public attention (Schecter, 1982; Tierney, 1982). As a result, "wife abuse" has been transformed from a private, largely invisible matter to one viewed as a social problem for which appropriate remedies should be sought. Further, there have been numerous reforms in the legal, governmental, and social service response to battered women (Gelb, 1983; Pagelow, 1984; Tierney, 1982).

Researchers, by providing statistical evidence documenting the extent of wife abuse, have played a critical role in making it a social issue. Social scientists have been particularly important in surveying this problem. Their statistics on the extent of woman battering are cited to legitimate concern in books, professional journals, and the popular press. The most frequently cited researchers are Straus, Gelles, and Steinmetz, who among them have published more on this subject than any other social scientists (Gelles, 1974, 1979, 1983, 1985; Gelles & Straus, 1988; Straus, 1976, 1980a, 1980b, 1980c; Straus & Gelles, 1986; Straus et al., 1980). Their figures demonstrating that over 2 million Americans had been physically abused by a spouse (Straus et al., 1980, p. 34) are frequently cited, as is their belief that "a marriage license is a hitting license" (Straus,

1980a). Other social scientists frequently cited include Dobash and Dobash (1979), Pagelow (1984), and Russell (1982).

Although publicly the facts and analyses these researchers present are assumed to be given, social scientists themselves differ sharply both in their view of the facts and in their analyses of the causes of violence. The purpose of this chapter is to examine two major social science perspectives on the study of physical abuse of husbands and wives. One perspective will be referred to here as the *family violence approach,* which is the name used by its proponents. Those who take this perspective view violence between husbands and wives, which they call "spouse abuse," as part of a pattern of violence occurring among all family members (Gelles, 1974, 1979, 1983, 1985; Gelles & Straus, 1988; Straus 1980a, 1980b, 1980c; Straus et al., 1980). The other perspective is called here the *feminist approach.* Feminists place male-female relations at the center of their analysis and view inequality between men and women as a key factor in violence (Bowker, 1986; Dobash & Dobash, 1979; Pagelow, 1987; Russell, 1982; Stanko, 1985; Stark, Flitcraft, & Frazier, 1979; Yllö, 1988).

In this chapter, I compare the basic premises, methodology, and conclusions of these two perspectives with respect to their views of women and gender. I argue that each perspective treats women differently, and therefore each has consequences for our scholarly understanding of the meaning of the physical abuse of women by male intimates. Although both perspectives emphasize the importance of women's subordinate position in creating violence, family violence researchers believe it is only one of several contributing factors. For feminist writers, women's subordination is central in their analyses of violence. After comparing the two perspectives, I argue that the feminist perspective portrays the realities of battering more accurately. I conclude this article with directions for future research.

FAMILY VIOLENCE PERSPECTIVE

Straus, Gelles, and Steinmetz have published the largest body of social science research on domestic violence (see Gelles, 1974, 1979, 1983, 1985; Gelles & Straus, 1988; Steinmetz, 1977, 1977-1978; Straus, 1973, 1976, 1979, 1980a, 1980b, 1980c; Straus & Gelles, 1986; Straus et al., 1980). They began to work in this area soon after the battered women's movement brought the issue to public attention, and they have been substantially funded by the U.S. National Institutes of Mental Health. They have trained many researchers, and their methodology has been used by researchers in different parts of the United States (Straus & Gelles, 1986, p. 470).

Both the theoretical approach of these researchers and their data lead them to name the problem one of family violence. They believe that all family members carry out and are victims of violence. They base their claims on their data showing an equivalent amount of violence committed by both husbands and wives toward each other, physical violence of parents toward children and children toward elders, and sibling abuse (Straus, 1979, 1980c, 1983). As will be described, they believe family violence originates in wider social norms condoning violence and in the structure of the contemporary family.

Straus, Gelles, and Steinmetz have written extensively on the topic of violence between male and female intimates, which they call *spouse abuse*. Their research findings and conclusions about spouse abuse are based on data they have collected with the Conflict Tactics Scales (CTS), an instrument that asks one member of a couple, drawn from a random sample of married people composed one half of men and one half of women, to fill out a form indicating if or how many times he or she performed specific actions during the previous 12 months (Straus, 1979). This survey instrument asks about conflicts between husbands and wives in the previous year and measures conflict resolution on a continuum from nonviolent tactics (calm discussion) to the most violent tactics (use of a knife or gun).

Using this scale, Straus et al. (1980) obtain the following results: 12.8 percent of the husbands commit these acts toward their wives, and 11.7 percent of the wives commit them toward their husbands (p. 36). According to Straus et al. (1980), whereas "traditionally men have been considered more aggressive and violent than women," looking at the couples in which the husband was the only one to use violence and those in which both used violence, "the most common situation was that in which both used violence" (p. 36). Of those couples reporting any violence, 49 percent were in situations in which both were violent. For the year previous to the study, a comparison of the number of couples in which only the husband was violent with those in which only the wife was violent shows the figures to be very close: 27 percent of the husbands committed violent acts compared with 24 percent of the wives (p. 37). On the basis of this study, a member of the research team concluded that there was a battered husband syndrome, which had not previously been recognized and which deserved attention (Steinmetz, 1977-1978).

Feminist researchers (Berk, Berk, Loseke, & Rauma, 1983; Dobash & Dobash, 1979; Pleck, Pleck, Grossman, & Bart, 1977-1978; Russell, 1992) criticized this study for its failure to measure how much of women's violence was in self-defense or who was injured by the violence. These criticisms will be described in more detail in the next section. After 10 years, Straus and Gelles (1986) repeated the survey with almost no change in the methodology. This time they found an increase in violence on the part of wives. They again conclude:

> The violence rates . . . reveal an important and distressing finding about violence in American families—that in marked contrast to the behavior of women outside the family, women are about as violent within the family as men. (p. 470)

Straus et al. (1980) conclude that violence is an all-pervasive feature of family life:

> A fundamental solution to the problem of wife-beating has to go beyond a concern with how to control assaulting husbands. It seems as if violence is built into the very structure of the society and the family system itself. . . . It [wife-beating] is only one aspect of the general pattern of family violence, which includes parent-child violence, child-to-child violence, and wife-to-husband violence. (p. 44)

Their analysis, as well as their use of the terms *family violence* and *spouse abuse,* rather than *battering* or *wife abuse,* indicate that it is the family, not the relationship between women and men, that is their central unit of analysis (Gelles, 1985; Gelles & Straus, 1988).

Straus et al. (1980), Gelles (1985), and Gelles and Straus (1988) isolate three causes of violence in the contemporary U.S. family. First is the structure of the family. They believe that the contemporary U.S. family is subject to serious stresses from difficult working conditions, unemployment, financial insecurity, and health problems, which cause family members to be violent to one another. This structural proclivity to violence is exacerbated by the large amount of privacy accorded the contemporary U.S. family, privacy that allows family violence to go unchecked by outside scrutiny or control (Gelles, 1985; Gelles & Straus, 1988).

Second, these authors believe that the family, borrowing from the society at large, accepts violence as a means of solving conflict. They see evidence of the cultural acceptance of violence in television programming, folklore, and fairy tales (Straus, 1980b), and in surveys showing widespread public acceptance of violence. In their own survey, one of four wives and one third of husbands thought that "a couple slapping one another was at least somewhat necessary, normal, and good" (Gelles & Straus, 1988, p. 27). Their survey also found that 70 percent of those surveyed thought that slapping a 12-year-old child was either necessary, normal, or good (1988, p. 27).

Straus (1983) and Straus et al. (1980) believe that families socialize children into violence by the widely accepted practice of punishing children with physical force. They report that men who saw their parents attack each other are 3 times as likely to hit their wives and 10 times more likely to "abuse" their wives (with a weapon). They also find that many more men who report being hit as teenagers hit their wives, compared to those who were not hit as teenagers. They conclude, "Each generation learns to be violent by being a participant in a violent family—Violence begets violence" (1980, p. 121). Other researchers have pursued this line of inquiry and have concluded that men learn abusive behavior from their families of origin (Browne, 1987, p. 31).

Straus et al. (1980) also frequently cite sexism as a factor in family violence and believe that there are some differences in the violent behavior and experiences of women and men. They state that despite the high rate of violence by wives, "It would be a great mistake if that fact distracted us from giving first attention to *wives as victims* as the focus of social policy" (p. 43). The reasons they give are the following: (a) husbands have higher rates of the most dangerous and injurious forms of violence; (b) because men are physically stronger, women may be more seriously injured than men; (c) husbands repeat their violent acts more than wives do; (d) some of the women's acts of violence may be in self-defense; (e) there are many acts of violence toward pregnant women, and thus the fetus or unborn child is in danger also; and (f) for economic and social reasons women have fewer alternatives to leaving a violent situation than do men. In other words, women are as responsible as men for causing violence, but because women are more victimized by violence, they deserve some special consideration.

Straus et al. (1980) also state that the sexist organization of society and its family system is one of the fundamental factors in the high level of wife beating, and they cite the power of men over women, at the societal level and in the family, as a cause of violence. They claim that "Violence is used by the most powerful family member as a means of legitimizing his or her dominant position" (p. 193). After dividing families into those that are "wife dominant," those that are "husband dominant," and those that are "democratic," Straus et al. conclude that wives are more likely to be beaten in homes in which power is concentrated in the hands of the husband and that, similarly, husbands are more likely to be beaten by their wives in wife-dominant homes. They claim that the least amount of battering occurs in democratic households. They conclude:

> It seems that violence is used by the most powerful family member as a means of legitimizing his or her dominant position. Even less powerful members of the family tend to rely on violence as a reaction to their own lack of participation in the family decision-making process. (p. 193)

Thus, although Straus et al. raise the issue of the use of power by husbands and wives, they assume that power can as equally be held by a wife as by a husband.

The policy recommendations of Straus et al. follow from their perspective. To reduce violence in the home, they recommend changing norms that legitimize and glorify violence in society and in the family. They suggest public awareness campaigns, gun control, abolition of the death penalty and corporal punishment, and the reduction of violence in the media. They also recommend reducing violence-provoking stresses created by society, such as unemployment, underemployment, and poverty. They advocate integrating families into a network of kin and community and the provision of adequate health and dental care. Finally, in keeping with their view of marital inequality as a factor in family violence, they recommend changing the sexist character of society and the family (Straus et al., 1980; see also Gelles & Straus, 1988).

THE FEMINIST PERSPECTIVE

Some of the work of feminist researchers on violence, such as Dobash and Dobash's book *Violence Against Wives* (1979), has become influential and well known, and feminist social scientists are frequently cited in scholarly and popular sources. Feminist social scientists focus on a variety of substantive issues and themes, but they make certain common assumptions that challenge the family violence perspective (Bowker, 1986; Pagelow, 1981; Russell, 1982; Stanko, 1985; Stark et al., 1979).

First, for acts of violence in heterosexual couples, feminist researchers argue against the claim that men and women engage in equal amounts of violence. They argue that data proving such an equivalence of violence, particularly data based on the CTS, are flawed. The scale does not ask what acts were done in self-defense, who initiated the violence, or who was injured. In their view, the validity of the scale is undermined because the continuum of violence in the scale is so broad that it fails to discriminate among very different kinds of violence (Dobash & Dobash, 1979; Stark & Flitcraft, 1985). If these questions were asked, the picture would be clear—overwhelmingly, men abuse women (Breines & Gordon, 1983; Dobash & Dobash, 1979; Gubman & Newton, 1983; Pleck et al., 1977-1978; Russell, 1982; Saunders, 1988). These researchers believe that when women engage in acts of violence, they do it primarily in self-defense. Others criticize the findings of CTS because they do not take into account male-female differences in self-reporting; men are more likely to underreport their violent acts than women are.

Feminist researchers support their point of view with official crime statistics and data from the criminal justice system and hospitals. The National Crime Survey of 1982 reported that 91 percent of all violent crimes between spouses were directed at women by husbands or ex-husbands, whereas only 5 percent were directed at husbands by wives or ex-wives (cited in Browne, 1987, p. 7). Analyzing police records from Scotland, Dobash and Dobash (1979) found that when gender was known, women were targets in 94 percent and offenders in 3 percent of the cases. Also examining police records, Berk et al. (1983) found that in 94 to 95 percent of cases, it is the woman who gets injured, and that even when both partners are injured, the woman's injuries are nearly three times as severe as the man's. Data from hospitals (Kurz, 1987; McLeer & Anwar, 1989; Stark et al., 1979) show women to be overwhelmingly the injured party. These data challenge the argument for the battered husband syndrome (Pagelow, 1985; Pleck et al., 1977-1978).

Feminist researchers believe that men use violence as a way to control female partners, citing interview data from men and women that demonstrate that battering incidents occur when husbands try to make their wives comply with their wishes. Using data from interviews with 109 battered women, Dobash and Dobash (1979) demonstrate how over the course of their marriages, batterers increasingly control wives through intimidation and isolation, findings confirmed by other interview studies (Pagelow, 1981; Walker, 1984). Violence, therefore, is just one of a variety of controls that men try to exercise over female partners; others are anger and psychological abuse (Adams, 1988; Dobash & Dobash, 1979; Mederos, 1987). Interviews with batterers (Adams, 1988; Dobash & Dobash, 1979; Ptacek, 1988) show that men believe they are justified in their use of violence by their wives' behavior or by what they feel are acceptable norms.

Second, feminist researchers point out that both historically and in the present, major institutions have permitted and condoned the use of physical abuse by husbands to control wives. In the United States, in the early 19th century, some state laws specifically approved wife beating. The first law in the United States to recognize a husband's right to control his wife with physical force was an 1824 ruling by the Supreme Court of Mississippi permitting the husband "to exercise the right of moderate chastisement in cases of great emergency" (quoted in Browne, 1987, p. 166). This and similar rulings that followed in courts in Maryland and Massachusetts were based on English common law, which gave a husband the right of "correction" of his wife, although he was supposed to use it in moderation.

In 1971 wife beating was made illegal in Alabama. The court stated:

> The privilege, ancient though it be, to beat her with a stick, to pull her hair, choke her, spit in her face or kick her about the floor, or to inflict upon her like indignities, is not now acknowledged by our law. . . . The wife is entitled to the same protection of the law that the husband can invoke for himself. (quoted in Browne, 1987, p. 167)

A North Carolina court made a similar decision in 1874 but limited the kinds of cases in which the court should intervene:

> If no permanent injury has been inflicted, nor malice, cruelty nor dangerous violence shown by the husband, it is better to draw the curtain, shut out the public gaze, and leave the parties to forget and forgive. (quoted in Browne, 1987, p. 167)

Until recent legal reforms were enacted, the "curtain rule" was widely used by the legal system to justify its nonintervention in wife-abuse cases. Although the law and the nature of marriage have changed dramatically since the early 20th century, feminists argue that important social and legal norms still support the use of violence against women as a means of control in marriage.

Despite the U.S. ideology of spousal equality in contemporary marriage, feminists claim that marriage still institutionalizes the control of wives by husbands through the structure of husband-wife roles. As long as women are responsible for domestic work, child care, and emotional and psychological support, and men's primary identity is that of provider and revolves around work, the husband has the more important status and also controls the majority of issues and decisions in the family. It is through such a system, coupled with the acceptance of physical force as a means of control, that, in the words of the Dobashes (1979), the wife becomes an "appropriate victim" of physical and psychological abuse. Feminists argue further that the use of violence for control in marriage is perpetuated not only through norms about a man's rights in marriage but through women's continued economic dependence on their husbands, which makes it difficult to leave a violent relationship. This dependence is increased by the lack of adequate child care and job training, which would enable women to get jobs with which they could support themselves.

Currently, no U.S. jurisdiction legally permits a husband to strike his wife, and attempts have been made to increase the arrest rate of offenders (Browne, 1987). But changing the attitudes of police, prosecutors, and judges is difficult; many still hold the view that woman battering is a family affair (Berk & Loseke, 1981) and classify assaults against women as misdemeanors rather than criminal offenses (Tong, 1984). Thus, enforcing new laws may prove to be difficult.

Hospitals and medical personnel can be reeducated about woman battering, yet battering is either invisible or a low priority (Kurz, 1987; Kurz & Stark, 1988; McLeer, Anwar, Herman, & Maquiling, 1989; Stark et al., 1979). Because mental health personnel and social workers tend to define the problem as one of individual pathology (Davis, 1987; Ferraro, 1983; Johnson, 1985), every case has to be assessed separately, and there are few routines for addressing male violence toward women and girls.

The social acceptance of violence as a means of control of women leads some feminist researchers to question the thesis that violence is transmitted primarily through pathological family patterns. They claim that the data confirming that witnessing abuse in one's family of origin produces later abusive behavior is not invariably predictive, pointing out that there are many who witness abuse and do not become abusers (Breines & Gordon, 1983; Dobash & Dobash, 1979). Stark and Flitcraft (1979) contradict the claim that those who are abused as children are more likely to be batterers, arguing that the Straus data are based on subgroups of such varying size that the conclusions are misleading. Stark and Flitcraft conclude that "for every abuser who has been hit as a youngster, two have not been hit" (p. 168) and that "the vast majority of persons from violent childhoods do not become abusive and that the vast majority of woman batterers do not come from violent families of origin" (p. 168). Thus, although the theory that violent behavior is learned in childhood and thereby transmitted from one generation to another has empirical support, feminist researchers believe that other factors, particularly norms and practices of male dominance, are even more important in accounting for why some males adopt violent behavior.

Feminist policy recommendations are to make women more economically independent in order to give them alternatives to violent marriages (Dobash & Dobash, 1979; Pagelow, 1987; Stark et al., 1979). Feminists also favor reforms to make institutions more responsive to battered women and public education campaigns to arouse support for those reforms.

COMPARISON OF KEY ASSUMPTIONS

In this chapter, I have compared the family violence and the feminist perspectives with respect to their views of the origins and causes of physical abuse of wives by husbands, its prevalence, the transmission of violence from one generation to another, and recommended policy changes. Some might argue that the two perspectives are relatively similar and have only minor differences of emphasis. For example, they could point to the fact that the family violence perspective focuses not only on stresses in the family and norms of violence in U.S. culture as causes of family violence but on sexism as well.

But from a feminist perspective, the question whether sexism is "a" factor or "the" factor at the root of violence is critical and reveals basic differences in assumptions about gender. One such difference is that family violence researchers use the family as their primary unit of analysis, whereas feminists place male-female relations at the center of their analysis. Further, family violence researchers make the assumption that although not completely equal, U.S. men and women have a fair amount of equality in marriage (Straus & Gelles, 1986), whereas feminists believe that in general, U.S. women have fewer resources and less power than men. Finally, for family violence researchers, violence is the primary problem to be explained, whereas for feminists an equally important question is why women are overwhelmingly the targets of violence.

Feminists view the two approaches as significantly different because they believe that male dominance must be a central aspect of an analysis of violence in the family. When male dominance is not a central feature of the analysis, as in the family violence perspective, feminists believe that women come to be seen as one of several groups of victims, not particularly different from other victims of family violence. Feminists believe that comparing wife abuse to child abuse, elder abuse, and sibling abuse—as family violence researchers do—deflects attention from women. Some feminists (Russell, 1982; Stanko, 1985; Wardell, Gillespie, & Leffler, 1983) argue that battering should be compared with related types of violence against women, such as rape, marital rape, sexual harassment, and incest, not just with other types of family violence. They argue that these acts of violence against women share common characteristics as products of male dominance.

Feminists believe that the decontextualized family violence perspective denies a central element of women's experience by deflecting attention from one of the key places where women's oppression occurs —in the family (Breines & Gordon, 1983; Dobash & Dobash, 1979; Russell, 1988; Saunders, 1988; Stark & Flitcraft, 1979). As a result, feminists believe that the family violence perspective encourages individualistic explanations of the behavior of targets and aggressors. Arguing that violence is transmitted by the family through "social heredity" (Straus et al., 1980, p. 112) leads to a view of the family as shaped more by psychological and pathological processes than by social and historical family and gender structures. Similarly, although family violence researchers emphasize the social origins of the stress that they say is related to violence—stress resulting from unemployment, bad working conditions, and inadequate income and health care—the emphasis on coping with stress further suggests individual and family pathology.

Some feminists argue there may in fact be a relationship between different kinds of family violence but that without a feminist perspective on the family, researchers may fail to identify the most important dynamics of these relationships—particularly child abuse. There is increasing evidence that when women are battered, children are abused (Bowker, Arbitell, & McFerron, 1988; Stark & Flitcraft, 1985). Child abuse has traditionally been assumed to be caused by inadequate mothering. Mothers do abuse children, including mothers who are battered women (Gayford, 1975; Roy, 1977; Straus et al., 1980). But there is increasing evidence that men who abuse their wives also abuse their children.

Bowker et al. (1988), who found that 70 percent of wife beaters also physically abused their children, argue that the most important cause and context of child abuse is current abuse of a woman by a male intimate. They also found that the severity of wife beating predicted the severity of child abuse and that the greater the degree of husband dominance, the greater the likelihood of child abuse. Similarly, Stark and Flitcraft (1985), in their review of medical records, found that children whose mother is battered are more than twice as likely to be physically abused as children whose mother is not battered. They also believe that purposive violence by male intimates against women is the most important context for child abuse. In sum, for feminists, family violence is a direct outcome of men's attempts to maintain control over the powerless members of the family—women and children.

The framework one chooses for investigating different types of violence in the family has serious implications for policy, as well as theory. For example, in the case of child abuse, at the present time in the United States there are court cases in which both mother and child have been abused by the father, yet the mother's parental rights are being terminated for "failure to protect the child." Obviously, the degree of the mother's culpability for criminal neglect or other charges can be decided only on a case-by-case basis. But it is very important to make distinctions between women who are or are not engaging in child abuse themselves and those who are and are not being abused themselves, in order to avoid further punishing abused women by taking away their children (Susan McLeer, M.D., personal communication, December 1, 1988; Susan Schecter, M.S.W., personal communication, November 19, 1988).

Feminist researchers fear that the family violence perspective contributes to the adoption of social policies that fail to address the inequality between women and men. They fear, for example, that practitioners will increasingly counsel battered women in an individualistic framework, advising them to solve their personal problems without taking into account the context of power in the family (Adams, 1988; Stark et al., 1979). They also believe that research that identifies the problem of wife battering as one of family violence and spouse abuse contributes to society's denial of male violence against women (Breines & Gordon, 1983; Dobash & Dobash, 1979; Russell, 1988).

DIRECTIONS FOR FUTURE RESEARCH

Feminist researchers should demonstrate how male dominance produces male violence against women on an ongoing, everyday basis (Hood, 1989). A fruitful method for achieving this goal would be to investigate how major institutions, through their ideologies and practices, define the abuse of women by male intimates and respond to women who have experienced abuse. Researchers should focus both on institutionwide policies and practices and on the labeling and processing of abused women by front-line workers who have the most contact with abused women. In studying the institutional response to violence, it would be profitable to compare responses to the range of violence against women, including rape, marital rape, sexual harassment, and incest (Stanko, 1985; Wardell et al., 1983). From a feminist perspective, an institution that is central in the labeling and processing of woman battering is the legal system. Traditionally, the legal system has defined woman battering as a private, family matter and has been instrumental in enforcing its privatization. Although new laws have criminalized woman battering, the critical question is whether these laws will be enforced. A recent study suggests that even police who receive training in how to make a criminal response to woman battering cases may continue to view battered women as unfortunate victims of personal and social problems such as poverty, and in the absence of strong police department support, view arrests as low priority and not part of their "real" work (Ferraro, 1989). To the extent that these laws are not taken seriously, the legal system will continue to treat the problem of woman battering as an individual one and return battered women to the private sphere.

Another key institution in the defining and processing of battering is the medical system. Stark et al. (1979) argue that because of patriarchal medical ideologies and practices, medical practitioners fail to recognize woman battering and instead label battered women as having psychological problems. Stark et al. claim that these actions serve to perpetuate battering relationships and argue that the medical system duplicates and reinforces the patriarchal structure of the family. Kurz (1987) has documented how individual staff in emergency rooms come to define battered women as not "true" medical cases, but "social" ones, and feel they make extra work and trouble for medical practitioners. This study also documents how after they receive training in how to respond to woman battering, medical emergency-room workers have a higher rate of recognition and intervention with battered women. But battered women who do not look like "typical victims" are frequently not recognized as battered. They are sent back home, without any recognition of or attention to their battering.

A study of major institutions must include institutions other than the family in which males learn violence, such as the military (Russell, 1989), sports (Messner, 1989), fraternities, and male bonding rituals. Sanday (1991) has studied the ways in which fraternity practices and rituals, in promoting loyalty to a brotherhood of men, legitimate gang rape and other types of violence against women (see also Martin & Hummer, Chapter 8). Kanin (1984) suggests that the college date rapists he studied came from a more highly sexualized subculture than non-date-rapists. We need a major reexamination of those norms of male-female intimate and family relationships that promote and condone violence. One approach would be to place the study of woman battering in the context of other strategies of power and control in male-female relationships. Mederos (1987) suggests that there is a continuum of strategies that husbands use to control wives, from anger to emotional abuse to physical violence.

We would also profit from an understanding of women's responses to violence and women's control strategies in intimate relationships. There are strong indications that men and women see violent acts differently (Adams, 1988). Some argue that women minimize and rationalize the violence done to them (Greenblat, 1983). Several studies (Dobash & Dobash, 1979; Ferraro & Johnson, 1983; Mills, 1985) have documented a progression in women's outlook from an initial view of the violence as an aberrant, occasional event to a view of the violence as a serious problem. Mills (1995) describes how the women she interviewed minimized the problematic aspects of their husband's violence by ignoring it and focusing on the positive aspects of their relationship with their husband or by justifying their husband's behavior as beyond his control. As the violence in these relationships increased, however, the women became increasingly anxious. But women's perceptions that something is wrong must be validated by someone outside the situation in order for them to develop a new definition of the situation as one in which they are victims of physical abuse.

In the case of men, some argue that batterers have either a set of explanations by which they deny their abusive behavior or a set of rationalizations by which they legitimize their violent behavior (Okun, 1986; Ptacek, 1988). Understanding these control strategies would provide a greater understanding of power in marriage, of the origins of violence, and of the possibilities of reducing male violence toward female intimates.

A focus on power in the family also provides an opportunity to examine changes in rates of violence along with changes in family power. For example, it is widely accepted that when wives work, they increase their power in the family (Collins, 1988; Scanzoni, 1982). Does male violence against women increase or decrease as a result of this shift in power? Does it make a difference whether the wife works with mostly women or mostly men?

Finally, it would be very useful to have cross-cultural data on rates of violence and variations in institutional responses to violence. In a cross-cultural study of rape, Sanday (1981) found that a combination of economic and cultural factors contributes to variations in rates of rape. In societies in which women are included in religious and cultural institutions and in which women's economic and reproductive contributions are recognized, there is less violence and rape against women. Cross-cultural data would provide useful information on the relative importance of a variety of factors influencing all the forms of violence against women: norms and practices of male domination, norms of violence, cultural productions, and economic and family systems.

REFERENCES

Adams, D. (1988). Treatment models of men who batter. In K. Yllö & M. Bograd (Eds.), *Feminist perspectives on wife abuse* (pp. 176-199). Newbury Park, CA: Sage.
Attorney General's Task Force on Family Violence. (1984). Washington, DC: Department of Justice.
Berk, R., Berk , S. F., Loseke, D., & Rauma, D. (1983). Mutual combat and other family violence myths. In D. Finkelhor et al. (Eds.), *The dark side of families: Current family violence research* (pp. 197-212). Beverly Hills, CA: Sage.
Berk, S. F., & Loseke, D. (1981). "Handling" family violence: Situational determinants of police arrest in domestic disturbances. *Law and Society Review, 15,* 317-346.
Bowker, L. H. (1986). *Ending the violence.* Holmes Beach, FL: Learning Publications.
Bowker, L. H., Arbitell, M., & McFerron, J. (1988). On the relationship between wife beating and child abuse. In K. Yllö & M. Bograd, (Eds.), *Feminist perspectives on wife abuse* (pp. 158-174). Newbury Park, CA: Sage.
Breines, W., & Gordon, L. (1983). The new scholarship on family violence. *Signs: Journal of Women in Culture and Society, 8,* 490-531.
Browne, A. (1987). *Battered women who kill.* New York: Free Press.
Collins, R. (1988). *Sociology of marriage and the family.* Chicago: Nelson-Hall.
Davis, L. V. (1987, July/August). Battered women: The transformation of a social problem. *Social Work,* pp. 306-311.
Dobash, R. E., & Dobash, R. (1979). *Violence against wives.* New York: Free Press.
Ferraro, K. J. (1983). Negotiating trouble in a battered women's shelter. *Urban Life, 3,* 287-306.
Ferraro, K. J. (1989). Policing woman battering. *Social Problems, 36,* 61-74.
Ferraro, K. J., & Johnson, J. M. (1983). How women experience battering: The process of victimization. *Social Problems, 3,* 325-339.
Gayford, J. (1975). Wife battering: A preliminary survey of 100 cases. *British Medical Journal, 1,* 194-197.

Gelb, J. (1983). The politics of wife abuse. In I. Diamond (Ed.), *Families, politics, and public policy* (pp. 250-264). New York: Longman.

Gelles, R. (1974). *The violent home: A study of physical aggression between husbands and wives.* Beverly Hills, CA: Sage.

Gelles, R. (1979). *Family violence.* Beverly Hills, CA: Sage.

Gelles, R. (1983). An exchange/social control theory. In D. Finkelhor et al. (Eds.), *The dark side of families: Current family violence research* (pp. 151-165). Beverly Hills, CA: Sage.

Gelles, R. (1985). *Intimate violence in families.* Beverly Hills, CA: Sage.

Gelles, R., & Straus, M. (1988). *Intimate violence.* New York: Simon & Schuster.

Greenblat, C. S. (1983). A hit is a hit is a hit . . . Or is it? Approval and tolerance of the use of physical force by spouses. In D. Finkelhor et al. (Eds.), *The dark side of families: Current family violence research* (pp. 235-260). Beverly Hills, CA: Sage.

Gubman, G., & Newton, P. (1983). *When two are too many: The configuration of a battering incident.* Paper presented at meeting of the American Sociological Association, Detroit, MI.

Hood, J. (1989, May 16). Why our society is rape-prone. *The New York Times,* p. 23.

Johnson, N. (1985). Police, social work and medical responses to battered women. In N. Johnson (Ed.), *Marital violence* (pp. 109-123). London: Routledge & Kegan Paul.

Kanin, E. (1984). Date rape: Unofficial criminals and victims. *Victimology, 9,* 94-108.

Kurz, D. (1987). Responses to battered women: Resistance to medicalization. *Social Problems, 34,* 501-513.

Kurz, D., & Stark, E. (1988). Not-so-benign neglect: The medical response to battering. In K. Yllö & M. Bograd, (Eds.), *Feminist perspectives on wife abuse* (pp. 249-266). Newbury Park, CA: Sage.

Martin, P. Y., & Hummer, R. (1989). Fraternities and rape on campus. *Gender & Society, 3,* 457-473.

McLeer, S., & Anwar, R. (1989). A study of battered women presenting in an emergency department. *American Journal of Public Health, 79,* 65-66.

McLeer, S., Anwar, R., Herman, S., & Maquiling, K. (1989). Education is not enough: A systems failure in protecting battered women. *Annals of Emergency Medicine, 18,* 651-653.

Mederos, F. (1987). *Theorizing continuities and discontinuities between "normal" men and abusive men: Work in progress.* Paper presented at the Third National Family Violence Research Conference, University of New Hampshire, Durham.

Messner, M. (1989). When bodies are weapons: Masculinity and violence in sport. *International Review of the Sociology of Sport 25*(3), 203-220.

Mills, T. (1985). The assault on the self: Stages on coping with battering husbands. *Qualitative Sociology, 8,* 103-123.

Okun, L. (1986). *Woman abuse.* Albany: State University of New York.

Pagelow, M. D. (1981). *Woman-battering: Victims and their experiences.* Beverly Hills, CA: Sage.

Pagelow, M. D. (1984). *Family violence.* New York: Praeger.

Pagelow, M. D. (1985). The "battered husband syndrome": Social problem or much ado about little? In N. Johnson (Ed.), *Marital violence* (pp. 172-195). London: Routledge & Kegan Paul.

Pagelow, M. D. (1987). *Application of research to policy in partner abuse.* Paper presented at the Family Violence Research Conference for Practitioners and Policymakers, University of New Hampshire, Durham.

Pleck, E., Pleck, J. H., Grossman, M., & Bart, P. B. (1977-1978). The battered data syndrome: A comment on Steinmetz' article. *Victimology: An International Journal, 2,* 680-684.

Ptacek, J. (1988). Why do men batter their wives? In K. Yllö & M. Bograd, (Eds.), *Feminist perspectives on wife abuse* (pp. 133-157). Newbury Park, CA: Sage.

Roy, M. (1977). A current study of 150 cases. In M. Roy (Ed.), *Battered women: A psychosociological study of domestic violence* (pp. 25-44). New York: Van Nostrand Reinhold.

Russell, D.E.H. (1982). *Rape in marriage.* New York: Macmillan.

Russell, D.E.H. (1988). Foreword. In K. Yllö & M. Bograd (Eds.), *Feminist perspectives on wife abuse* (pp. 7-9). Newbury Park, CA: Sage.

Russell, D.E.H. (1989). Sexism, violence, and the nuclear mentality. In *Exposing nuclear phallocies* (pp. 63-74). New York: Pergamon.

Sanday, P. R. (1981). The socio-cultural context of rape: A cross-cultural study. *Journal of Social Issues, 37,* 5-27.

Sanday, P. R. (1991). *Fraternity gang rape: Sex, brotherhood, and privilege on campus.* New York: New York University Press.

Saunders, D. G. (1988). Wife abuse, husband abuse, or mutual combat? In K. Yllö & M. Bograd (Eds.), *Feminist perspectives on wife abuse* (pp. 90-113). Newbury Park, CA: Sage.

Scanzoni, J. (1982). *Sexual bargaining.* Chicago: University of Chicago Press.

Schecter, S. (1982). *Women and male violence.* Boston: South End.

Stanko, E. A. (1985). *Intimate intrusions.* London: Routledge & Kegan Paul.

Stark, E., & Flitcraft, A. (1985). Woman battering, child abuse and social heredity: What is the relationship? In N. Johnson (Ed.), *Marital violence* (pp. 147-171). London: Routledge & Kegan Paul.

Stark, E., Flitcraft, A., & Frazier, W. (1979). Medicine and patriarchal violence: The social construction of a "private" event. *International Journal of Health Services, 98,* 461-491.

Steinmetz, S. (1977). *The cycle of violence: Assertive, aggressive, and abusive family interaction.* New York: Praeger.

Steinmetz, S. (1977-1978). The battered husband syndrome. *Victimology: An International Journal, 2,* 499-509.

Straus, M. (1973). A general systems theory approach to a theory of violence between family members. *Social Science Information, 12,* 105-125.

Straus, M. (1976). Sexual inequality, cultural norms, and wife-beating. *Victimology, 1,* 54-76.

Straus, M. (1979). Measuring intrafamily conflict and violence: The Conflict Tactics (CT) Scales. *Journal of Marriage and the Family, 41,* 75-88.

Straus, M. (1980a). The marriage license as a hitting license: Evidence from popular culture, law, and social science. In M. Straus & G. Hotaling (Eds.), *The social causes of husband-wife violence* (pp. 39-50). Minneapolis: University of Minnesota Press.

Straus, M. (1980b). A sociological perspective on the prevention of wife beating. In M. Straus & G. Hotaling (Eds.), *The social causes of husband-wife violence* (pp. 211-234). Minneapolis: University of Minnesota Press.

Straus, M. (1980c). Victims and aggressors in marital violence. *American Behavioral Scientist, 23,* 681-704.

Straus, M. (1983). Ordinary violence, child abuse, and wife beating: What do they have in common? In D. Finkelhor et al. (Eds.), *The dark side of families: Current family violence research* (pp. 213-234). Beverly Hills, CA: Sage.

Straus, M., & Gelles, R. (1986). Societal change and change in family violence from 1975 to 1985 as revealed by two national surveys. *Journal of Marriage and the Family, 48,* 465-479.

Straus, M., Gelles, R., & Steinmetz, S. (1980). *Behind closed doors: Violence in the American family.* Garden City, NY: Doubleday.

Tierney, K. (1982). The battered women movement and the creation of the wife beating problem. *Social Problems, 29,* 207-220.

Tong, R. (1984). *Women, sex and the law.* Totowa, NJ: Rowman & Allenheld.

Walker, L. E. (1984). *The battered woman syndrome.* New York: Springer.

Wardell, L., Gillespie, D. D., & Leffler, A. (1983). Science and violence against women. In D. Finkelhor et al. (Eds.), *The dark side of families: Current family violence research* (pp. 69-84). Beverly Hills, CA: Sage.

Yllö, K. (1988). Political and methodological debates in wife abuse research. In K. Yllö & M. Bograd (Eds.), *Feminist perspectives on wife abuse* (pp. 28-51). Newbury Park, CA: Sage.

19 "Our Hearts Are Collectively Breaking": Teaching Survivors of Violence

JANET LEE
Oregon State University

> For all of us who have experienced such awful things as rape, violence, incest, our hearts are collectively breaking.
>
> —A survivor's voice

Violence against women is one of the most enraging, disturbing, and painful components of any introductory women's studies course. As teachers, when we attempt to politicize the personal on this issue, facing the pain and poignancy of such an endeavor, we are faced with questions, responsibilities, and concerns. In this chapter, I focus on the effects of such a course for survivors in terms of the potential for their feeling more powerful about themselves and the world, and discuss ways in which teachers might be able to be more effective in the classroom to help survivors heal themselves.

The classroom experience I describe here occurred when I was teaching an introductory women's studies course, "Woman, Self and Others," at Mankato State University during the winter term 1988, with a group of mainly returning and nontraditional students. The course was a general education, 10-week survey of the impact of sexist, heterosexist, ageist, classist, ableist, racist, and anti-Semitic social institutions on women's

AUTHOR'S NOTE: I would like to thank all the women whose voices and stories I have shared here. Also thanks to my teaching assistant, Shelly Owen. This chapter is an abridged version of a much longer paper by the same title, available upon request from Janet Lee, Women Studies, Oregon State University, Corvalis, OR, 97331-6208.

270

lives. Core topics included the content and impact of cultural messages, women's domestic and market work, art and creativity, women's history and social movements, the politics of interpersonal relationships, lesbianism, reproductive rights and women's health, and violence against women. The class met once a week for 4 hours.

Mankato State University is the second-largest state college in Minnesota. It attracts a white, predominantly rural, working- to middle-class population of mainly Scandinavian and German background and has a relatively conservative student body. But it is well known for its praxis-oriented Women's Studies Department, which offers both bachelor's and master's degrees. Five or six sections of the introductory course are taught each quarter, and usually there are waiting lists for enrollment. Classes are closed at 35 students to facilitate the short lecture and discussion format that has been found to be most conducive to student participation, learning, and empowerment.

Feminist pedagogy is based on the belief that personal and academic knowledge are complementary. We encourage this fusion through the use of "integrative learning journals" (Berry & Black, 1987), student-facilitated class sessions, and small-group work, which place personal experiences in broader political contexts and emphasize the constructedness of our culture. Such pedagogy aims at facilitating both compassion and critique as we grapple with systems of privilege and oppression and encourage personal and social action. It means dealing with issues of power in the classroom as we attempt to foster the skills of critical thinking and respect for others.

Of the 21 students enrolled in the course, all were white women; 15 were mothers, 10 married and 5 divorced; and 6 had never married. They were of rural working- to middle-class background, except for one young woman from an urban, upper-middle-class family. The 6 never-married nonmothers were the "traditional" college students under 23 years old. The other 15 women were all mothers, married or divorced, ranging in age from early 20s to late 40s. Among them, these women had 38 children, from preschoolers to young adults. Most of these non-traditional students also had jobs outside the home. None of the students identified themselves as lesbians.

One intent of this class was to raise consciousness and impart knowledge of the pervasiveness of violence against women, as well as help students place their everyday experiences with this issue into a broader political context. We devoted one class session to the issue of violence against women and integrated the concept into other sessions, so that it was open for ongoing dialogue throughout the term. On the topic of women's wage labor, for example, we discussed sexual harassment and evaluated the university's current stance and guidelines for dealing with the problem. In focusing on language, sexuality, body imagery, and the effects of the media on the construction of "femininity," we were also talking about and sharing information and perspectives on violence.

CLASS SESSION ON VIOLENCE

During the specific session devoted to misogyny and violence, we covered rape, battering, incest, and pornography. Students had read "Rape Information," put out by a local crisis service on the aftereffects of this experience on survivors and the reactions of others—friends, lovers, and health care and law enforcement personnel. We watched the short movie *Rethinking Rape* (1985) about the need to understand rape as a violent crime that has its roots in the way our gender roles are organized, and we referred to Diane Herman's article "The Rape Culture" (1989). Students had also read pieces by Butler (1985) on incest and by Walker (1979) on battered women. During the morning, we had guests who talked about their experiences as survivors; the phone numbers of the local crisis centers, the student counseling center, and the local shelter for battered women were written on the board.

We watched a slide show on pornography put together by graduate students in Women's Studies and discussed the article the class had read by Russell and Lederer, "Questions We Get Asked Most Often" (1980). The slide show depicted pornography outlets located in the local Minneapolis area and was accompanied by a script critiquing pornography and relating it to issues of violence against women. Time for reflection and cooling down is always needed after this slide show, and we enjoyed some music by Ferron.

There was a lot of personal sharing in the classroom from students who talked of their own experiences, accompanied by tears and hugs. There were also many unsolicited personal accounts in journals. Over two thirds of the class wrote of their direct or indirect personal relationship to violence and the extent of their fear and rage. Each one of these women had been a survivor of more than one form of abuse.

Of the 21 students enrolled in the course, 10 wrote in their classroom journals about experiencing physical or sexual abuse as children or as adults. Among these 10, 3 women shared experiences of incest and 1 of being sexually assaulted as a child by a teacher, 5 of having been raped or sexually abused as adults, and 6 of having been physically abused as an adult and 4 as a child. Ten women said that they felt that they had been verbally or psychologically abused in relationships, 7 mentioned forms of harassment as workers or as students, and 5 wrote of experiences of violence described by relatives or friends. Given the potential for denial and underreporting, these figures illustrate the enormity of the problem of sexual terrorism in our society.

The session devoted to violence against women was very painful and draining, yet seemed to bond the class together. There was much respect for the strength of the survivors who shared their experiences, a respect that the survivors themselves could feel and use to grow. It would have been preferable to have had more time to spend on this topic and to have been able to stagger it over several days so that the students could process and reflect on the issues. But in many ways, the long block of time added to the intensity of the session. Students were not distracted by subsequent classes and everyday happenings; they were saturated with the topic and visibly moved. Even class members who did not identify as survivors were concerned, angered, scared, and wanted to see things change, especially on the issue of pornography.

For a teacher, it is always difficult to end such a session without feeling anxious about the aftereffects of such an intense morning on students. One survivor of violence said she would have liked "a few extra moments at the end of the session to reach out to others for support—even just time to sit in silence or tears." At this point, prose, poetry, music, and a session on self-defense could be especially empowering.

EMPOWERMENT

At the end of the 10-week term, when we had developed a sense of ease and trust with each other, I asked the students to complete a self-evaluation survey that consisted mainly of open-ended questions about the effects of the course on them and if and how they felt they had grown or changed. The self-evaluation survey had two questions on empowerment. One asked students to rate themselves on a continuum, showing how they felt when they came into the class and how they saw themselves at the end of the course. The second asked students if they felt more or less empowered generally as a result of the course, and to explain in what areas and in what ways they felt more or less empowered. In an attempt to have some negotiation of meaning as well as facilitating a sense of collaboration, I used "member checks" (Guba &

Lincoln, 1981), where I asked some of the women whose experiences I am sharing here to comment on, edit, and otherwise help negotiate the validity of the descriptions and analyses I had drawn.

All but one student (who had not talked of being a survivor of violence) said they felt more powerful at the end of the class than they had coming into the course. The survivors of violence were more affected by the class than the other students. Their average self-evaluated empowerment score was 1.9 before the class and 3.8 after it (1 was low and 5 high), compared to 2.6 and 3.8 for those who had not experienced violence. The survivors tended to be somewhat older and more conscious of themselves and the world, as well as more easily able to integrate classroom material with minimal resistance.

The students said the source of their increased feeling of empowerment was twofold: One came from the knowledge, "facts," and information they received in the class during discussion, lectures, movies, and panels; and the second from the feeling of unity and solidarity with other women in the classroom. Both survivors and other students mentioned these issues, but the survivors emphasized the point about feeling support and solidarity from the group more than the other students did. They mentioned an increased acceptance and liking of themselves as well as a feeling of having more control over their own lives and increased assertiveness in relationships with others.

I also asked the survivors if the class had helped them deal with the experiences of being abused. Nine of 10 said emphatically yes. They felt that being able to talk of their experiences helped and that the feeling that they were not alone was especially healing. The classroom was reported as a "safe place" by several. Many indicated that the journal was also a safe place to share feelings and discuss issues. The one student who felt that the class had not helped her handle being a survivor said that although the class had had a positive effect on her generally, "As a class I don't think it could have helped. I think I just need to see a counselor. I'm afraid to put my problems on the table in front of these people because I guess I'm just scared."

In contrast, "Alice," a mother in her 40s and survivor of much pain in her life, shared her feelings. She had experienced physical abuse as a child, incest, and rape, as well as having lived with psychological abuse and the threat of battering. She wrote in her journal:

> Before I felt things were wrong, but if you said something it was like I had
> nothing to base it on. I just felt it. Now I feel if something is said on TV or

in the paper about women and I know it's wrong and I can say it's wrong. I don't even feel I have to defend myself to disagree. Having facts and discussing in class, you do feel more empowered.

"Jill," a married woman with one child, who was struggling to regain her sense of self and agency in the world after having survived incest, rape, and psychological abuse, emphasized that it was the feeling of not being alone in one's pain that was so freeing. She wrote in her journal:

> I feel much more empowered. I know now the experiences and oppression I have felt are things felt by other women also—that I am not alone in seeing women as being treated unfairly. I feel empowered knowing my reality is valid—and that women can be strong together and change our world.

Women who did not identify themselves as survivors also appreciated the sharing of opinions and solidarity that developed during this class. They wrote: "Just knowing that others have the same feeling about things has really made me feel more empowered"; "I realized how many women feel the way that I do"; "The people [in class] cared. What I had to say was important."

"Solidarity" also came through in the words of several women who wrote that part of the source of feeling better about themselves was their ability to help other women in similar situations or to help educate the other women in the class who were just beginning to understand the issues surrounding violence against women. "Jane," a divorced mother who had been raped and physically beaten wrote:

> They say those who bear the mark of great pain are never really free—they owe a debt to those who still suffer. And this is how I look upon my experiences and if my story, my life can give another power, then it all hasn't been for nothing.

TEACHING ABOUT VIOLENCE
AGAINST WOMEN IN THE CLASSROOM

The impact of women's studies courses on students includes both integration of feminist values and resistance when oppositional education or counterhegemonic knowledge contradicts everyday knowledge. This group of mainly returning women, with their rich variety of life experiences, had so little resistance mainly because feminism made sense to them. It helped them understand their pasts and explained present situations. They grasped the issues and shared openly because they were in a small, homogeneous group and were willing to place their experiences in a broader political context. For a teacher, it is exciting to be a part of this discovery of the power of our own authenticity.

Feminist pedagogy taps into students' important everyday and personal experiences and gives them new information and knowledge that politicizes these experiences in a compassionate and useful way. It is most important that course content draw connections between institutional structures and personal experience. This type of critical thinking must be a self-reflexive process grounded in everyday life.

Ways to facilitate such learning may include the integration of community events into the curriculum. Students in the course were given credit for attending campus or community events on woman abuse and other issues, or for volunteering at local agencies. Guests who share their personal stories are more effective than formal lecturing, and the use of local community literature and resources that focus on social action makes the issues more real for students. It is often enlightening for students to realize that there have been successful national and international social movements dedicated to eradicating violence against women, as well as local activities in their hometown. Also important are phone numbers for local crisis centers, battered women's shelters, and counseling centers.

Feminist pedagogy can help facilitate a supportive atmosphere in which students feel safe and validated by teachers and each other. The classroom can be a place where students can take risks for their own self-growth as well as practice ways of working together on mutual goals. In the class I taught, survivors shared their stories of fear, guilt, shame, anger, and denial; and they expressed the realities of living in a misogynist world. They were able to act as role models, as survivors and not as victims, validating themselves as well as teaching others. In that sense they were leaders.

This group of students became friends and experienced a feeling of community. They connected with each other practicing the interrelationships between autonomy and mutuality. A buddy system and the use of internal partners helped, as did maximal student involvement and trust-building group work to promote discussion and listening skills. Obviously, class size is a factor here. The physical absence of men in the classroom helped this definition of safe, female-defined space and greatly facilitated self-disclosure. Feminist educators should take seriously the twofold commitment of promoting individual agency through the empowerment and education of students and attempting to subvert patriarchal institutional structures. We will probably always have survivors of woman abuse in our classrooms; and we need to be sensitive to these needs, these experiences, and current situations so that we may empower ourselves and each other.

REFERENCES

Berry, E., & Black, E. (1987). The integrative learning journal. *Women's Studies Quarterly, 15,* 59-64.

Butler, S. (1985). *Conspiracy of silence: The trauma of incest.* San Francisco: Volcano.

Guba, E., & Lincoln, Y. (1981). *Effective evaluation.* San Francisco: Jossey-Bass.

Herman, D. (1989). The rape culture. In J. Freeman (Ed.), *Women: A feminist perspective* (pp. 20-44). Palo Alto, CA: Mayfield.

Rethinking rape. (1985). [Film, 26 min. color, 16mm]. Seattle: Film Distribution Center.

Russell, D.E.H., & Lederer, L. (1980). Questions we get asked most often. In L. Lederer (Ed.), *Take back the night: Women on pornography* (pp. 23-29). New York: William Morrow.

Walker, L. (1979). *The battered woman.* New York: Harper & Row.

20 The Politics of Research and Activism: Violence Against Women

MICHELLE FINE
CUNY/Graduate Center

S*cene 1*. I am in my office, and a colleague enters, quite excited about his new data. He explains:

> We surveyed over 1,000 students on this campus and can predict with a great degree of reliability what individual factors cause young men to be sexually violent with young women—hypersexual socialization, homophobia, and negative attitudes toward women. But here's our problem. We can't predict which women are likely to be attacked by men. Maybe we didn't use the right variables.

I explained that you cannot predict which young women are particularly vulnerable because on a college campus, individual characteristics do not distinguish women about to be victimized from those lucky enough to survive campus life unscathed.

Scene 2. I am in a hospital emergency room with Altamese Thomas. She is a young African-American woman, just gang-raped, bruised, but still a bit drunk. I am a young white woman, a rape crisis volunteer, a psychologist, and a feminist. Our conversation goes something like this:

AUTHOR'S NOTE: An earlier version of this chapter was presented as a keynote address to the Canadian Research Institute for the Advancement of Women, Quebec, November 1988. This chapter reflects many conversations with Julie Blackman, Barbara Hart, Susan Ostoff, Lynn Phillips, Susan Schecter, and Jacqui Wade about the possibilities and paradoxes of activist research. They all deserve thanks, but no responsibility for the conclusions reached. Appreciation also to Judith Lorber for rapid and careful editing.

278

MF   Altamese, the police will be here to speak with you. Are you interested
(3:00 a.m.): in prosecuting? Do you want to take these guys to court?
AT: No, I don't want to do nothin' but get over this. When I'm pickin'
            the guy out of some line, who knows who's messin' around with
            my momma, or my baby. Anyway nobody would believe me. Can
            I wash now?
MF   Once the exam is over you can wash and brush your teeth. First we
(3:30 a.m.): need to wait for the doctor for your exam. Wouldn't your friends
            testify as witnesses?
AT: Where I live, nobody's gonna testify. Not to the police. Anyway,
            I'm a Baptist and I know God is punishing him right now. He done
            bad enough and he's suffering.
MF   Maybe if we talked about the rape you would feel better.
(4:00 a.m.):
AT: You know, I don't remember things. When I was little lots of bad
            things happened to me, and I forget them. My memory's bad, I don't
            like to remember bad stuff. I just forget. When I was a young child,
            my momma told me about rape and robberies. I told her she was
            wrong. Those things happen in the movies, not here. When I saw
            such things on the streets I thought they was making a movie. Then
            one day a lady started bleeding, and I knew it was not a movie.
MF   Do you think maybe you would like to talk with a counselor, in a
(4:30 a.m.): few days, about some of your feelings?
AT: I've been to one of them. It just made it worse. I just kept thinking
            about my problems too much. You feel better when you're talking,
            but then you got to go back home, and they're still there. No good
            just talking when things ain't no better.
MF: Is there anyone you can talk to about this?
AT: Not really. I can't tell my mother, not my brothers either. They
            would go out and kill the guys. My mother's boyfriend, too. I don't
            want them going to jail 'cause of me.
MF: You said you sometimes meet with a social worker. Can you talk
            with your social worker?
AT: She's the one who took away my kids. If they take my baby, I would
            kill myself. I ain't gonna get myself in trouble, all I got is my baby,
            and she already thinks I'm a bad mother. But I love my babies and
            I try hard to take care of them. I just don't understand why men have
            to rape. Why do they have to take, when they could just ask?
MF: How about one of your teachers at college? Can you talk to them?
AT: Those teachers think I'm stupid. Sometimes they call on me, and I
            don't answer. When you got problems, your mind is on the moon.
            He calls on you, and you don't know what he's saying. They treat
            you like a dog, and you act like a dog.

MF   Soon you will get to leave here and go home, where you'll feel safe.
(5:30 a.m.):
AT: It ain't safe there. I live in the projects with my baby. I can't go back
                there now. It feels safer here . . . I hurt so much.
MF   Can I call you next week just to see how you're doing?
(7:00 a.m.):
AT: Sure.

All that I knew, as feminist, psychologist, and as volunteer counselor, was rendered irrelevant by this exchange. My personal and professional ways of coping could not apply smoothly to the material conditions of Altamese Thomas's life. Even 2 hours into our conversation, I still did not quite understand it. Then I thought about how a more traditional psychologist might have seen her: learned helplessness, external locus of control, resistant to the mental health system, cynical about institutions of criminal justice, perhaps depressed. What Altamese Thomas offered was a realistic appraisal of the slim likelihood that a poor African-American woman would get a hearing in the mental health or "justice" systems. Critical of social inequities, she was ambivalent about men, cops, sexuality, and the state. And she was tolerant of me. Before me was a woman who was taking control of an uncontrollable life.

THE INDIVIDUALISTIC RESEARCH BIAS

In this chapter, I offer a critique of the individualistic research bias that my colleague unwittingly voiced in his research on date rape, that could have easily perverted the story Altamese Thomas had to tell about stranger rape, and that threads through much scholarship on violence against women. Although many progressive and feminist researchers have come to understand most poignantly the power of injustice through the lives and words of *individuals* like Altamese Thomas, the individualistic research bias that extracts women (and men) from their social contexts has inadvertently invaded the study of violence against women, yielding unfortunate consequences for social theory and social movements.

To focus on the individual, although it may be practically useful given our access to women but not their domestic contexts, contributes to a discourse that finally blames individual survivors, for the source of social inequity is sought inside their bodies and minds. Not only does such an approach decontextualize a woman from her political, social, and personal worlds, but it systematically renders oblique the structures of patriarchy, racism, classism, and advanced capitalism that have sculpted what appear to be the "conditions" or "choices" of her life.

The individualistic research bias not only fails to undermine prevailing ideologies that hold individuals—especially women—responsible for their own misery but usually grants these ideologies scientific legitimacy. Women who claim they have been violently attacked by men are typically suspect. Social science research that focuses on qualities of such a woman's life may unwittingly reinforce the belief that she is the locus of her social ills. Changing *her* then appears to be the best solution to institutionalized violence against women.

Finally, individualistic research is situated in a most problematic relationship to social movements. In the case of violence against women, such research not only fails to advance the cause of the battered women's, anti-rape, and anti-sexual harassment movements but often works against them by creating easily assimilated images of women as victims, powerless, unable to fend for themselves, or even masochistic. Such research reinforces hegemonic beliefs that support male violence against women and facilitates secondary institutional victimization by courts, hospitals, schools, therapists, and social agencies. Women who love too much, who are seen as helpless, addicted to violence, or even unaware of their options (as if there were so many), do not lend themselves easily to grass-roots demands for mandatory arrest laws, privileged consideration in custody battles, acquittal in homicide cases, or even feminist individual and group therapies.

TOWARD A TRANSFORMED RESEARCH AGENDA

If feminists developed activist research projects studying the institutionalization of violence against women, rather than individualistic projects on characteristics of battered women, we would have to reconsider both the research questions we ask and the contexts in which we ask them.

The Questions Asked

Five categories of questions come to mind that feminist activist researchers may want to address over the coming years. Through these questions we can seek to understand the politics of gender, power, and violence inside distinct contexts: women's diverse consciousness, intimate relationships, feminist agencies, the battered women's movement, and the institutional structures that sustain violence against women.

On Transforming Consciousness. We know a lot about how women feel about male violence, experience it, and make sense of it (see Blackman, 1989; Browne, 1986; Fine & Gordon, 1989; Schechter, 1985; Walker, 1988). But analyses of women's political consciousness, in which gender braids with class, race, disability, sexual orientation, and community, still remain wanting. That is, we do not know much about how women's consciousness flows over historic and personal time— through self-blame, "ignoring," "tolerating," moral outrage, collective action, legal remedy, flight, or violent revenge. Such shifts in consciousness and resistance need to be understood longitudinally, and not only for different groups of women in differing social contexts but also for the women and men who sit on juries deciding the fates of battered women accused of murder, and those who become psychotherapists, provide health care, and serve as policymakers who legislate, render legal judgments, and determine which research and service projects will be funded.

An example of research on the micropolitics of social consciousness can be found in a study in progress in women's responses to the term *battered woman.* Susan Schechter, Lynn Phillips, and I have been interviewing diverse groups of women survivors of male violence about their self-descriptions. We are learning, perhaps ironically, that women who have been abused often distance themselves from precisely those labels feminists use to heighten public recognition of how gendered domestic violence is. One young woman recently commented:

> Not me. I'm not a battered woman. Battered women have bruises all over their bodies. Two broken legs. And he's not a batterer, not like I seen them. No, he just hits me too much.

By popularizing the category *battered woman* and by portraying her usually as powerless and innocent, activists have staked out important but problematic political territory. We need to understand the consequences, for women themselves, of this political act of naming. Adult and adolescent women who feel that they do not fit the category—because they do not feel helpless, they hit back, or they are ambivalent about their lover or the relationship—may resist the category upon which activists rely. We need to know how survivors and nonabused women interpret such politically charged categories and what kinds of home-grown categories they carve to capture and preserve their own experiences.

On Women's Relationships. A second scene for activist research concerns the politics of intimacy, selfishness, and separation in women's personal relationships. Women's lives are situated inside relationships—for better or worse. Given this aspect of women's social realities, it is important to understand how women manage to do *for self,* while still doing *for others.*

An analysis of narratives authored by students at the University of Pennsylvania on their experiences of sexual harassment reveal subtle nuances in how young women translate abuse within existing relationships. Linda Brodkey and I found the young women to be not at all reluctant to name the harassment per se but extremely resistant to naming a faculty member as responsible, that is, getting him in trouble formally or informally, especially when his career or marriage might be threatened (Brodkey & Fine, 1989). Battered women are often similarly situated, with even more to lose, in the ambivalence of their relationships. Research is needed to understand how women who remain inside abusive relations, temporarily or permanently, can imagine doing something for themselves. Research on the disrupting politics of women's "selfishness" is clearly on the horizon.

In Activist Settings. A third scene for activist research may involve battered women's shelters. Women who work in or with shelters know the struggles and pains that saturate those sites. Trying to pick up the pieces of a race-, class-, and gender-stratified society, in which housing and health care are inadequate, in which alternatives to violent homes are few, the staff of shelters are beleaguered and frustrated. Feminist researchers need to be inside those shelters, conducting research that enables paid workers and volunteers to feel empowered, to have a grounded sense of their import, and to experience a sense of success in work with little gratification.

In the mid-1980s, the Hilton Foundation solicited an evaluation proposal to assess qualitatively their network of shelters, safe homes, and hotlines in rural Tennessee and to conduct quantitatively a cost-benefit analysis of the effectiveness per woman and child. Jacqui Wade and I competed successfully for the evaluation grant but insisted on the inclusion of another study that would document what it costs per woman and child *not* to provide services.

In our effort to catalog the import of services, we asked the battered women and their children, "What would happen to you/your children if no shelter existed?" They provided rich and tragic responses: broken bones; time off from school; I would be in foster care; my children would be taken away; time missed from work; destroyed furniture; I would have killed him—or he would have killed me.

We next asked the women and staff to define what they thought success meant and what the women needed from the shelters in order to survive. The women in residence offered the following indicators of success: to keep him out as late as possible; to get the kids to bed before he gets violent; to be able to call a friend when he is about to go off; to leave so that he knows that when I come back I can leave again. In contrast, many shelter workers described success as that imaginary leaving when the woman never returns and is never bothered by him again. Although they knew this to be unattainable in rural Tennessee, anything short of it nevertheless seemed like a failure.

The rural women who had survived violence in their homes and fled, like Altamese Thomas, grappled with the material and psychological realities of poverty, sexism, and classism; with ambivalence surrounding love, hate, and emotional connections; with the tensions of doing "for self" while still being a "good woman." Leaving for good, with no further connections, was an option identified by very few of the survivors. One woman explained, simply, that on Friday nights every woman in her community gets beaten. "Work's out. The men drink. And we get beat. That's Friday night." Survival meant finding periodic respite.

As a result of our collaborative research with shelter staff and residents, a set of conversations were launched in a few of these settings in which more sensitive and dialectic images of *success* and *empowerment* came to be woven between staff and residents. Although tensions were often high between staff and residents, who espoused very different conceptions of heterosexuality, gender, entitlement, the family, religion, and the appropriate use of violence, the discussions represented an ongoing attempt to fill the yawning cavity that often separates these two groups.

Our research also found that although Hilton's project officer was quite committed to these shelters, safe homes, and hotlines being multiracial, rarely were the residents or the staff racially or ethnically diverse. After much conversation, and with some reservation, we recommended to Hilton that a separate shelter be established to respond to the needs of African-American women and that the staff from that shelter be invited to join the statewide coalition (cf. Matthews, 1989). In this case, doing collaborative research meant having the ability to merge agendas between practitioners and ourselves creatively, but also to split voices when necessary.

The Battered Women's Movement. Research is sorely lacking on the politics of social movements against violence against women. Multivoiced and contradictory though they may be, we have little social history to document their complexity (see Schechter, 1985, for a counterexample). An example of a slice of such work comes from Lynn Phillips (1988), who, through interviews with survivors and staff at a series of shelters and agencies in the urban Northeast, has been studying what administrators, staff, and residents mean by the term *empowerment*. She has discovered rich contradictions that typically remain unresolved and therefore confusing at the level of practice.

For some, empowerment seems to mean that the women survivors in residence—women who have been treated terribly for years, who arrive seeking refuge—autonomously identify what they need, which often means safety, sleep, and a television set. But to other staff, these goals seem much too limited and not at all empowering. Some argue that empowerment means launching an autonomous life by pursuing education, paid employment, child care, and housing. And in response to this image, others complain that it sounds too much like the Salvation Army, that is, too moralistic. Phillips's work reminds us that central to the battered women's movement are questions asking: Who decides who needs what? And what happens when the answers diverge dramatically by race, class, age, experience, and politics?

Unlike the situation a decade ago, when there seemed to be little space for imagining activist-researcher collaboration, today this space has been opened by practitioners and activists who seek critical analyses of their own work and by researchers who have committed to the practice and politics of feminist scholarship.[1] In particular, activist women have initiated important research on the battered women's movement, seeking to redress racism, homophobia, and residual reluctance to deal with disabled battered women. Some have examined the impact of long-advocated laws and policies, such as automatic arrest, which moves violent men out of their homes and seems to reduce recidivism but may actually intimidate women so that fewer seek help; others have investigated the role of formerly battered and currently battered women in the formulation of movement policies and politics (Activist Research Task Force members, personal communications); and still others have struggled through strategies for representing in court battered women who have killed their abusers (Ostoff, 1988).

The Structures of Abuse: Institutionalized Violence Against Women. The most basic knowledge we need is how social and economic institutions sustain and multiply the kinds of violence women experience (Blackman, 1989; Garfield, 1989; Kurz, 1989; Ostoff, 1988; Ritchie, 1989, Schechter, 1985; Stanko, 1985). Only when the dense institutional supports that socialize for male violence, obscure it from public scrutiny, and multiply its effects by doubly victimizing women are revealed, can women's individual psychologies and forms of resistance be fully understood as socially, politically, and institutionally embedded.

REFLECTIONS

Individualistic research on violence against women typically "makes science" of a sweeping and prevailing discourse that holds women responsible for domestic abuse. Such research, at best, positions individual women as the site for remedying such violence. At worst it suggests that these women are themselves the source of the problem. In this chapter, I have offered alternative images for how feminist scholars might conduct research so as to nurture counterdiscourses that focus popular and policy attention back onto institutions that perpetrate, sustain, and exacerbate violence against women.

If feminist scholars do move to reinstitutionalize our work on violence against women, we must be sure to collect the diverse voices of women, harmonious and disharmonious, across races, ethnic groups, classes, disabilities, sexualities, communities, and politics, and together with activists, create forums in which ideas, nodes of agreement, and fault lines of dissension can be aired, studied, resolved, or worked around. In the absence of such collaboration, feminist scholarship will retreat (if unwittingly) toward individualism, to be ignored, or perhaps worse, used against those women whose social contexts we seek to transform.

NOTE

1. An activist research network has grown out of the battered women's movement and has begun to investigate questions of ethics, politics, methods, and collaboration. For

information about the Activist Research Task Force or the National Coalition Against Domestic Violence, contact Pat Kuta and Donna Garske, 1717 Fifth Avenue, San Rafael, CA 94901.

REFERENCES

Blackman, J. (1989). *Intimate violence.* New York: Columbia University Press.

Brodkey, L., & Fine, M. (1988). Presence of mind in the absence of body. *Journal of Education, 170*(3), 84-89.

Browne, A. (1986). *Women who kill.* New York: Free Press.

Fine, M., & Gordon, S. (1989). Feminist transformations of/despite psychology. In M. Crawford & M. Gentry (Eds.), *Gender and thought* (pp. 146-174). New York: Springer Verlag.

Garfield, G. (1989, August). *Boarder babies: Institutionalized violence against women of color.* Paper presented at the annual meeting of the American Psychological Association, New Orleans.

Kurz, D. (1989). Social science perspectives on wife abuse: Current debates and future directions. *Gender & Society, 3,* 489-506.

Matthews, N. (1989). Surmounting a legacy: The expansion of racial diversity in a local anti-rape movement. *Gender & Society, 3*(4), 518-532.

Ostoff, S. (1988, August). *Strategies for justice: Working with battered women who kill.* Paper presented at the annual meeting of the American Psychological Association, Atlanta, GA.

Phillips, L. (1988). *Opening conversation: An internal evaluation of the House of Ruth's shelter program.* Unpublished manuscript.

Ritchie, B. (1989, August). *Battered women of color in the emergency room: Institutionalized violence.* Paper presented at the annual meeting of the American Psychological Association, New Orleans.

Schechter, S. (1985). *Women and male violence.* Boston: South End.

Stanko, E. A. (1985). *Intimate intrusions: Women's experience of male violence.* London: Routledge & Kegan Paul.

Walker, L. (1988, August). *Justice for battered women who kill: Theory research, service, activism, expert testimony.* Respondent in panel at the annual meeting of the American Psychological Association, Atlanta, GA.

About the Contributors

Pauline B. Bart is Professor of Sociology in the Department of Psychiatry, University of Illinois at Chicago. Trying to demystify the world for women, she has written about depressed middle-aged women in "Portnoy's Mother's Complaint," a feminist illegal abortion collective in "Seizing the Means of Reproduction," and women who were attacked and avoided rape in *Stopping Rape: Successful Survival Strategies*, as well as other articles on violence, feminist theories, and health. She also co-authored the *Student Sociologists' Handbook*. Her work is grounded in women's experience as she attempts to lessen women's subordination, for which violence is the linchpin. She tells the truth and pays the consequences.

Christina Bevilaqua, worked as a counselor and court advocate for battered women and victims of sexual assault at Rape Victim Services of Edgewater Uptown Community Mental Health Center and Women's Services of the YWCA of Metropolitan Chicago after receiving a master's degree in social work from the University of Chicago. Currently, she is introducing herself to members of the women's community in Providence, Rhode Island, her brand-new home.

Mary Scott Boria, M.S.W., is Director of Women's Services, Metropolitan YWCA of Chicago. She directs a comprehensive program for survivors of sexual assault and a domestic violence counseling program in the Chicago area. Prior to that, she was Director of the Chicago Sexual Assault Services Network, a coalition of 30 organizations in Chicago.

Lisa D. Brush is a doctoral candidate in sociology and a Family Policy Fellow with the Institute for Legal Studies at the University of Wisconsin—Madison, where she teaches self-defense and assault prevention and practices traditional Japanese karate. Her current research combines her passions for feminism and state theory in a history of the "problems" and "needs" of single mothers as they have been constructed in 20th-century U.S. welfare reform debates. Previous publications include works on women and privatization in Great Britain under Thatcher. She fights back.

Jane Caputi is Associate Professor of American Studies at the University of New Mexico in Albuquerque. She is the author of *The Age of Sex Crime* (1987), a feminist analysis of serial sex murder, and collaborated with Mary Daly on *Webster's First New Intergalactic Wickedary of the English Language* (Beacon, 1987). Currently she is writing a new book, *Gossips, Gorgons, and Crones: Female Powers at the Ends of the Earth.*

Patricia Hill Collins is an Associate Professor of Afro-American Studies at the University of Cincinnati and winner of the 1992 C. Wright Mills Award for her book *Black Feminist Thought: Knowledge, Consciousness, and the Politics of Empowerment.*

Andrea Dworkin is the author of *Intercourse, Pornography: Men Possessing Women*, and the novels *Mercy* and *Ice and Fire*. With the lawyer Catharine A. MacKinnon, she co-authored an ordinance defining pornography as a civil rights violation against women. She lives in New York City.

Kathleen J. Ferraro is Associate Professor of Justice Studies and Women's Studies at Arizona State University. She is a scholar/activist/ survivor of male violence and the mother of two children. She is currently working on a book summarizing 13 years of work on woman battering.

Michelle Fine is Professor of Psychology at the CUNY Graduate Center. She is the author of *Disruptive Voices: the Possibilities of Feminist Research* (1992) and coeditor (with Lois Weis) of *Beyond Silenced Voices: Race, Class and Gender in U. S. Schools.*

Helen Gualtieri ("Elena" to some) is the mother of a 4-year-old daughter, Amaranta; a social worker; feminist; and "part-time" political activist. She divides her time and energy among single-parenting, sharing quality time with her little girl, and working at Women's Services with battered women and survivors of sexual assault.

Judith Herman, M.D., is Associate Clinical Professor of Psychiatry at Harvard Medical School and Director of Training at the Victims of Violence Program in the Department of Psychiatry at Cambridge Hospital, Cambridge, MA. She received her medical degree at Harvard Medical School and her training in general and community psychiatry at Boston University Medical Center. She is the author of *Trauma and Recovery* (1992) and *Father-Daughter Incest* (1981). She is a founding member of the Women's Mental Health Collective, a woman-controlled clinic in Somerville, MA, and has lectured widely on topics of child sexual abuse and violence against women.

Yolanda Hernandez received her M.A. from DePaul University and is currently employed at Women's Services of the Chicago Metropolitan YWCA as a Crisis Counselor. She has been working at Women's Services for 2 years and feels strongly committed to the empowerment of women.

Robert A. Hummer is a Ph.D. candidate in sociology with a focus on population studies and ethnic/race relations. He has a paper in press on intra-Hispanic diversity and infant mortality and is completing his dissertation on the relationship between race and infant mortality in the United States. He is also conducting research (with Patricia Yancey Martin) on varsity athletes' treatment of women on the college campus.

Jamie A. Jimenez has been a counselor at Women's Services, Metropolitan YWCA, for the last 5 years. She currently works with women and adolescent girls who are survivors of incest or sexual assault.

Demie Kurz is Co-Director of Women's Studies and has an appointment in the sociology department at the University of Pennsylvania. She writes on issues of gender and the family, including issues of domestic violence.

Janet Lee is Director of Women Studies at Oregon State University in Corvallis. She teaches a variety of women's studies courses and is involved in campus and community issues to improve women's lives. She is currently working on a book, *Blood Stories: Body Politics and the Phenomenology of Menarche*, that explores the meaning of menarche for women in the context of a society that devalues them and their bodies. She is a mother of three children.

Catharine A. MacKinnon, Professor of Law at the University of Michigan, has written *Sexual Harassment of Working Women,* an analysis which made sexual harassment illegal as sex discrimination and defined equality not as sameness but as lack of hierarchy. With Andrea Dworkin, she has written an ordinance making pornography a violation of civil rights and has profoundly influenced Canadian jurisprudence. She has written *Feminism Unmodified: Discourses on Life and Law* (1987) and *Toward a Feminist Theory of the State* (1989) as well as *Pornography and Civil Rights: A New Day for Women's Equality* with Andrea Dworkin.

Joseph Marolla is Chairperson of the Sociology/Anthropology department at Virginia Commonwealth University. He received his Ph.D. from the University of Denver in 1975 and has been on the faculty at Virginia Commonwealth since that time. He is the author of a number of articles and chapters in the areas of self-esteem, education, and rape and violence.

Patricia Yancey Martin is Daisy Parker Flory Alumni Professor of Sociology at Florida State University, Tallahassee. She is writing a monograph on the politics of rape processing at the community level and conducting a study of the policies and strategies that help women managers and employees in large U.S. corporations. She is also conducting research (with Robert Hummer) on varsity athletes' treatment of women on the college campus.

Nancy A. Matthews is a sociologist who studies and teaches in the areas of inequality, social movements, and the social construction of gender and sexuality. She is the author of *Managing Rape: The Feminist Anti-Rape Movement and the State* (forthcoming), a study of the transformation of rape crisis organizations in Los Angeles, CA, in the 1970s and 1980s. She is currently Project Manager for a study of law school education at the American Bar Foundation in Chicago.

Eileen Geil Moran is Research Associate with the Michael Harrington Center for Democratic Values and Social Change at Queens College of the City University of New York. For 3 years she directed a shelter for battered women and their children. Along with Pauline Bart, Patricia Miller, and Elizabeth Stanko, she co-edited the special issue of *Gender & Society* on violence against women.

Beth E. Schneider is Associate Professor of Sociology and Women's Studies at the University of California, Santa Barbara. Her research on the sexualization of the workplace has been published in a variety of sociology journals and feminist studies books. Her current work focuses on women's place in the AIDS crisis and the politics of AIDS education in public schools. She has served on the Council of the Sex/Gender Section of the American Sociological Association and as chair of the Sociologists' Lesbian and Gay Caucus and the Sexual Behavior Division of the Society for the Study of Social Problems.

Diana Scully is Director of the Women's Studies Program and Associate Professor of Sociology at Virginia Commonwealth University. She is the author of two books, *Men Who Control Women's Health: The Miseducation of Obstetrician-Gynecologists* (1980) and *Understanding Sexual Violence: A Study of Convicted Rapists* (1990). She is President-Elect of the Southeastern Women's Studies Association and a member of the Coordinating Council of the National Women's Studies Association.

Carole J. Sheffield is Professor of Political Science and Women's Studies at the William Paterson College of New Jersey. She was a founding member of the college's Women's Studies program and currently serves as its director. She is the author of "Sexual Terrorism," which serves as the basis for her research and lectures on issues of violence against women. Her current work focuses on violence against women on college campuses.

Erin Sorenson, M.S.W., A.C.S.W., is currently a Social Worker working with sexually abused children and their families. She is also a Ph.D. candidate and lecturer at the University of Chicago. She recently co-authored a chapter in N. Barker's forthcoming book *A Multi-DIsciplinary Guide to Child Abuse.*

364.1555
BZ83 LINCOLN CHRISTIAN COLLEGE AND SEMINARY   86923

Elizabeth Anne Stanko, Reader in the Department of Law, Brunel University, UK, has been a pioneer of feminist criminology on both sides of the Atlantic. She is the author of *Everyday Violence* (1990) and *Intimate Intrusions* (1985) and editor of texts on gender and crime. She has written widely on the subject of violence against women. Her current focus is on positive crime prevention against violence. She is examining the daily operations of inner-city policing in a study funded by Islington Council, London.

Joanne Stato is an Italian-American lesbian and mother of three children, residing in the nuclear-free municipality of Takoma Park, MD. She was office coordinator, collective member, and frequent contributor to the feminist newsjournal *off our backs* from 1988 to 1991. She is a songwriter and musician, and is preparing to release *St. Botolph Street,* her first recording of original songs.

Carole Warshaw, psychiatrist/internist and formerly emergency room physician at Cook County hospital, is currently Behavioral Science Director of the Primary Care Internal Medicine Residency there. She is Co-Director of Hospital Crisis Intervention Project, a collaborative effort of the Chicago Abused Women Coalition and Cook County Hospital, to provide training for health care providers and services for battered women. Her current research interests include the impact of abuse on gender identity and the life course and the effect of doctor-patient dynamics on patient care.

Deborah Weber is Intake Coordinator for the Metropolitan YWCA's Children's Program and provides individual and group counseling to sexually abused children. She believes women everywhere hold fragments that can be woven together in dreamwork and poetry, and in doing so, women become more than visionkeepers: They become creators.

Kathleen Z. Young teaches anthropology at Western Washington University in Bellingham and is completing a dissertation on Croatian ethnic identity at Simon Fraser University in Burnaby, British Columbia.